The Complete
Home Baking
COLLECTION

SIMON & ALISON **HOLST**

The Complete
Home Baking
COLLECTION

SIMON & ALISON **HOLST**

Published by Hyndman Publishing
325 Purchas Road
RD 2 Amberley 7482

ISBN: 978-0-9922471-9-5

TEXT: © Simon & Alison Holst

DESIGN: Dileva Design

PHOTOGRAPHY: Lindsay Keats
except: pages 12, 14, 18, 19, 23, 29, 35,
43, 49, 52, 61, 64, 66, 67, 68, 69, 89, 95,
97, 100, 102, 111, 228, 229, 231 and 252
Sal Criscillo. © Hyndman Publishing
except page 84 © Bateman

HOME ECONOMISTS: Simon & Alison
Holst, Michelle Gill

FOOD STYLIST: Simon Holst

STYLING & PROPS: Pip Spite

The recipes in this book have
been carefully tested by the authors.
The publisher and the authors have
made every effort to ensure that the
instructions are accurate and safe
but they cannot accept liability for
any resulting injury or loss or damage
to property whether direct
or consequential.

ABBREVIATIONS USED:

ml	millilitre	°C	degrees Celsius
tsp	teaspoon	°F	degrees Fahrenheit
Tbsp	tablespoon	cm	centimetre
g	gram	mm	millimetre

ACKNOWLEDGEMENTS:

We would like to thank the following firms:

- Alison's Pantry for high quality dried fruit, fruit mixtures, crystallised fruit, nuts, seeds, etc., used in recipe development and photographs.

- Benniks Poultry Farm, Buller Road, Levin for RSPCA approved barn-laid eggs.

For information about other Holst titles, visit
www.holst.co.nz or www.hyndman.co.nz

For information about kitchen utensils which Simon and Alison find invaluable,
visit www.holst.co.nz

Contents

Introduction

Judging by the number of specialty shops and television programmes devoted to it, baking is having a massive resurgence in popularity. However, for many, producing your own baked goods can seem a little intimidating in the face of the near perfect creations showcased in the media. But, the truth of the matter is, baking needn't be intimidating. By trying and practising these 'tried and true' recipes, you will soon see that you can produce delicious treats at home — often for a fraction of the cost that you could buy the same product for.

We've always enjoyed baking (both as cooks and consumers!) in our family and some of the recipes in this collection have been made and enjoyed by four generations, while others are more recent favourites. New or old, we are delighted to be able to share these with you.

We wanted this to be our 'baking bible'. It contains over 250 recipes, so we hope we've managed to include something for everyone. There are:

- cakes, perfect just for snacking or to mark a special occasion
- little cakes, scones, slices and squares; perfect for lunchboxes or a nostalgic high tea
- sweet and savoury muffins, for something quick and easy
- biscuits and crackers, from simple mix-in-the-pot classics to macaroons
- breads and buns, from quick 'baking powder' breads to classic yeasted favourites
- festive treats for Christmas and Easter
- gluten-free goodies, because they're so often requested
- and fillings and icings to top it all off!

Regardless of whether you are new to baking or a 'well-seasoned' old hand, we are certain that you will find enough tasty recipes in here to fill your cake tins and lunchboxes, delight your family and friends, or just enjoy over a hot drink.

Have fun and happy baking!

Simon & Alison Holst

Measurements

For consistently good results when you use the recipes in this book, please measure the ingredients carefully. Most recipe ingredients have been measured rather than weighed, and the quantities given in level (standard) cup and spoon measures.

A set of 'single capacity' measuring cups will enable you to measure all your dry ingredients quickly, easily, and accurately. (It is harder to measure fractions of a cup accurately when you use only a one cup measure.) We use one cup, half cup and quarter cup measures, measuring three quarters of a cup using half and quarter cup measures. Occasionally you may see ⅛ cup (ground coffee) measures. These little measures hold 2 tablespoons (15ml) and are useful at times, but are not essential.

All the dry ingredients you measure should fill the measures, but should not be heaped up above the rim. The only ingredient which is PRESSED into a measure is brown sugar. It should hold its shape like a sandcastle when it is turned out of its measure.

Flour measurements are especially important when you are baking. Too much flour will make your baking dry and stodgy. When you measure flour, first stir it with a fork or whisk in its original container. Spoon the stirred flour into your measure and level it off with the edge of a knife. NEVER bang or shake the measure to level off the flour in it, or it will compact again and you will finish up using more flour than intended.

We used to measure liquids in clear, graduated measuring cups, but we now find it more practical to use the same single capacity cups that we use for dry ingredients. You should fill the measuring cup so that it is brimming full. Don't carry a brimming full cup from one side of your kitchen to the other, or you will spill it, and your measuring will not be accurate!

If you get into the habit of measuring dry ingredients before you measure liquid ingredients, you will not have to wash and dry your measures before you finish measuring. Do not measure dry ingredients in a measure which is wet after measuring liquids or some will remain in the cup and the amount you use will not be large enough.

Because household spoons vary so much in size, we always use a set of metric measuring spoons. One tablespoon holds 15ml, and 1 teaspoon holds 5ml. (Australian measuring tablespoons hold 20ml, not 15ml. If you have Australian measuring spoons, use 3 teaspoon measures instead of the (larger) tablespoon. The Australian measuring teaspoon holds 5ml, as the New Zealand one does.)

Unless stated otherwise, don't use heaped spoon measures in any of these recipes, since a heaped spoon holds about twice as much as a level spoon. Incorrect amounts of baking powder, baking soda and salt can really spoil your baking.

Unless you are an experienced cake baker, you should read the suggestions and information on these pages. Having said this, no two ovens are exactly the same, so you will need to use your judgment too. Judging cooking times gets easier as you cook more. For your first few cakes it is a good idea to gently press the centre of the cake a few times as it cooks, so you can see and feel the way the texture changes as cooking progresses.

Cake pans:

It is often possible to make a cake, even if you don't have a pan of the specified size. To a large extent, the cooking time depends on the depth of the cake. A mixture cooked in a 20cm square pan will be deeper than the same mixture put in a 23cm square pan, so it will take longer to cook. Both will probably work, as long as you take the cakes out when they are ready (i.e. when the centres spring back when pressed, and when a skewer poked deeply into the centre comes out clean, without any uncooked mixture clinging to the bottom of it).

Similarly, if you use a round pan instead of a square pan the same size across, the round cake you make will be deeper than the same mixture cooked in the square pan, and will probably take longer to cook.

Ring cakes usually cook faster than solid cakes because the centre is closer to the edges and heats and cooks faster. You can stand an empty (fairly narrow) can in the centre of a round pan to make a ring pan, if you like. I sometimes make a cake mixture in two loaf pans instead of one pan. It is a good idea to check the volume of the different pans you

have, by seeing how many cups of water each one holds.

If you do not own cake pans, but like the idea of baking cakes, look around! Take a measuring tape with you and try second-hand shops and car boot sales before you look in larger supermarkets, and shops such as The Warehouse. Expanding pans mean that you can make cakes of different sizes in the same pan.

Usually, darker coloured and heavier weight pans cook faster, and give a browner crust than silvery pans.

Flour:

I have used standard (plain) flour for most of the lighter cakes. For fruit cakes you can choose between using standard flour or high-grade (bread) flour. If I have it in the house, I prefer to use the high-grade flour because it supports the dried fruit better than standard flour. If you have had trouble in the past with fruit sinking to the bottom half of the cake, use high-grade flour for your fruit cakes as well as for your bread.

Some of the recipes in this book call for self-raising flour. One cup of self-raising flour contains the equivalent of two teaspoons of baking powder, which is twice as much as is generally used in cakes. If you like the texture this flour gives your cakes, leave out the baking powder and use half self-raising and half plain flour to get the proportion of 1 teaspoon of baking powder to 1 cup of flour. This is the amount usually used in many cakes. (Do not make this substitution for fruit cakes which require little or sometimes no raising agent.

Cornflour Sponge – recipe page 37

Apricot & Almond Cake

Despite its odd ingredients, this cake is wonderful, and makes a great special-occasion dessert. Don't crush the biscuits and almonds too finely for this recipe, or the cake will be too firm and dry.

For a 21cm ring cake:

140g slivered almonds

75g (20) Snax biscuits or other crackers

2 tsp baking powder

½ cup dried apricots, chopped

3 large egg whites

1 cup sugar

1 tsp vanilla essence

extra apricots and toasted almonds for garnish

1 Preheat the oven to 180°C (170°C fanbake), with the rack just below the middle. Coat a 21cm ring pan evenly with non-stick spray and line its base with baking paper or a Teflon liner (or prepare 2 loaf pans, about 11 x 22cm).

2 Toast the almonds lightly by heating them gently in a frypan over low heat, or in a sponge roll pan under a grill. (Do not let them get any darker than straw colour.) Put the nuts in a plastic bag with the crackers. Bang the bag with a rolling pin until the crackers are broken into small pieces but are not as fine as dry breadcrumbs, or as they would be if crushed in a food processor. Add the baking powder and chopped apricots.

3 In a large, grease-free bowl, beat the egg whites until the peaks turn over. Add the sugar and beat again until the peaks stand up when the beater is removed. Beat in the vanilla essence. Fold the crumb mixture into the meringue, then spoon the mixture into the prepared pan.

4 Bake for 30 minutes, then run a knife around the pan and carefully tip cake out onto a rack. When cold, place on a flat serving plate. Decorate with whipped cream, and garnish with the extra nuts and chopped apricots. Leave 2–3 hours before serving.

Walnut Torte

Ground walnuts and biscuit crumbs replace the flour in this cake which is always popular — it makes a wonderful dinner partly finale, alone or with fresh berries, or fruit.

For a 23cm square cake:

½ cup fine sweet biscuit crumbs
(8–10 digestive biscuits)

125g walnuts

1 cup sugar

3 large eggs, at room temperature

❶ Preheat the oven to 160°C (150°C fanbake), with the rack just below the middle. Line a 23cm square cake pan with baking paper.

❷ Crumb the biscuits using a food processor or bang then roll them in a plastic bag using a rolling pin, until all the crumbs are fine.

❸ Preferably using a food processor, finely chop the walnuts with half the sugar.

❹ In another bowl, beat the eggs until thick, then add the remaining sugar and beat until very thick. Fold the crumbs, nut mixture and egg mixture together.

❺ Pour into the prepared pan and bake for 30–40 minutes or until the centre springs back when gently pressed. Leave to cool before removing from pan. Serve in squares, dusted with icing sugar, topped with whipped cream and extra chopped walnuts. Serve fresh berries or sliced ripe peaches alongside the cake, if desired.

Date & Walnut Cake

You can't actually see the fruit and nuts in this delicious cake because they are so finely chopped. Serve it for dessert or for a special occasion, with coffee. (You need a food processor and beater to make it.)

For a 23cm round or ring cake:

1 cup (150g) chopped dates

1 cup (90g) walnut pieces

½ cup sugar

2 Tbsp standard (plain) flour

1 tsp baking powder

2 large eggs

1 tsp vanilla essence

NOTE: Use good-quality dried fruit and nuts, especially walnuts. This cake may be made ahead and frozen. It is best decorated within three hours before serving. Do not expect a high cake — this cake is meant to be fairly flat!

1 Preheat the oven to 180°C (170°C fanbake), with the rack just below the middle. Line the base of a 23cm round cake pan (or a ring pan of the same diameter) with baking paper and spray sides with non-stick spray.

2 Measure the dates and nuts into a food processor. Add half of the sugar and all of the flour and baking powder, then process until dates and nuts are as fine as rolled oats.

3 In another bowl, beat the egg whites with half (2 tablespoons) of the remaining sugar, until their peaks turn over when the beater is lifted from them.

4 Beat egg yolks in another bowl, with the rest of the sugar and vanilla essence until thick and creamy.

5 Combine the three mixtures, folding them together lightly, and turn mixture into the prepared pan.

6 Bake for about 30 minutes, or until the centre springs back when pressed. Leave for 10 minutes then turn onto a rack to cool. Serve topped with whipped cream, quark or ricotta, decorated with an interesting selection of chopped dried fruit and nuts, such as dates, dried apricots, walnuts and pecans.

Apricot Filling:

about 8–10 dried apricots

about 12 almonds

¼ cup desiccated coconut

¼ cup sugar

4–5 Tbsp sherry or orange juice

few drops almond essence, optional

Cake:

½ cup sour cream

1 large egg

½ cup sugar

few drops each of vanilla and almond essence

1 cup self-raising flour

⅛ tsp baking soda

¼ tsp salt

1 Tbsp orange juice or milk

Holiday Surprise Cake

Although we love the almondy apricot filling given here, during the festive season we sometimes make this cake, replacing this apricot filling with Christmas mincemeat (see page 251), and find that the resulting cake is equally popular.

1 Preheat the oven to 190°C (or 180°C fanbake), with the rack just below the middle. Coat a 20cm ring pan with non-stick spray. (Line the bottom of the pan with a ring of baking paper as an extra precaution, if you like.)

2 For the filling, finely chop the apricots, almonds, coconut and sugar together in a food processor. Add the sherry (or juice) and essence and process until the mixture forms a paste. Remove from processor.

3 For the cake, measure the sour cream, egg, sugar and essences into the unwashed processor. Process briefly to mix, then add the unsifted remaining ingredients and process briefly again. The mixture should be runnier than a normal cake batter. Pour it into the prepared pan. Drop teaspoons of the filling evenly onto the batter, in a ring, so it does not touch the sides of the pan.

4 Bake for 25 minutes, or until top is golden brown and centre feels firm when pressed. (As the cake bakes, the filling sinks and should be completely, or nearly all covered and surrounded by the batter.) Leave cake on a rack for about 5 minutes, then run a knife around the pan and turn the cake out carefully. Serve warm or cold, preferably on the day of baking, dusted with icing sugar, or drizzled with Lemon Icing (see page 253). Sprinkle icing with lightly toasted sliced almonds, if desired.

For a 20–23cm square cake:

Topping:

50g cold butter, cubed

½ cup sugar

¼ cup + 2 Tbsp standard (plain) flour

½ tsp ground cinnamon

Cake:

finely grated zest of 1 orange

¾ cup sugar

50g butter, softened

1 large egg

½ cup orange juice

¼ cup water

2 cups self-raising flour

½ tsp salt

1–2 cups fresh or partly thawed blueberries

Blueberry & Orange Coffee Cake

Coffee cakes are an American 'invention'. They are made to be eaten, preferably warm, with coffee. Make this one with fresh or (partly thawed) frozen blueberries at any time of the year.

1. Preheat the oven to 180°C (170°C fanbake), with the rack just below the middle. Line a 20 or 23cm square pan with baking paper or coat with non-stick spray.

2. Finely chop the topping ingredients together in a food processor (or rub together by hand). Set aside the crumbly mixture while you make the cake.

3. For the cake, put the orange zest and sugar in a large bowl or food processor. Add the butter and the egg, then mix or process until combined. Pour in the orange juice and water, without mixing. Measure the flour and salt into a sieve over the bowl, then shake them in. Mix everything until just blended.

4. Pour the batter into the prepared pan and sprinkle the blueberries evenly over the surface. Press them down gently, then sprinkle evenly with the topping.

5. Bake for about 45 minutes, or until a skewer comes out clean. Cool slightly before cutting into squares. Serve warm, dusted with icing sugar.

VARIATION: When partly cooled, drizzle with Lemon Glaze (see page 255).

Peachy Coffee Cake

The canned peaches in this cake brighten cold winter days. Serve it with morning coffee or for dessert.

For a 23cm square cake:

Topping:

¼ cup sugar

1 Tbsp cinnamon

¼ cup chopped nuts of your choice

Cake:

425g can of sliced peaches

100g butter

2 large eggs

½ cup sour cream

1 tsp vanilla essence

½ tsp almond essence

1 cup sugar

2 cups self-raising flour

1. Preheat the oven to 180°C (170°C fanbake), with the rack just below the middle. Line a 23cm square cake pan with baking paper or spray with non-stick spray.

2. Mix the topping ingredients together and put aside. Drain the peaches, reserving the liquid.

3. Melt the butter in a large pot or microwave-safe bowl. Remove from heat. Add the eggs, sour cream, essences, sugar and 2 tablespoons of the peach juice. Beat thoroughly with a fork or eggbeater, then fold in the sifted flour.

4. Spoon about half the mixture into the prepared cake pan, then sprinkle with half the topping mixture. Spoon on the remaining mixture, then arrange drained peaches on top. Sprinkle the peach layer with the remaining topping.

5. Bake for 30 minutes, or until a skewer in the centre comes out clean. Serve warm.

Chocolate Apple Cake

This versatile cake is just as popular served with a mid-morning coffee, as it is packed in lunch boxes, or served warm for dessert.

For a 23cm cake:

Crunchy Topping:

¼ cup brown sugar

2 Tbsp standard (plain) flour

1 tsp ground cinnamon

25g cold butter, cubed

2 Tbsp chopped walnuts

Alternative Topping:

¼ cup slivered almonds

Cake:

2–3 tangy apples

125g butter, melted

1 large egg

1 cup sugar

1½ cups standard (plain) flour

2 Tbsp cocoa

1 tsp ground cinnamon

1 tsp baking soda

1. Preheat the oven to 190°C (180°C fanbake), with the rack just below the middle. Line a 23cm square or round cake pan with baking paper, a Teflon liner, or coat with non-stick spray.

2. Prepare the topping in a food processor, using the metal chopping blade to chop everything together briefly, or rub the ingredients together by hand. Set aside.

3. Chop unpeeled apples in the (unwashed) food processor (or grate them into a bowl). Add remaining ingredients in the order given, sieving the last four ingredients onto the others, if mixing by hand. Mix briefly, until ingredients are combined. (Always check baking soda for lumps by pressing it with a spoon against the palm of your hand before adding it with other ingredients.) Turn mixture into the prepared cake pan. Sprinkle with topping mixture or with slivered almonds.

4. Bake for about 25–30 minutes or until the centre springs back when pressed. Cool in the pan for a few minutes before turning out. Serve with whipped cream or ice-cream.

NOTE: For best flavour, choose apples which are tangy, not just sweet. Cox's Orange, Braeburn and Granny Smith are favourites for this cake.

Dutch Apple Cake

Alison has been making variations of this delicious pudding for decades. She has always called it Dutch Apple Cake — authentic or not, it is a good, cheap and easily made pudding. It looks attractive too — children will love arranging the pieces of apple for you, and then enjoy watching the batter rise around the apple as it bakes. Don't overcook it, as it tends to dry out and, although it's good served with cream or ice cream, it's particularly good with the lemon sauce.

For 6 servings:

1½ cups standard (plain) flour

2 tsp baking powder

¼ tsp salt

¼ cup sugar

50g butter, cubed

1 large (size 7) egg

½ cup milk

2 large apples (Braeburn are ideal)

½ tsp ground cinnamon

2 Tbsp sugar

Lemon Sauce (see page 27)

1 Preheat the oven to 200°C. Sift the flour, baking powder and salt into a food processor, add the sugar and butter and process until the mixture resembles coarse breadcrumbs. Add the egg and the milk then process to mix. (The dough should be firmer than a 'conventional' cake batter.)

2 Spread the mixture into a baking paper-lined and/or non-stick sprayed 20cm square or 23cm round ovenware dish or cake pan.

3 Peel and core the apples and cut them into quarters then each quarter into four. Poke these pieces, rounded (skin-side) surface up, into the dough as close together as possible. Mix together the cinnamon and sugar and sprinkle this thickly over the surface of the pudding.

4 Bake at 200°C for 25–30 minutes or until cake is firm in the centre.

5 Serve the apple cake hot or warm with cream or ice-cream and Lemon Sauce (see page 27).

Sharon's Banana Cake

Sharon was a charming young English photographer who came to stay with Alison for a few months, some years ago. In her luggage was her handwritten cookbook of favourite recipes. Alison would often come home to a sparkling clean kitchen, the smell of this banana cake made from over-ripe bananas from our fruit dish, and a note saying 'Out photographing, have a good evening'. We hated her leaving!

For 2 loaves or 1 cake:

125g butter

1½ cups sugar

3 large eggs

2½ cups self-raising flour

4 medium-sized ripe bananas, peeled

1 Preheat the oven to 180°C (170°C fanbake), with the rack just below the middle. Line one large (23cm) cake pan, or two smallish (20cm) loaf pans with baking paper, or coat with non-stick spray.

2 Soften (but do not melt) the butter. Use a food processor, electric mixer or hand-beater to combine the butter and sugar. Mix until light coloured and creamy. Beat in the eggs, one at a time, adding a spoonful of the measured flour between each egg so the mixture does not curdle.

3 Mash the bananas with a fork, then fold by hand or briefly process half the bananas and half the flour into the mixture in the food processor or bowl. Repeat with the rest of the bananas and flour. Spoon the mixture into the cake pans. Do not fill more than two-thirds full.

4 Bake for about 45 minutes for two loaves, and slightly longer for one large cake, until a skewer pushed into the middle of the cake comes out clean. Leave to stand for 5 minutes before removing from the pan. Eat within a few days.

Chocolate Banana Cake

This cake is moist, soft and well-flavoured with a light texture. It is delicious served warm, before it cools completely, and is best eaten within a couple of days. We don't think you'll find this difficult!

For two 23 x 10cm loaves or one 21cm ring cake:

200g butter, softened

1½ cups sugar

1 tsp vanilla essence

2 large eggs

1 cup (about 2) ripe, mashed bananas

½ cup buttermilk or ½ cup milk + 1 tsp white wine vinegar

2 cups standard (plain) flour

3 Tbsp cocoa

1 tsp baking powder

¾ tsp baking soda

1 Preheat the oven to 180°C (fanbake 170°C), with the rack just below the middle. Line two 23cm loaf pans or one 21cm ring pan (see Note) with baking paper.

2 In a food processor or mixer, mix the butter, sugar and vanilla essence until fluffy. Add the eggs, one at a time, beating well after each addition. Mix banana with the buttermilk (or the milk and vinegar).

3 If using a food processor, pour the banana mixture over the butter mixture, then measure the dry ingredients on top. Process in brief bursts to mix everything. If mixing any other way, sift the dry ingredients together. Fold half the banana mixture and half the sifted dry ingredients through the butter mixture with a stirrer or rubber scraper. Repeat with remaining ingredients. Stop mixing when everything is combined.

4 Bake for 30–40 minutes, or until a skewer in the middle comes out clean and the centre springs back when pressed. Dust the top with icing sugar before serving or, when cold, ice with Chocolate Icing (see page 252). Do not store the iced cake in a sealed container, or the top may become sticky.

NOTE: As this mixture is a little big for some ring pans, use extra strips of paper (held in place with a little butter or non-stick spray), to make the sides higher, before lining the base.

For a 25cm cake:

½ cup canola or other oil

3 large eggs

3 cups grated carrot

1½ cups standard (plain) flour

1 cup brown sugar

1 tsp baking soda

1½ tsp baking powder

2 tsp ground cinnamon

2 tsp ground mixed spice

½ tsp salt

½ cup raisins, optional

½ cup chopped walnuts, optional

Cream Cheese Icing:

½ cup cold cream cheese

1 tsp vanilla essence

1–1¼ cups icing sugar

Carrot Cake

A good carrot cake is hard to go past. This one is nice enough to enjoy un-iced (try serving it as a dessert, warm from the oven with ice-cream on the side). However, if you're willing to make a little extra effort, the icing definitely adds another dimension.

1 Preheat the oven to 180°C. Non-stick spray a 25cm round springform pan (or you can use 2 x 20cm round tins).

2 Measure the oil into a large bowl, break in the eggs and whisk until well combined. Add the grated carrot and stir until well mixed.

3 Sift in the flour, brown sugar, baking soda, baking powder, spices and salt. Sprinkle with the raisins and nuts (if using), then stir until evenly mixed.

4 Pour the batter into the pan, then bake for 25–30 minutes or until a skewer inserted in the centre comes out clean (smaller cakes will cook more quickly, 20–25 minutes).

5 Remove the cake from the oven, allow to cool in the pan for a few minutes before turning out onto a rack to cool completely.

6 To make the icing, combine the cold cream cheese and vanilla essence in a food processor. Sift in the icing sugar (start with the smaller quantity) and process just enough to mix thoroughly.

Food Processor Apple Cake

For a 20cm cake:

2 medium apples (preferably tart), unpeeled and quartered

1 cup sugar

1 large egg

100g butter, melted

1 cup standard (plain) flour

1 tsp ground cinnamon

1 tsp mixed spice

pinch ground cloves, optional

1 tsp baking soda

½ cup chopped walnuts

There are times when you want something straightforward and no-fuss for weekend snacking or to please everyone for dessert — and hopefully to use for lunches the next day.

1 Preheat the oven to 180°C (170°C fanbake), with the rack just below the middle. Line a 20cm square pan with baking paper or coat with non-stick spray.

2 In a food processor, chop the apples into pieces the size of peas. Quickly, before the apples can brown, add the sugar, egg and melted butter and process just enough to mix them through the apple. Without sifting anything, measure the remaining ingredients on top of the apple mixture. Mix briefly, using the pulse button, then spoon the mixture into the prepared cake pan.

3 Bake for 45–60 minutes, or until the centre springs back when pressed and a skewer comes out clean. Leave for 5–10 minutes before turning out. Dust with icing sugar before serving.

Microwaved Banana Cake

For a 21cm ring cake:

125g butter, melted

1 cup packed brown sugar

1 Tbsp white wine vinegar

2 large eggs

2–3 very ripe bananas, mashed

1 cup wholemeal flour

¾ cup standard (plain) flour

1 tsp baking soda

¼ cup milk

As long as you ice this cake, it won't look as if it was cooked in a microwave. We find it a good standby to have a few cakes which we can microwave when our regular ovens are out of action for any reason. This is one of them!

1 In a fairly large microwavable mixing bowl, melt the butter on High (100% power) for 1½ minutes. Add the brown sugar, vinegar and eggs, then beat with a fork or rotary beater until well mixed.

2 Stir in the mashed bananas. Sprinkle the wholemeal flour over the surface. Add the flour and baking soda, which have been sifted together, and the milk. Fold everything together, using a stirrer or a rubber scraper.

3 Turn into a non-stick sprayed or lightly buttered microwave ring pan. Cover pan lightly with a paper towel.

4 Microwave on Medium-High (70% power) for 10–12 minutes, or until the centre is firm. Leave for about 2 minutes before turning out onto a piece of baking paper.

5 Ice with Cream Cheese Icing (see page 253) and sprinkle with chopped walnuts, if desired.

Elizabeth's Carrot Cake

Alison's granddaughter Elizabeth, when aged 12, liked this cake so much she would get out her food processor and make it by herself! It is always very popular and is certainly a great way to eat carrots! (Use a food processor for grating and mixing if you have one.)

For a 20cm square cake:

2 cups finely grated carrots

2 large eggs

1 cup brown sugar

¾ cup canola (or other) oil

1 tsp vanilla essence

1 tsp grated lemon zest

1¼ cups standard (plain) flour

2 tsp ground cinnamon

2 tsp mixed spice

1 tsp baking soda

1 tsp salt

1. Preheat the oven to 180°C (170°C fanbake), with the rack just below the middle. Line the sides and bottom of a 20cm square cake pan with two strips of baking paper. (Each strip should cover two opposite sides and the bottom.)

2. Grate the carrots finely, using a food processor or hand grater. Set aside. Process or beat the eggs, brown sugar, oil, vanilla essence and lemon zest together until thick and smooth. Add the grated carrot and mix in thoroughly.

3. Measure the flour, cinnamon, mixed spice, baking soda and salt into a sieve over the (food processor) bowl and shake in. Process briefly or fold together, without over-mixing, then pour into the lined pan.

4. Bake for 45 minutes or until the centre feels firm and a skewer pushed deep in the middle comes out clean. (The cake may rise up in the middle, but it is still fine!) Cool in the pan for 15 minutes, then carefully transfer to a rack.

5. When cold, ice with Lemon Icing (see page 253). Let icing set before cutting cake.

Pineapple Carrot Cake

The sharing of favourite recipes is a longstanding New Zealand tradition. Alison praised this cake in a cafeteria in Christchurch, years ago. Next thing she knew, the owner had brought over the recipe, telling Alison it was her most popular cake. She never knew the lady's name, but remembered her kindness whenever she make it!

For a 23cm cake:

1 cup wholemeal flour

1 cup standard (plain) flour

1 cup sugar

2 tsp ground cinnamon

1½ tsp baking soda

1 tsp salt

½ cup chopped walnuts

2 cups (250g) grated carrot

3 large eggs

1 cup canola oil

1 tsp vanilla essence

225g can crushed pineapple

1. Preheat the oven to 160°C (150°C fanbake), with the rack just below the middle. Line the sides and bottom of a 23cm baking pan with baking paper.

2. In a large bowl, mix the first eight ingredients. In another bowl, beat the eggs, oil, vanilla essence and pineapple (including liquid) with a fork.

3. Stir both mixtures together, mixing until just combined. Pour the cake mixture into the prepared pan, levelling the top.

4. Bake for about 45 minutes until the centre feels firm and a skewer inserted into the middle comes out clean. Leave to stand for 5 minutes before removing from the pan.

5. When cold, ice with Cream Cheese Icing (see page 253) and sprinkle with chopped walnuts, if you like.

Light Carrot Cake

Because carrots are inexpensive and available all year round, this cake, which is moist and has a good colour, is a good standby!

For a 23cm round or 20cm square cake:

2 large eggs

½ cup canola or other flavourless oil

1 cup packed brown sugar

2 tsp ground cinnamon

2 cups (250g) grated carrots

½ tsp baking soda

2 cups self-raising flour

1 tsp salt

1 Preheat the oven to 180°C (170°C fanbake), with the rack just below the middle. Line a 23cm round, or 20cm square cake pan with baking paper.

2 In a medium-sized bowl or food processor, beat or mix the eggs, oil and brown sugar until well combined and light in colour. Add the cinnamon and grated carrot and mix in. Add the sifted baking soda, flour and salt, stirring or pulsing until just combined. Pour or spoon the mixture into the prepared cake pan.

3 Bake for 45 minutes or until the centre springs back when pressed, a skewer inserted into the middle comes out clean and the cake shrinks away from the sides of the pan. Leave to stand for 5 minutes in the pan before transferring to a cooling rack.

4 When cold, ice with Lemon Icing (see page 253).

NOTE: If using a food processor, grate the carrots in it before starting to process the cake. (Remove carrot but don't wash the bowl before the cake mixing.)

Rhubarb Cake

For a 23cm square cake:

150g butter, softened

¾ cup sugar

3 large eggs

1½ cups standard (plain) flour

2 tsp baking powder

¼ cup milk

Topping:

500g rhubarb

½ cup sugar

1 Tbsp standard (plain) flour

1 tsp ground cinnamon

icing sugar

If you have a clump of rhubarb at the bottom of your garden, do try this cake! If not, consider planting a young rhubarb plant or two. Rhubarb requires very little care — and provides you with fresh fruit for many months, year after year. All you need to do is pull off its outer stalks and discard its leaves, leaving it to grow more of both. Our friend Hilary makes this cake often because her family enjoys it so much. For a special treat she sometimes replaces some of the rhubarb with a cup of frozen raspberries — the combination is delicious!

1 Preheat the oven to 190°C (180°C fanbake), with the rack just below the middle. Line a 23cm square (preferably loose-bottomed) cake pan with baking paper.

2 In a food processor or bowl, beat the butter and sugar together, then mix in the eggs, one at a time. Stir in the dry ingredients alternately with the milk, until both are combined. Spoon the cake mixture into the prepared baking pan, in 16 spoonfuls, without spreading these out.

3 To make the topping, cut the rhubarb into 5mm lengths. Toss these pieces in the sugar, flour and cinnamon in a bowl, then sprinkle the mixture over the dough so that much of the rhubarb is in the batter rather than on top of it. Sprinkle any remaining sugar mixture over the batter.

4 Bake for 40–45 minutes, until the centre is golden brown, and springs back when pressed. Cool in the pan for 15 minutes, then remove from the pan, and remove the paper at the sides of the cake. Sprinkle the top of the cake evenly with icing sugar, using a fine sieve.

5 Serve warm or reheated, cut in squares or rectangles, preferably with a little cream, yoghurt or vanilla ice-cream.

Rhubarb Coconut Cake

For a 23cm cake:

½ cup canola oil

½ cup plain or fruit-flavoured yoghurt

2 large eggs

1½ cups sugar

½ tsp salt

1 tsp vanilla essence

1½ cups self-raising flour

1½ cups coconut thread

1–1½ cups (150–200g) rhubarb

Topping:

2 Tbsp sugar

½ tsp ground cinnamon

Simon first made this cake several years ago, and was surprised then (given the tartness of rhubarb) by how much his children enjoyed it. Since then, almost every time they see rhubarb, they ask him if he will make it for them! Fortunately it is easy to make so he's happy to indulge them when he can.

1. Preheat the oven to 180°C), with the rack just below the middle. Line the bottom of a 23cm round pan with baking paper then spray the sides with non-stick spray.

2. Measure the oil and yoghurt into a food processor or large bowl. Add the eggs, sugar, salt and vanilla essence. Process (or whisk) until the mixture looks pale and creamy.

3. Measure the flour and coconut thread into the food processor bowl, then process in short bursts (or mix by hand) until everything is just combined.

4. Cut the rhubarb into 5–7mm thick slices.

5. Pour or spoon the batter into the prepared pan, then sprinkle the sliced rhubarb evenly over the top.

6. To make the topping, combine the sugar and cinnamon in a small bowl, then sprinkle over the top of the cake.

7. Bake at 180°C for 50–60 minutes or until a skewer inserted into the centre comes out clean. Remove from the oven and leave to cool in the pan for 5–10 minutes before turning out onto a rack to cool completely.

8. Serve as is or with a little softly whipped cream or yoghurt on the side.

Lemon Yoghurt Cake with Lemon Sauce

This is a great 'go to' recipe! It is very quick and simple to prepare and, most importantly, makes a delicious, moist cake. Because it contains oil rather than butter, it is very easy to mix, either in a food processor or in a bowl. Served warm with the lemon sauce, it makes a great dessert or it is equally enjoyable cooled then dusted with icing sugar and served with tea or coffee, or packed in lunches.

For a 21cm ring cake (8–10 servings):

1½ cups sugar

zest of 2 lemons

2 large eggs

½ cup canola or other light vegetable oil

½ tsp salt

1 cup yoghurt

2–3 Tbsp lemon juice

1½ cups self-raising flour

Lemon Sauce:

zest and juice of 1 lemon

1 Tbsp golden syrup

2 Tbsp sugar

¾ cup hot water

2 Tbsp custard powder

¼ cup cold water

1 tsp butter

1 Preheat the oven to 190°C (or 180°C if using fanbake).

2 If you are using a food processor, put the sugar into the (dry) bowl with the metal chopping blade. Peel all the yellow peel from the lemons, using a potato peeler, and add to the bowl. Run the machine until the lemon peel is finely chopped through the sugar.

3 Add the eggs, oil and salt and process until thick and smooth, then add the yoghurt and lemon juice and blend enough to mix. Use any kind of yoghurt — plain, sweetened or flavoured (if you use flavoured yoghurt, choose a flavour that will blend with the colour and flavour of the lemon). Add the flour and process just enough to combine with the rest of the mixture.

4 To mix by hand, grate all the coloured peel from the lemons into a large bowl. Add the sugar, eggs and oil, then whisk together. Add the salt, yoghurt and lemon juice and mix again. Sift in the flour, then mix gently until just combined.

5 Pour the cake mixture into a non-stick sprayed and floured ring pan (which holds 7 cups of water). Bake for 30 minutes, or until the sides start to shrink, the centre springs back when pressed, and a skewer comes out clean. Leave to cool for about 10 minutes before carefully turning out onto a rack.

6 Serve sprinkled with a little icing sugar, and topped with whipped cream, if you like. Alternatively, serve with the lemon sauce.

7 To make the lemon sauce, combine the lemon zest and juice, golden syrup, sugar and hot water in a jug or bowl. In another small bowl, mix custard powder with cold water, then stir this into the lemon mixture. Microwave for about 2 minutes, stirring once or twice, until the sauce thickens and boils, then stir in butter.

Lemon Sherry Cake

For a 21cm ring cake or a 22 x 11cm loaf pan:

100g butter

½ cup sugar

2 large eggs

zest of 2 lemons

1½ cups self-raising flour

¼ cup sherry

Lemon Glaze:

2–3 Tbsp sugar

2–3 Tbsp sherry

2–3 Tbsp lemon juice

This is an interesting cake — quickly made and delicious served warm for dessert, soon after it is made. It is also very good cold, after the syrup has had plenty of time to soak through the cake. You will find, if you make it frequently, that the thickness of the final batter varies with the warmth of the butter used. If the batter looks thicker than a normal butter cake mixture, add extra sherry to thin it down — it makes the cake taste even better.

1 Preheat the oven to 180°C (170°C fanbake), with the rack just below the middle. Line a 21cm ring pan or a 22 x 11cm loaf pan with baking paper or coat with non-stick spray.

2 Melt the butter in a pot until liquid. Remove from heat and add sugar, eggs and grated lemon zest. Stand the pot in cold water and beat with a rotary or electric beater for about 30 seconds. Add the flour and sherry and beat briefly again with the beater, only until the flour is dampened — do not beat until smooth. If the mixture will not drop from a spoon, add extra sherry until it will. Spread mixture in the prepared ring pan.

3 Bake for 20–30 minutes, or until a skewer in the centre comes out clean and the sides start to shrink away from the pan.

4 While the cake is baking, make the glaze. Mix together the sugar, sherry and lemon juice (the sugar will not dissolve completely). Use the larger quantities for a moister cake.

5 As soon as the cake comes out of the oven, poke it all over the surface with a skewer, and spoon or brush the glaze over it. If you do this before the cake is removed from its pan, it should be left for about 10 minutes before it is turned out.

6 Serve warm or cold with whipped cream or yoghurt.

VARIATIONS: Replace sherry in the glaze with brandy, whisky, orange liqueur or extra lemon juice. Replace the sherry in cake batter with lemon juice diluted with equal quantities of water.

Orange Cake

Make this cake by the conventional creaming method or use a food processor. Serve it with coffee or tea at any time of the day, or dress it up! Produce it warm for dessert, in slices topped with drained mandarin segments and lightly whipped cream flavoured with orange liqueur.

For a 21cm ring cake or several small cakes:

1 large or 2 small oranges

1 cup sugar

125g butter

3 large eggs

1 cup self-raising flour

¾ cup standard (plain) flour

water

1 Tbsp lemon juice

1 Preheat the oven to 180°C (170°C fanbake), with the rack just below the middle. Line a 21cm ring pan with baking paper or coat well with non-stick spray.

2 Thinly peel the orange with a vegetable peeler. Put the peel in a food processor with the sugar and process until finely chopped.

3 Add the softened (but not melted) butter and the eggs, and process until thoroughly mixed. Measure in the flours, then add the juice from the orange/s, made up to ½ cup with water, and the lemon juice. Process briefly, just enough to mix, then spoon into the prepared ring pan.

4 Bake for 35–50 minutes, until a skewer inserted into the middle comes out clean. Leave to stand for 5–10 minutes, then remove from the pan.

5 Transfer to a rack, and dust generously with icing sugar or, when cool, spread with Cream Cheese Icing (see page 253).

Orange, Olive Oil & Polenta Cake

This simple cake makes an interesting dessert and a good conversation starter! The idea of using extra virgin olive oil in a cake may seem a little odd, but it adds to the fruity flavour while the polenta gives an interesting, slightly crunchy texture. It is good served dusted with icing sugar and a little lightly whipped cream or, if you want to give it an extra lift, try it drizzled with a little of the orange syrup as well.

For a 23cm cake (8–10 servings):

zest and juice of 1 orange

½ cup extra virgin olive oil (or other vegetable oil)

2 large (size 7) eggs

½ tsp salt

1 cup sugar

1¼ cups self-raising flour

½ cup instant polenta

Orange Syrup:

zest and juice of 1 orange

½ cup sugar

1 Preheat the oven to 180°C.

2 Zest the orange and place the zest in a large bowl. Squeeze the juice from the orange and make it up to half a cup with a little water if required.

3 Add the orange juice, oil and eggs and salt to the bowl and whisk to combine. Measure in the sugar then whisk again until the mixture looks pale and creamy.

4 Measure in the flour and polenta and stir to combine.

5 Pour the batter into a baking paper-lined and non-stick sprayed 23cm round cake pan and bake for 25–30 minutes. Leave to cool for 5–10 minutes in the pan before removing and cooling completely on a rack.

6 Dust with icing sugar just before serving with a little lightly whipped cream, yogurt or ice-cream. Alternatively, drizzle with the orange syrup.

7 To make the orange syrup, place the orange zest and juice in a small pot or microwave-safe bowl. Stir in the sugar. Heat, stirring occasionally, on the stovetop or in the microwave until the mixture boils and the sugar dissolves. Cool a little before serving alongside the cake.

Apricot & Cardamom Cake

This easy-to-make cake contains a can of apricot purée. Made in a large fluted (bundt) cake pan, it is truly spectacular, but it can also be cooked in a plain ring pan or loaf pans, with extra mixture cooked in muffin tins. (To check size, fill tins with measured water to see how much they hold.)

For a 25cm round bundt cake:

250g butter

1½ cups sugar

445g can apricot pulp

finely grated zest of ½ lemon

2 tsp vanilla essence

2 tsp ground cardamom, optional

2 Tbsp lemon juice

3 large eggs

2 cups standard (plain) flour

1 cup (140g) ground almonds

2 tsp baking powder

1 tsp baking soda

½ cup chopped dried apricots

icing sugar

1 Preheat the oven to 180°C (170°C fanbake), with the rack just below the middle. Spray a 25cm (10 cup capacity) fluted bundt pan (or 2 smaller pans of the same total capacity), thoroughly with non-stick spray, then dust with sieved flour. Bang and turn pan to coat evenly, then tip off excess flour. Do this carefully so the cake will come out cleanly.

2 Cube butter and heat in a large pot or microwave-safe bowl until just melted. Take off the heat and mix the cake in the same container. Add the sugar, apricot pulp (2 cups) and the next five ingredients (including eggs). Beat with a fork or whisk until well combined.

3 Sieve the flour, ground almonds, baking powder and baking soda into the pot or bowl, then tip in any almond left in the sieve. Add the dried apricots then fold everything together. (Mixture is thinner than a normal creamed cake.) Fill cake pan two-thirds full with the mixture, to allow room for rising.

4 Bake for about 45 minutes (or less if using smaller tins) until centre feels firm and a skewer pushed to the bottom comes out clean. Leave to cool for 5 minutes in the pan, then transfer to a cake rack. Dust with icing sugar when cool.

5 Serve with grapes, strawberries, etc. and whipped cream, or apricot yoghurt mixed with whipped cream. Eat fresh, refrigerate for several days, or freeze for a couple of months.

Gingerbread

For a 23cm square cake:

100g butter

½ cup packed brown sugar

½ cup boiling water

½ cup golden syrup

2 large eggs

2 cups standard (plain) flour

1 tsp baking powder

½ tsp baking soda

2 tsp ground ginger

1 tsp ground cinnamon

Gingerbread is a good standby. We like it because it is quick and easy to mix, cooks in 20–30 minutes, and requires ingredients which we keep on hand. Fresh gingerbread can be cut and eaten like cake. Not-so-fresh gingerbread can be buttered. Reheated gingerbread makes excellent hot puddings especially if you use your imagination with toppings. Try whipped cream and chopped nuts, or yoghurt and sliced banana over a layer of raspberry jam. Top it with warm or cold apple purée, hot lemon sauce, or warm, thickened blackcurrants. This gingerbread is light in colour.

1 Preheat the oven to 200°C (190°C fanbake), with the rack just below the middle. Line a 23cm square cake pan with baking paper or coat with non-stick spray.

2 Cut the butter into small squares and put it into a large bowl with the brown sugar. Pour the boiling water over it (to melt the butter) then measure the golden syrup with the same hot wet ½ cup measure.

3 Add the eggs and beat the mixture with a rotary or electric beater until the butter has melted and the egg is mixed in thoroughly. Sift in the dry ingredients and beat briefly to combine. (The flour should be measured lightly into the measuring cup, not compressed.) Pour the fairly thin mixture into the prepared cake pan.

4 Turn the heat down to 180°C (170°C fanbake) as soon as you put the gingerbread in the oven. Bake for 20–25 minutes, until the centre springs back when pressed, and a skewer inserted into the middle comes out clean. Leave to cool for 5 minutes in the pan, then transfer to a cooling rack.

5 Serve in any of the ways suggested above.

Fresh Ginger Cake

This wonderful, spicy cake is best eaten warm, topped with lightly whipped cream.

For a 21cm ring cake:

125g butter

1 tsp grated lemon zest

½ cup hot water

½ cup packed brown sugar

½ cup golden syrup

1 large egg

1 Tbsp finely grated fresh ginger

1¾ cups standard (plain) flour

1 tsp baking soda

1 tsp grated nutmeg

¼ tsp ground cloves

½ tsp ground cinnamon

1 Preheat the oven to 180°C (170°C fanbake), with the rack just below the middle. Line a 21cm ring pan with baking paper.

2 Cut the butter into 16 cubes, put in a pot, add the lemon zest and pour over the hot water. Heat until the butter melts, then remove from the heat. (Do not let the mixture boil.) Cool to bath temperature.

3 Whisk in the brown sugar, golden syrup, egg and ginger, and cool to lukewarm by standing pot in cold water.

4 Add the sifted dry ingredients and mix with a whisk or beater until the mixture is relatively free of lumps, without mixing more than you need to. Pour into the prepared ring pan.

5 Bake for 40 minutes, until a skewer inserted into the middle comes out clean. Cool in the pan for about 5 minutes, then transfer to a serving plate.

6 Dust lightly with icing sugar and serve warm, plain or with fresh fruit and lightly whipped cream.

Three Minute Sponge

This quickly made cake has a texture between that of a sponge and a butter cake. It will keep for several days — if it gets the chance!

For a 20–23cm cake:

1¼ cups sifted standard (plain) flour

½ cup sugar

3 large eggs

¼ cup milk

50g butter, melted

2 tsp baking powder

1 Preheat the oven to 180°C (170°C fanbake), with the rack just below the middle. Line a 20cm square or a 23cm round cake pan (or a 21cm ring pan) with baking paper.

2 Combine the first five ingredients in the small bowl of an electric mixer. Beat at medium speed for 3 minutes. Reduce speed to lowest setting and add the baking powder. Pour into the prepared pan.

3 Bake for 15–20 minutes or until the cake shrinks from the sides of the pan and the centre springs back when pressed. Stand cake in pan on cooling rack until cool enough to handle then turn out onto the rack.

4 When cold, split and fill with Mock Cream (see page 255), if desired, and ice with Lemon or Orange Icing (see page 253).

VARIATION:

Orange Cake: Add the finely grated zest of 1 orange with the baking powder. Save part of the orange juice for Orange Icing (see page 253) and use the remaining juice to replace some of the milk.

Orange Chocolate Cake: Proceed as for orange cake. Add 3–4 Tbsp finely grated chocolate with the baking powder. Grate more chocolate over the Orange Icing (see page 253).

Passionfruit Cake: Add the pulp of 1 passionfruit after the baking powder is added. Ice with Passionfruit Icing (see page 253).

Three Minute Chocolate Sponge

Some people can 'throw together' three minute sponges which are perfect each time, while others have trouble. If you come into the second category, don't worry too much — try another next time!

For a 20cm round or a 21cm ring cake:

75g butter, melted

3 large eggs

¾ cup sugar

2 Tbsp milk

1 cup less 2 Tbsp standard (plain) flour

2 tsp baking powder

2 Tbsp cocoa

1 Preheat the oven to 175°C (165°C fanbake), with the rack just below the middle. Line a 20cm round or a 21cm ring pan with baking paper or coat with non-stick spray.

2 Melt the butter in a bowl big enough to hold the whole mixture. Add the eggs, sugar and milk to the melted butter. Sift in the carefully measured flour, baking powder and cocoa.

3 Using an electric beater, or a good hand beater, beat until the mixture is well mixed, looks creamy and is slightly paler in colour, about 1–3 minutes. Turn into the prepared cake pan.

4 Bake for 20 minutes or until the centre springs back when pressed.

5 Dust with icing sugar or ice when cold with Chocolate Icing (see page 252).

Cornflour Sponge

Take care not to overcook this cake, since the baking time required will vary with the colour, material and size of the baking pan, and different ovens. Remove the sponge from the oven as soon as the centre springs back when pressed, even if it has only cooked for 10 minutes. If you leave the sponge in the pan for a few minutes after cooking, you finish up with a softer texture.

For a 20–23cm cake:

3 large eggs

½ cup caster sugar

¼ cup cornflour, stirred

¼ cup standard (plain) flour

1 tsp baking powder

1 Preheat the oven to 190°C (180°C fanbake), with the rack just below the middle. Line a 20–23cm square cake pan with baking paper.

2 Separate the eggs. Beat the whites in an absolutely clean bowl until they form soft peaks. Add the sugar and beat until the peaks are stiff. Add the yolks and beat just enough to blend them with the whites. Sift the cornflour, flour and baking powder together two or three times for extra lightness. Add to the egg mixture in two or three parts. Fold in carefully but thoroughly after each addition. Turn the mixture into the prepared cake pan.

3 Bake for 15–20 minutes, or just until the centre springs back when lightly pressed. Leave to cool in the pan for 2–3 minutes, then transfer to a cake rack.

4 Top with whipped cream and decorate with halved strawberries, sliced kiwifruit or passionfruit pulp.

Lemon (or Orange) Cream Cake

For a 20cm square or 21cm ring cake:

2 large eggs

1 cup sugar

1 cup cream

finely grated zest of 2 lemons or 1 large orange

1 cup (130g) standard (plain) flour

1 cup (130g) self-raising flour

2 Tbsp lemon or orange juice

This cake is a cross between a sponge cake and a buttercake. Cream replaces butter, so there is no need to bother with softening or creaming, and the ingredients are easy to combine.

1 Preheat the oven to 180°C (170°C fanbake), with the rack just below the middle. Coat either pan thoroughly with non-stick spray, then dust liberally with flour, banging pan to remove excess, or line the bottom and sides of the square pan with two, crossed lengths of baking paper, each 20cm wide.

2 Put the eggs, sugar and cream in a medium-sized bowl and beat until the sugar has dissolved and the mixture has thickened slightly. Grate onto it the zest from the lemons or orange then stir in the sifted flours and the juice until the mixture is thick and smooth. (Make sure that you do not add extra flour to this cake. Stir the flour with a fork to aerate and lighten it before measuring it, then spoon it lightly into the measuring cups without banging cups or compacting the flour.) Pour the mixture into the prepared pan.

3 Bake for 25–40 minutes or until the centre springs back when pressed and a skewer inserted into the middle comes out clean.

4 Dust cake with icing sugar or ice it with Lemon or Orange Icing (see page 253). Eat cake within two or three days.

Yoghurt Cake

For two 23 x 10cm loaves:

75g butter, melted

1 cup sugar

2 large eggs

1 tsp vanilla essence

1½ cups standard (plain) flour

1 tsp baking soda

¼ tsp salt

300g plain yoghurt

Our grandmothers knew that a pound cake was a good basic cake to serve plain, or with sweetened fruit for dessert. Few young cooks today make pound cakes like this, because they consider them to be rather heavy and rich. Here is a much lighter version of a plain cake that is delicious served alone or with berries. We like to make the quantity given below, making two loaves. Use one straight away, and freeze the other.

1 Preheat the oven to 180°C (170°C fanbake), with the rack just below the middle. Line two 23 x 10cm loaf pans with baking paper.

2 Melt butter just until it is liquid but not hot. Measure the sugar, eggs and vanilla essence into a food processor, add the melted butter and process to mix thoroughly.

3 Sift in the flour, baking soda and salt, add the yoghurt, and process very briefly, until just combined. The mixture will be airy and puffy. Do not beat it or you will lose some of its lightness. Handle it as little, and as gently, as possible. Turn mixture into the prepared loaf pans. Or, to mix without a food processor, use a beater to combine the first four ingredients, then fold in the sifted dry ingredients and the yoghurt, taking care not to over-mix.

4 Bake for 30 minutes, or until the centre springs back when lightly pressed, and a skewer comes out clean.

5 This cake is nicest eaten the same day it is baked (or thawed), with the top dusted with icing sugar. Try slices topped with fresh berries, with extra yoghurt or lightly whipped cream.

Pavlova

That the pavlova should score so highly on a list of favourite New Zealand desserts was hardly a surprise! Everybody's grandmother probably had her own secret recipe, but here's our favourite version — it's a simplified version where everything goes into the mixer at once, but still works very well. (This isn't an enormous mixture, but you can double it if you want.)

For 1 large pavlova:

1 cup caster sugar

2 tsp cornflour

¼ tsp salt

1 tsp wine vinegar

½ tsp vanilla

½ cup (3–4) egg whites

1. Preheat the oven to 100°C.

2. Using standard, level cups and spoons for everything, measure the caster sugar, cornflour and salt into a clean, dry bowl. (Any traces of fat in the bowl or on the beater will stop eggs beating up.) Stir together. Add the vinegar and vanilla, then measure and add the egg whites, taking care to get absolutely no yolk in the mixture.

3. Beat with an electric mixer at high speed for about 15 minutes, until a thick, non-gritty meringue forms. When you lift out the mixer blades, the peaks should stand up stiffly, or just bend over at their tips.

4. Cover a baking sheet with baking paper, then pile the mixture onto this into a round shape about 25cm across.

5. Bake for 60 minutes, then turn off the oven and leave for 30 minutes longer. Take out of oven after this time.

6. Leave unwrapped, in a cool place, up to two days.

7. To serve, top with whipped cream. Decorate traditionally with strawberries, kiwifruit or passionfruit or use other fruit. Drizzle chocolate topping over strawberries if desired.

VARIATIONS: For a larger, taller pav use double quantities. Pile on baking paper or bake in a paper-lined round 20 or 23cm pan. Bake for 1¼ hours and leave in oven for 15 minutes longer.

NOTE: Because ovens vary, cooking times may need slight changes. Pavlovas with space below the crust and compacted middles have been cooked for too long. If centres are not completely set, cook a little longer next time. Fan bake for the first 10 minutes if you have this option. If fan baking for the whole time, lower temperature by about 10°C.

Strawberry Pavlova Roll

Don't despair if you can't make a pavlova! This pavlova roll is not only quicker (cooking in 10 minutes) but looks really interesting and impressive! You can eat this roll half an hour after it goes into the oven, if necessary, although it is really best to allow an hour, in case it takes longer to cool than you think it will. You need to wait until it is cool before rolling it up, but this usually takes only 10–20 minutes.

For about 6 servings:

4 large egg whites

⅛ tsp salt

½ cup caster sugar

½ tsp vanilla essence

250–300 ml cream

fresh strawberries

❶ Preheat the oven to 180°C (or 170°C fanbake) with the rack just below the middle. Line a sponge roll pan (about 33 x 23cm) with baking paper.

❷ Separate the eggs, putting the whites into the (clean and grease-free) bowl of an electric beater. Add the salt, sugar and vanilla essence and beat everything together at high speed until the mixture is stiff, and the peaks stand upright, with only a small tip turning over when the beater is lifted from them. Spread the mixture evenly over the lined sponge roll pan.

❸ Bake for about 10 minutes, until the surface is a light golden brown, the centre springs back when pressed with an oiled finger, and the mixture has puffed up. Do not overcook, since overcooked rolls shrink excessively. Take from the oven, and turn upside down onto a sheet of baking paper, which has been wiped over very lightly with soft butter then sprinkled with caster sugar. Lift away the paper which was on the bottom of the baking pan.

❹ While the meringue cools, whip the chilled cream. When roll is cold, spread the upper surface (the bottom of the cake) with half the stiffly whipped, cold cream. Cover the surface of the cream with sliced strawberries, if desired, and then roll up using the paper under the cake to help you. It is usual to roll the meringue up, starting from a short side, forming a short, fat roll, but you can make a long thin roll if this suits you better.

❺ Place the roll join down on a rectangular plate or board. Put the remaining whipped cream in a forcing bag (or plastic bag with the corner cut out) and pipe it decoratively along the top of the roll, then decorate with strawberries. To serve, cut slices with a thin, sharp or serrated knife.

NOTE: This mixture should not be overcooked. Since ovens vary, be prepared to experiment, using shorter times if first cooked mixture shrank excessively. Replace the strawberries with passionfruit pulp or other flavourings, if desired.

Strawberry & Coconut Cake

For a 23cm round cake (8–10 servings):

400–500g (2 regular punnets) strawberries, hulled and sliced

150g butter, softened

¾ cup lightly packed brown sugar

2 large (size 7) eggs

1 tsp vanilla essence

1 tsp ground cinnamon

1½ cups self-raising flour (or 1½ cups plain flour + 3 tsp baking powder)

1 cup (100g) fine desiccated coconut

½ cup milk

We came up with this cake trying to think of something a little different to make with strawberries. While perfect fresh berries are great 'as is' or halved and served with a little cream, you can sometimes end up with a punnet of two that are slightly beyond their best for eating. These are perfect for a cake like this.

1 Preheat the oven to 180°C (or 160°C if using fanbake). Spray a 23cm round cake pan with non-stick spray and line with baking paper.

2 Put the butter and brown sugar in a food processor and process until soft and creamy. Add the eggs, vanilla essence and cinnamon and process just enough to mix.

3 Measure in the self-raising flour (or flour and baking powder) and the coconut. Pour the milk over the mixture, then pulse briefly or stir by hand to combine.

4 Spoon about two-thirds of the batter mixture into the prepared pan and spread evenly. Scatter the sliced strawberries over this, then drop spoonfuls of the remaining batter over the berries.

5 Place the cake in the middle of the oven and bake for 40–50 minutes or until a skewer inserted into the middle comes out clean.

6 Leave to cool in the pan for a few minutes before lifting out and leaving to cool to about room temperature before dusting with icing sugar.

7 Serve with softly whipped cream or ice-cream. Best eaten within a day or two of baking.

100g butter

½ cup sugar

2 large egg yolks

¼ tsp almond essence

½ tsp vanilla essence

1 cup standard (plain) flour

1 tsp baking powder

2 Tbsp desiccated coconut

¼–½ cup glacé cherries

¼ cup milk

Meringue topping:

2 large egg whites

5 Tbsp sugar

¼ tsp almond essence

1 tsp cornflour

1 cup desiccated coconut

¼–½ cup glacé cherries

NOTE: To cut this cake neatly, use a sharp serrated knife. If the meringue sticks or breaks, dip the knife in hot water first.

Coconut Cherry Meringue Cake

This is a really popular cake — everybody comes back for another piece! The base is mixed first, then the meringue topping is made and spread over the base before it is baked.

1 Preheat the oven to 160°C (150°C fanbake), with the rack just below the middle. Line a 21cm ring pan with baking paper. (To avoid turning the cooked cake upside-down onto its meringue topping, put four long strips of baking paper crosswise into the empty ring pan under the baking paper to use as 'slings' to lift the cooked cake out.)

2 Beat the softened (but not melted) butter with the sugar in a food processor or bowl, until light coloured. Separate the eggs and put the whites aside in a clean bowl big enough to beat them in later.

3 Add the yolks, almond essence and vanilla essence to the butter mixture and beat again.

4 Measure the flour, baking powder, coconut and cherries (halved, if desired) into another container and toss with a fork. Tip these ingredients and the milk onto the creamed mixture, and fold in or process briefly, until mixed. Drop this mixture in blobs into the prepared ring pan and spread as evenly as possible.

5 For the topping, use a clean beater to beat the egg whites until foamy. Add the sugar and beat until the peaks stand up without turning over when the beater is removed. Add the essence, cornflour and coconut, and beat briefly or fold in to mix. Spread over the uncooked base, and decorate with the cherries cut in pieces or left whole.

6 Bake for 45–55 minutes, until the top is a light golden brown, and the sides start to shrink from the pan. Leave to stand for 10 minutes, then remove carefully from the pan.

7 When cold, store on a flat plate in a lightly covered container, at room temperature, for up to a few days. Refrigerate, tightly covered, for longer storage.

Kirsten's Chocolate Cake

Alison's daughter Kirsten is well known for the hundreds of perfect cakes she has made from this recipe over the years.

For a 23cm round cake:

125g butter

½ cup golden syrup

2 large eggs

1½ cups milk

1 cup sugar

2 cups standard (plain) flour

¼ cup cocoa powder

2 tsp baking powder

2 tsp baking soda

1 Preheat the oven to 180°C (170°C fanbake), with the rack just below the middle. Line the bottom of a 23cm round cake pan (see note below) with baking paper and non-stick spray its sides.

2 Melt the butter in a pot, then remove from the heat. Dip a measuring cup in hot water and use this to measure the syrup. Add the syrup to the butter and set aside. Put eggs, milk and sugar in a food processor or large bowl. Process or whisk until well mixed.

3 Measure the flour, cocoa, baking powder and baking soda into a sieve over the food processor or bowl, and shake in. Process in very short bursts, or stir until just mixed, then add the cooled melted butter and syrup. Mix or process briefly again. (Do not over-mix!) Pour mixture into the pan.

4 Bake for 40 minutes or until the centre feels firm and a skewer inserted into the middle comes out clean. Cool on rack.

5 If you like, cut cake in half and fill with whipped cream. Dust with icing sugar, or ice with Chocolate Icing or Chocolate Cream Icing (see page 252).

NOTE: If you prefer, bake this cake in a rectangular 23 x 33cm pan or two 20cm round tins.

Caramel Chocolate Marble Cake

For a 21cm ring cake:

125g butter

¾ cup sugar

2 rounded household dessertspoons golden syrup

2 large eggs

1 tsp vanilla essence

2 cups standard (plain) flour

½ tsp baking soda

2 tsp baking powder

½ cup milk

2 Tbsp cocoa

2 Tbsp extra milk

Caramel icing:

½ cup packed brown sugar

2 Tbsp milk

1 Tbsp butter

¼ tsp vanilla essence

about 1 cup icing sugar

This quick stir-in-a-pot mixture was a standby of mine when Kirsten was a baby. Attractive because of its 'marbling' yet straightforward and quite economical, it is best eaten within two days. Its icing is optional but yummy.

1 Preheat the oven to 180°C (170°C fanbake) with the rack just below the middle. Line a 21cm ring pan with baking paper or non-stick spray.

2 Warm the butter, sugar and golden syrup gently in a pot until the sugar dissolves. Do not boil. Stand the pot in cold water until lukewarm, then beat in the eggs and vanilla essence with a fork. Sift in the dry ingredients, pour in the first measure of milk, and stir with a stirrer/scraper to mix.

3 Spoon half the mixture into the prepared ring pan. Sift the cocoa onto the remaining mixture, pour on the extra milk, then stir to mix. Drop this in spoonfuls on top of the mixture in the pan. Leave the chocolate mixture in 'blobs' or run a knife through it to mix it slightly.

4 Bake for 30 minutes or until a skewer inserted in the middle comes out clean.

5 To make the icing, warm together the sugar, milk and butter until sugar dissolves. Let mixture boil for 30 seconds. Cool to lukewarm then stir in vanilla essence and icing sugar. Add extra icing sugar or hot water to mix to an icing consistency.

6 Pour or drizzle the icing over the cold cake while icing is still warm. Top with chopped walnuts, if you like.

Five Minute Chocolate Mug Cake

For 2 small cakes:

¼ cup sugar

1 large egg

2 Tbsp canola or other light oil

2 Tbsp cocoa powder

¼ cup self-raising flour

¼ cup milk

¼ tsp vanilla essence

pinch of salt

Yes, that is chocolate mug, not mud, cake. This is our version of a recipe that we were emailed, where the mixture was stirred together, then baked in a coffee mug. We've moved away from this a little, but it's still amazing how you can get such a good result in a short space of time. Chocolate cake is only five minutes away any time of day!

❶ Measure the sugar into a small bowl, add the egg and oil and whisk until pale and creamy. Add the remaining ingredients and stir just enough to combine.

❷ Non-stick spray two microwave-safe teacups or two 250ml ramekins or teacups. Divide the mixture evenly between the prepared containers, then place them in the microwave.

❸ Cover with a square of baking paper or a paper towel, then cook on High (100% power) for 2½–3 minutes or until the centre of the cakes is firm. Remove the cakes from the microwave, then tip them out of the cups/ramekins. Cool on a rack for a few minutes or enjoy immediately.

❹ Some yoghurt, whipped cream or ice-cream make the perfect accompaniment.

Chocolate Roll

For a 20 x 30cm sponge roll pan:

3 large eggs, at room temperature

½ cup sugar

½ cup standard (plain) flour

2 Tbsp cocoa

1 tsp baking powder

1 Tbsp boiling water

Light and tender, this is quickly made, looks good and tastes delicious! Fill it with raspberry jam or berries and whipped cream.

❶ Preheat the oven to 230°C (220°C fanbake), with the rack just below the middle. Line a 20 x 30cm sponge roll pan with baking paper.

❷ Beat the eggs and sugar together until mixture is very thick and creamy. Measure flour, cocoa and baking powder into a sieve over the egg mixture, and gently shake them through it. Carefully fold them into the egg mixture, then add and fold in the boiling water. Pour and spread the mixture evenly into the prepared sponge roll pan.

❸ Bake for 8–10 minutes, taking it out as soon as the centre of the sponge springs back when pressed lightly with a finger.

❹ Working quickly, loosen the sponge from the sides of the pan, and turn it out on to a clean piece of fine cotton (muslin or a soft, old tea towel) that has been wet, then wrung out as dry as possible. Lift the baking paper off the sponge, and roll up the sponge and tea towel together, lightly but firmly. (Roll either way, depending whether you want a short thick or a long thin roll.)

❺ Stand the roll, still in towel, on a rack until cold, then unroll carefully. Spread the surface with raspberry jam and fresh whipped cream (or cream and berries) and roll up again (without the tea towel!) Sprinkle with icing sugar just before serving. (This cake is best eaten the day it is made, although slightly soft leftovers taste good the next day.)

Mix-in-a-minute Dark Chocolate Cake

Here is another easy, dark chocolate cake. It keeps for a few days, and you can use it in different ways, in one large or two smaller cake pans. Don't worry that the mixture seems rather runny, it 'comes right' as it cooks!

For a 30 x 20cm cake:

1½ cups sugar

¾ cup cocoa

1 tsp salt

1½ tsp baking soda

¼ cup + 2 Tbsp canola or other oil

1½ cups water

2 large eggs

1½ tsp vanilla essence

2 cups standard (plain) flour

❶ Preheat the oven to 180°C (170°C fanbake), with the rack just below the middle. Line a 30 x 20 cm baking pan or small roasting pan with baking paper or coat with non-stick spray.

❷ Put sugar, cocoa, salt and baking soda in a food processor, and pulse to mix. Add oil, water, eggs and vanilla essence to the dry mixture and process for about 20 seconds to combine well. Add flour and pulse briefly about 5 times again until just smooth. Pour the fairly thin mixture into the prepared baking pan.

❸ Bake for about 25 minutes, until a skewer inserted into the centre of the cake comes out clean. Cool cake in pan on a rack, then turn out or cut straight from pan.

❹ Ice as desired (see pages 252–255) or top pieces with whipped cream and fruit or berries.

Nice and Easy Chocolate Cake

Yet another quick, dark chocolate cake, which you mix with a fork! Decorate it with strawberries and cream for a special dessert.

For a 23cm cake:

1 large egg

1 cup sugar

¾ cup water

½ cup canola or other oil

1 Tbsp wine vinegar

1 tsp vanilla essence

1½ cups self-raising flour

3 Tbsp cocoa

½ tsp baking soda

½ tsp salt

1 Preheat the oven to 190°C (180°C fanbake), with the rack just below the middle. Line a 23cm square pan with baking paper or coat with non-stick spray.

2 Place egg, sugar, water, oil, vinegar and essence in a mixing bowl and stir thoroughly with a fork.

3 Shake remaining ingredients through a sieve, then stir until combined, using the fork or a stirrer/scraper. (Do not over-mix.) Pour into the prepared pan.

4 Bake for 30–40 minutes, until the centre springs back when pressed.

5 Serve topped with whipped cream and berries, sliced kiwifruit, etc. Or halve then sandwich the two pieces together with raspberry jam, and sprinkle with icing sugar.

Chocolate Stout Cake

While this cake is simple to make, it probably isn't really an 'everyday' chocolate cake, but rather it makes a large, moist and dark cake, that's perfect for a dinner party dessert or other special occasion.

For 10–12 servings:

125g butter

175g (1 cup) dark chocolate melts

½ cup plain unsweetened yoghurt

2 large eggs

330ml dark beer or stout

2 tsp vanilla essence

½ cup cocoa powder

1½ cups sugar

1½ tsp baking soda

½ tsp salt

2 cups flour

1 Preheat the oven to 180°C. Coat a 25cm spring-form pan with non-stick spray and line with baking paper.

2 Measure the butter and chocolate into a small pot and heat gently until melted. Whisk the yoghurt and eggs together in a large bowl, then add the stout, vanilla essence and the chocolate-butter mixture. Stir to combine.

3 Sift the cocoa powder, sugar, baking soda, salt and flour into the liquids, then stir until evenly mixed. Pour into prepared pan and bake for 45–60 minutes or until a skewer comes out clean.

4 Cool cake on a rack, then ice with Chocolate Sour Cream Icing (page 253).

5 Serve as is or with yoghurt or lightly whipped cream.

Chocolate Zucchini Cake

This unusual combination of ingredients makes a really delicious, large, moist, family cake which you can serve with pride. This recipe is especially useful for zucchini growers!

For a 25cm square cake:

125g butter, softened

1 cup brown sugar

¾ cup white sugar

3 large eggs

2½ cups standard (plain) flour

1 tsp vanilla

½ cup yoghurt, plain or flavoured

¼ cup cocoa

2 tsp baking soda

1 tsp cinnamon

½ tsp mixed spice

½ tsp salt

3 cups (350g) grated zucchini

½–1 cup chocolate chips or pieces

① Heat oven to 170°C (without fanbake), with rack just below the middle. Line a 25cm square cake pan with two strips of baking paper, so the bottom and all sides are covered.

② Beat the butter with the sugars in a food processor or with an electric beater until light and creamy. Add the eggs one at a time, adding a little of the measured flour with each egg to prevent the mixture curdling, and beating well after each addition. Add the vanilla and yoghurt and mix well.

③ Put aside half a cup of the measured flour and sift the rest with the other dry ingredients. Mix the grated zucchini into the egg mixture. Fold the sifted dry ingredients into the egg mixture without overmixing. The final mixture should be just wet enough to pour into the pan. If it seems too runny, fold in part or all of the reserved half cup of flour. (A cake with less flour is softer.)

④ Turn into the prepared baking pan. Sprinkle the surface with the chocolate chips. Bake for 30–45 minutes, or until the centre feels firm and a skewer comes out clean. Cut when cold. Store in the refrigerator up to 3 days.

Chocolate Orange Liqueur Cake

This wonderful cake owes its outstanding texture to a high proportion of dark chocolate and ground almonds. A 20cm cake will make 8–10 servings. You can freeze the second cake, or halve the recipe, if you like.

For one 23cm or two 20cm round cakes:

250g dark cooking chocolate

¼ cup orange liqueur

zest of 1 orange

1 cup caster sugar

250g butter, softened

6 large eggs, separated

¼ tsp citric acid

1 tsp water

1 cup ground almonds

¾ cup standard (plain) flour

Chocolate Orange Icing:

125g dark cooking chocolate

100g butter

1–2 Tbsp orange liqueur

❶ Break the chocolate into even-sized pieces. Melt it with the liqueur in a bowl over a pot of hot water, stirring until well combined. Set aside to cool.

❷ Preheat the oven to 180°C (170°C fanbake), with the rack just below the middle. Line a 23cm round cake pan (or 2 x 20cm round pans) with baking paper.

❸ Put the finely grated orange zest and three-quarters of the caster sugar in a food processor. Add the butter, process until light and fluffy, then beat in the egg yolks and the citric acid dissolved in the water. Add the cooled chocolate mixture, then the ground almonds and flour, and mix just enough to blend.

❹ In another bowl, beat the egg whites until they form soft peaks. Add the remaining caster sugar and beat until mixture forms peaks that turn over when you lift the beater. Do not over-beat. Carefully fold the chocolate mixture through the beaten egg whites. Pour the mixture into the cake pan/s.

❺ Bake for about 45 minutes for a 23cm cake and for about 30–40 minutes for the 20cm cakes, until the centre feels as firm as the edges, and a skewer pushed into the middle of the cake comes out clean. Leave for 10 minutes before turning out onto a wire rack.

❻ To make the icing, combine all ingredients and heat in a bowl over hot water until melted, then mix well. Cool before spreading on cake. Decorate as desired.

Orange 'Eating' Cake

This is the type of cake Alison's father called a good 'eating' cake. He meant that it was not a cake which was to be kept for special occasions, but could be snacked on when hunger pangs struck!

For a 20cm square or 23cm round cake:

1 orange or 2 tangelos

125g butter, softened

1 cup sugar

2 large eggs

1 tsp baking soda

½ cup water

1 tsp vanilla essence

2 cups standard (plain) flour

1 cup sultanas

1 Preheat the oven to 150°C (140°C fanbake), with the rack just below the middle. Line a 20cm square or a 23cm round cake pan with baking paper.

2 Halve the orange or tangelos and remove the seeds. Cut each half into quarters, remove and discard the central pith, then chop the rest finely, skin and all, using the metal chopping blade of a food processor. Tip the pulped fruit into another container.

3 Without washing the bowl or blade, process the butter, sugar and eggs, for about 20 seconds. Add to the bowl the baking soda dissolved in the water, the essence, flour and sultanas. Pulse in brief bursts, until everything is just combined. Add the pulped fruit and pulse until mixed in. Turn mixture into the prepared cake pan.

4 Bake for 1–1¼ hours, or until the cake springs back when pressed lightly in the centre, and a skewer comes out clean. Leave to stand for about 20 minutes before turning out of the pan and cooling completely on a cooling rack.

5 Store in a plastic bag in the refrigerator, or at room temperature in a container with a loose-fitting lid.

Aunt Lucy's Mistake

Aunt Lucy, the much-loved aunt of Alison's friend, Anne Gilkison, once muddled up a recipe in an absent-minded moment. The resulting cake, better than the original, was given the above name.

For a 20–23cm cake:

1 cup sugar

3 large eggs

200g butter, softened

¼ cup cocoa

¼ cup boiling water

1½ cups standard (plain) flour

2 tsp baking powder

1 cup desiccated coconut

½ cup milk

1 Preheat the oven to 180°C (170°C fanbake), with the rack just below the middle. Line a 20–23cm cake pan with baking paper or coat with non-stick spray.

2 Measure the sugar and eggs into a food processor and process until thick and creamy. Gradually add the softened (but not melted) butter and mix until well combined.

3 Measure the cocoa into a cup or small bowl, add the boiling water and stir until mixed. Put in the food processor and, without mixing, add the flour and baking powder. Process briefly to mix in the cocoa and flour, but do not over-mix. Add the coconut and milk and process again until just combined.

4 If you use an electric mixer, use the usual creaming method for the butter, sugar and eggs, beat in the cocoa mixture before you fold in the sifted flour and baking powder, then stir in the coconut and milk at the end.

5 Pour the cake mixture into the prepared cake pan. Bake for about 30 minutes, depending on the pan size, until the cake starts to shrink at the edge and springs back when pressed in the middle.

6 Ice with Chocolate Icing (see page 252).

'War' Cake

For a 30cm square cake:

125g butter

1 cup sugar

2 large eggs

1 cup golden syrup

1 cup marmalade

2 tsp instant coffee

1 cup water

600–800g sultanas (or a mixture of currants and sultanas)

2 tsp ground cinnamon

2 tsp mixed spice

2 tsp baking powder

about 5 cups standard (plain) flour

Alison loved the large cakes her mother made in a roasting pan, soon after the Second World War. They always contained some dried fruit and some marmalade, and went down really well in school lunches. She left it too late to get her mother's recipe, but this recipe, sent to Alison from Hokitika, where her mother's family once lived, has many similarities.

1 Preheat the oven to140°C (130°C fanbake), with the rack just below the middle. Line a 30cm square cake pan (or a roasting pan about 27 x 33cm) with baking paper.

2 Before you start mixing, look at the marmalade you intend to use. If you think it will not mix into the other ingredients easily, mix it with the instant coffee and a cup of boiling water at this stage. You might like to do this in a food processor, so you chop the peel finely, too.

3 In a large bowl, cream the butter and sugar, add the eggs and beat until light. Mix into this the golden syrup, the cool coffee, marmalade and water mixture, and the dried fruit.

4 Sift the spices and baking powder with 2 cups of flour, and stir them into the cake mixture. Fold in another 2 cups of well-stirred flour, then add as much more flour as you need to make a fairly wet cake batter. About 1 extra cup is usually needed.

5 Pour the mixture into the prepared pan. Bake for about 1½ hours, or until the centre of the cake feels firm, and a skewer inserted into the middle comes out clean. Overcooking will dry out the cake, so take care. Leave it to stand overnight, before cutting, for the flavour to develop.

6 Store the cake in the refrigerator in a plastic bag or airtight container. Plan to eat the whole cake within two or three weeks, since it is not rich enough to keep for long.

Boiled Pineapple Fruit Cake

For a 20cm round or square cake:

100g butter

1 cup sugar

450g can crushed pineapple

300g (2 cups) sultanas

200g (1½ cups) mixed fruit

1 tsp ground cinnamon

1 tsp mixed spice

½ tsp baking soda

grated zest and juice of 1 tangelo or ½ an orange

2 large eggs

1 cup self-raising flour

1 cup standard or high-grade flour

This very popular, two-egg cake is intended for eating soon after it is made, and finished within three weeks or so. Any boiled cake mixture requires care and attention to the recipe, however, since boiling not long enough, or adding the flour to a hot or warm mixture can result in a soggy or gluey cake. With reasonable care, this makes a lovely moist cake with a great flavour. Alison gave the recipe to her mother who, over the years, made dozens of these cakes as gifts for delighted friends.

1 Preheat the oven to 160°C (150°C fanbake), with the rack just below the middle. Line a 20cm round or square cake pan with baking paper.

2 Put everything except the eggs and flours in a 23cm saucepan. Bring to the boil, then boil gently, uncovered, stirring often, for 15 minutes. The mixture must boil fast enough to evaporate some of the juice, but not fast enough to burn the fruit. (If you are worried about this, measure the mixture as soon as it comes to the boil, then again at the end. It should lose half a cup of liquid.)

3 Stand the pot in a sink of cold water and leave until it is absolutely cold. (If you are impatient, your cake will be gluey!)

4 Beat the eggs until light coloured and thick then stir them thoroughly into the cold mixture. Next, sift or sieve the flours into the mixture and stir to combine without over-mixing. If the mixture looks too wet, add up to a ¼ cup more flour. Turn into the prepared cake pan.

5 Bake for 30 minutes, then turn oven down to 150°C (140°C fanbake). Bake for a further 1–1½ hours, until a skewer inserted in the middle comes out clean and the centre is springy when pressed. Remove from pan as soon as cake is cool enough to handle. Finish cooling on a rack.

6 Store, loosely covered, at room temperature or in a plastic bag in the refrigerator. (The cake may go mouldy if plastic-wrapped at room temperature.)

Boiled Fruit Loaf

This delicious loaf is really worth trying. It is very easy to make, and it keeps really well (it will last for one week or more stored in an airtight container or plastic bag kept in a cool place).

For about a 10 x 23cm loaf:

1 cup water

¾ cup sugar

1 cup sultanas or dried fruit

25g (2 Tbsp) butter

1 tsp ground cinnamon

1 tsp mixed spice

½ tsp ground cloves

½ tsp salt

1½ cups standard (plain) flour

1 tsp baking powder

½ tsp baking soda

① Turn the oven to 180°C (170°C fanbake).

② Put the first eight ingredients into a medium-sized pot. Bring to the boil, stirring occasionally, then simmer gently, uncovered, for 5 minutes. Stand the pot in a sink of cold water and cool to room temperature, stirring now and then. (This step is important!)

③ While you wait, sift or thoroughly stir the remaining ingredients together, and line the long sides and the bottom of a loaf pan with a strip of baking paper.

④ When the mixture in the pot is cold, carefully stir in the mixed ingredients. (Mix only enough to blend, since over-mixing causes the mixture to toughen and rise to a peak in the middle during cooking.)

⑤ Bake for 45–60 minutes, or until centre springs back when pressed and a skewer Inserted in the centre comes out clean.

⑥ If you can, leave it for 24 hours before cutting, so the loaf is firmer and easier to cut in thin slices. You may not, however, consider this essential!

Four-egg Easy Fruit Cake

This easily mixed cake is beautifully flavoured with fruit and nuts — no essences or spices are needed.

For a 23cm cake:

600g (4 cups) mixed fruit (see Note)

½ cup orange juice

200g butter, cut into 1cm cubes

1 cup brown or white sugar

about 1 cup walnuts or other nuts

4 large eggs

1 cup self-raising flour

1 cup wholemeal or standard (plain) flour

① Preheat the oven to 150°C (140°C fanbake) with the rack just below the middle. Line a square 23cm cake pan with two strips of baking paper so the base and sides are covered.

② Simmer the dried fruit in the orange juice in a large covered pot for about 5 minutes, stirring every now and then, until it soaks up all the juice. Lift off the heat and stir in the cubed butter and the sugar. (Pack brown sugar firmly into the cup.) Stir gently until butter melts and sugar loses its graininess, then stand pot in cold water to cool, stirring occasionally. Chop the nuts roughly (if they are in large pieces) and stir them into the cooling mixture in the pot.

③ When cooled to room temperature, add the eggs, beating them in with a fork or a stirrer. When thoroughly mixed, sprinkle the flours over the mixture in the pot and stir everything together. Pour mixture into the prepared cake pan and level the top.

④ Bake for 60–75 minutes, or until the centre feels firm and springs back when pressed, and a skewer inserted into the middle (to the bottom) comes out clean. Cool in pan.

⑤ For best flavour, leave two days before cutting. Top with bought or home-made icings, if desired (see page 254).

NOTE: Buy mixed fruit (fruit cake mix) or use a mixture of sultanas, currants and raisins.

Peter's Five-egg Birthday Cake

This is a lovely, dark, moist, fruity cake which Alison invented for her husband. Leave out any of the spices which you don't have — the flavour will still be great!

For a 23cm square or round cake:

500g each of sultanas, raisins, currants

½ cup sherry

zests of 1 lemon and 1 orange

1½ cups packed brown sugar

250g butter, softened

1 Tbsp treacle

5 large eggs

2 cups standard or high-grade flour

½ tsp each ground allspice, cardamom, cinnamon, cloves, coriander and nutmeg

1. One to two days before cake is to be made, put the (good-quality) dried fruits into a plastic bag with the sherry. Turn the bag every now and then and leave the bag in a warm place, until the fruit has absorbed all the sherry. (To speed up the soaking time, microwave the bag of fruit etc., until the contents are hot, then leave to cool, turning the bag over occasionally.)

2. When ready to make and bake your cake, preheat the oven to 150°C (140°C fanbake) with the rack just below the middle. Line the sides and bottom of a 23cm square or round cake pan with baking paper.

3. Remove the zest from the lemon and orange, using a microplane grater if you have one, and mix the zest with the sugar. (Or remove peel with a potato peeler and food process it with the sugar until finely chopped.) Add the butter, process until soft and fluffy, then add the treacle and mix again. Add eggs, one at a time, with a tablespoon of the measured flour between each.

4. In a very large bowl, mix the rest of the flour and the spices with the fruit. Tip the creamed mixture into the floured fruit and mix by hand, until soft enough to drop from your hand. If the mixture is dryer than this, add up to ¼ cup of extra sherry, orange juice or spirits. Tip the mixture into the prepared cake pan. Decorate top with almonds or cherries, if desired.

5. Bake for 1 hour, then lower the temperature to 140°C and bake for about 3 hours, until a skewer inserted into the centre comes out clean. Dribble or brush about ¼ cup of rum or brandy over the cake while it is hot, if you like. Leave an hour before removing from the pan.

Small Cakes

Although small cakes are delicious and very popular, if you are baking for the first time, I hope that you will start with biscuits and the more straightforward cakes, and gain some experience before you start on some of these small cakes! Having said this, there are really only four recipes which I suggest you leave until you have some baking experience: Cinnamon Oysters, Sponge Drops, Ginger Kisses and Cream Puffs. If you have a friend who 'has the right touch' with these, watch exactly what she does before you try them yourself!

The GOOD thing about these special little cakes is that after you HAVE mastered the recipes, you should be able to make them at the drop of a hat, and you will find them very useful for many occasions.

Always measure carefully so you use the amount intended for each recipe. Using a fork or whisk, stir the flour in its container before you start. Spoon it from its container into a dry cup measure, without packing it down or banging the measure to flatten the surface. Run the back of a knife along the top of the measure to remove excess. (If you have put too much flour into a measuring cup which has a rim above the desired marked amount, remove excess using a spoon, without shaking or banging the cup.) When you bang or shake a cup containing flour, you pack it down and will be adding more than is required for the recipe.

Butterfly Cakes – recipe page 61

Rich Chocolate Cupcakes

For 12 cupcakes:

150g butter, softened

¾ cup lightly packed brown sugar

3 large eggs

¾ cup self-raising flour

¼ cup cocoa powder

Chocolate Butter Cream Icing:

75g milk chocolate

75g soft butter, softened

1 cup icing sugar

These little cupcakes look and taste great — and they couldn't be much easier to make. All the ingredients (except the icing and decorations of course!) go in a bowl, you beat them for a couple of minutes, then you're done. They're very nice in their own right, but if you add the icing they really are something quite special.

1 Preheat the oven to 180°C. Line 12 muffin pans with decorative foil or paper cupcake liners.

2 Measure the softened butter, brown sugar, eggs, flour and cocoa powder into a large bowl. Beat for 2 minutes with an electric beater until the mixture is light and fluffy.

3 Divide the batter evenly between the muffin pans. Bake for 15–17 minutes or until firm in the middle. Remove from the oven and cool completely on a rack.

4 To make the icing, measure the broken chocolate into a small microwave-proof bowl. Microwave at Medium (50% power) for 1–1½ minutes, stirring every 30 seconds, or until the chocolate has just melted, then stir until smooth. Cream the softened butter and icing sugar together in a medium-sized bowl (this mixture will look very dry to start with, but should turn light and fluffy as you beat it), then add the melted chocolate and beat lightly to combine.

5 Spread or pipe the icing onto the cooled cupcakes.

Butterfly Cakes

For 12 cakes in large paper cups:

125g butter, softened

¾ cup caster sugar

finely grated zest of 1 orange

1 cup standard (plain) flour

2 large eggs

1 cup self-raising flour

¼ cup + 2 Tbsp milk

To decorate:

whipped cream

raspberry or strawberry jam

fresh strawberries or raspberries, optional

icing sugar

Whenever she sees these, Alison is reminded of her mother's afternoon tea parties where she served butterfly cakes and other delicate sweet treats on her finest china.

1 Preheat the oven to 170°C (160°C fanbake), with the rack just below the middle. Put pleated paper muffin cups in 12 medium-sized muffin pans. Measure out all the cake ingredients before you start cooking.

2 Mix the butter and the sugar together in the food processor, until cream coloured. Add the orange zest and about 2 tablespoons of the measured plain flour, and process again.

3 Add one of the eggs and another tablespoon of flour and process until the mixture is smooth. Repeat with the second egg and another tablespoon of flour. Tip the remaining flour on top of the mixture in the food processor and pour ¼ cup of milk over the flour. Process in bursts until the flour is incorporated, then add the extra milk and process briefly again. Do not over-mix at any stage.

4 Using two dessert spoons, spoon the mixture into the paper cases, using one spoon to help the mixture off the other. Each case should be about three-quarters full.

5 Bake for 15–20 minutes until cakes are golden brown, spring back when gently pressed, and a skewer inserted in the middle comes out clean.

6 When cool, cut the top off each cake carefully so the under-side of the part removed is cone-shaped, leaving a depression to fill with jam and vanilla-flavoured whipped cream. Carefully cut each removed top in half and arrange the two pieces, with the just-cut edges facing down, in the cream, rather like butterfly wings. Add a small piece of strawberry or a raspberry if you like, and dust with icing sugar.

NOTE: Store any unfilled cakes in an airtight container for several days or freeze. Ice with Orange Icing (see page 253) or dust with icing sugar.

Orange Syrup Cakes

This really easy cake recipe has become a standby dessert for our entire family! These little cakes are good as is, but if you've got time to soak them with the syrup, it transforms them into a really special dessert.

For 6 individual cakes:

1 cup sugar

½ cup canola (or other) oil

2 large eggs

finely grated zest of 1 medium orange

½ cup freshly squeezed orange juice

1 tsp vanilla essence

½ tsp salt

1½ cups self-raising flour

Orange Syrup:

¾ cup hot water

¾ cup sugar

finely grated zest of ½ an orange

1 Preheat the oven to 180°C (or 170°C if using fanbake). Coat six non-stick plain or fancy muffin tins or other moulds (each should hold 1 cup when full) with non-stick spray.

2 Measure sugar, oil, eggs and orange zest into a food processor and blend until pale and creamy. Add orange juice and vanilla essence and whiz again, then sieve in the salt and flour. Mix just enough to make a fairly smooth batter.

3 Divide the batter evenly (about ½ cup in each) between muffin tins (or other moulds). Bake for 12–15 minutes or until the cakes are golden brown and a skewer inserted into the middle of a cake comes out clean.

4 While the cakes cook, prepare the syrup by mixing the hot water, sugar and orange zest together in a small microwave-safe bowl. Heat for about 3 minutes on High (100% power), stirring occasionally, until the mixture boils and the sugar dissolves.

5 Remove cakes from the oven. Stand for 2–3 minutes before turning out onto a plate or tray and removing the tins. Drizzle the syrup evenly over the bottom and sides of the hot cakes (about 2 tablespoons per little cake).

6 Leave to stand for at least 1 hour (overnight, if possible), before cutting and serving with lightly whipped cream, ice-cream or yoghurt.

Chocolate Lamingtons

The mixture of boiled cocoa and raspberry jam give these Chocolate Lamingtons a particularly good flavour and colour.

For about 15 lamingtons:

350–400g bought unfilled 'slab' sponge

¼ cup cocoa

½ cup cold water

¼ cup raspberry jam

¾ cup hot water

2 cups icing sugar

about 1½ cups fine desiccated coconut

1 Cut the sponge into 5cm x 5cm squares.

2 Stir the cocoa and cold water in a small pot or microwave-safe jug, then heat until the mixture bubbles, darkens and thickens. Stir in the jam and hot water and bring back to the boil, then stir in the icing sugar to make a fairly thin mixture which will coat the sponge evenly.

3 Dip each sponge cube into the chocolate mixture, turning to coat evenly, then turn them in the coconut to coat. Leave the lamingtons on a cake rack to set, then refrigerate in airtight containers up to two days, or freeze.

4 To serve, split with a sharp serrated knife and fill with a teaspoonful of raspberry jam and whipped cream.

Pink Lamingtons

Raspberry jelly produces Lamingtons which are softer in texture than Chocolate Lamingtons. They are best eaten the day they are made.

For about 15 lamingtons:

350–400g bought unfilled 'slab' sponge

1 packet of raspberry jelly

1 cup boiling water

½ cup ice

about 1½ cups fine desiccated coconut

1 Cut the sponge into 5cm x 5cm squares. (Remove the brown top if you like.)

2 Stir the jelly crystals into the boiling water until they dissolve. Next, add ice. (To do this accurately, half fill a 1 cup measure with cold water, then fill with ice cubes, until the water begins to overflow. Discard all the water — you now have half a cup of ice cubes.)

3 Stir the ice into the hot jelly mixture until it melts. The jelly should now be starting to set. If not, stand it in a water and ice mixture.

4 When the jelly is the consistency of unbeaten egg white, dip each sponge cube into it, turning to coat evenly, then turn the cubes in the coconut to coat. Leave the lamingtons on a cake rack to set.

5 To serve, split with a sharp serrated knife and fill with a teaspoonful of raspberry jam and whipped cream.

Cinnamon Oysters

If you can master the art of making these, you'll be able to whip them up to impress no end of people! As a young mother, Alison would bake, fill and freeze a batch whenever she had a quiet moment. The day came, however, when she went to the freezer and found it 'oyster-less' — her three-year-old daughter and her friends had demolished the lot!

For 12–18 cinnamon oysters:

2 large eggs

pinch salt

½ cup less 2 Tbsp caster sugar

1 rounded household Tbsp golden syrup

½ cup standard (plain) flour

1 tsp ground cinnamon

¼ tsp ground ginger

½ tsp baking soda

1 Preheat the oven to 180°C (170°C fanbake), with the rack just below the middle. Coat a tray of shallow patty pans with non-stick spray.

2 Separate the eggs, put the yolks aside and beat the whites with a pinch of salt until foamy. Add the sugar and continue beating until the whites are stiff and the mixture forms peaks with tips that fold over when the beater is lifted from them.

3 Measure a slightly rounded tablespoon of the golden syrup using a household spoon dipped in hot water.

4 Add the golden syrup to the whites, and beat until well combined. Beat in the egg yolks.

5 Sift together the measured dry ingredients, and fold into the egg mixture with a stirrer/scraper or rubber scraper, taking care not to beat and lose air from the light mixture. Spoon rounded household tablespoons or dessertspoons of mixture into the prepared patty pans. Do not worry about making even shapes, since the mixture softens and spreads as it cooks.

6 Bake for 8–10 minutes, or just until the centres spring back when lightly pressed. The cinnamon oysters dry out, toughen, and shrink if over-cooked. Leave to cool slightly in the patty pans before removing, running a knife around them or gently turning to loosen them. Cool on a wire rack.

7 Using a sharp, serrated knife, cut horizontally through each 'oyster' leaving a hinge. Although the cinnamon oysters may seem tough and leathery at this stage, they soften once they are filled. Fill with plain or vanilla-flavoured, lightly sweetened whipped cream, and leave to stand for about an hour, until soft. Before serving, dust with sieved icing sugar.

Ginger Kisses

Alison came up with this recipe after deciding that she had spent a small fortune on the bought variety! You may need to make a few batches until you get them perfect.

For 18 sandwiched kisses, each 5cm across:

125g butter, softened

¼ cup + 2 Tbsp sugar

1 large egg

1 tsp ground ginger

1 tsp ground cinnamon

1 rounded household dessertspoon golden syrup

75g or ½ cup + 1 Tbsp standard (plain) flour

75g or ½ cup + 1 Tbsp cornflour

½ tsp baking powder

½ tsp baking soda

1 Preheat the oven to 220°C (210°C fanbake), with the rack just below the middle. Line a baking tray with baking paper.

2 This recipe requires accurate weighing/measuring. Put softened butter in a food processor with the next five ingredients and process until smooth and light coloured. (Measure the syrup with a spoon that has been heated in hot water. Have the spoon gently rounded, but not heaped to maximum capacity.)

3 Weigh or measure the dry ingredients carefully, directly into the food processor. (The half-cup measures should be filled precisely and levelled off completely. The spoon measures should also be level.) Process just until smooth.

4 Spoon the mixture into a piping bag with a plain nozzle, about 15mm wide, or shape small even blobs with a spoon. The piped mounds should be about the size of half a walnut shell. They rise a lot and need space between them. They will fill two oven trays.

5 Place the shaped kisses in the preheated oven. Turn heat down by 10°C as soon as the door is shut. Bake for about 5 minutes, until the kisses spring back when pressed. (Watch carefully, these burn easily. Reduce the heat if the bottoms brown before the centres are cooked.)

6 Sandwich together when cool with Mock Cream (see page 255). For more uniform kisses, sort into pairs of the same size. Put mock cream in a forcer bag with a smaller nozzle, and pipe a blob onto the centre one of each pair. Do not 'stick' the kisses together until you have used up all the mock cream as evenly as possible.

7 Store filled ginger kisses in a cool place, so the filling hardens.

NOTE: If kisses run all over the tray you have used too much butter or not enough flour. If they do not spread enough you have used too little butter or too much flour. Correct mistakes next time. The failures are quite edible!

Sponge Drops

These bring back happy memories of summer school holidays on a Southland farm. Every afternoon tea-time a huge platter of freshly made sponge drops would be put down in front of the dozen or so expectant faces — and this after a hearty (and always delicious) mid-day dinner!

For 10–12 filled sponge drops:

2 large eggs

¼ cup caster sugar

½ cup self-raising flour

extra caster sugar

about ½ cup cream, whipped

strawberry or raspberry jam

1 Preheat the oven to 180°C (170°C fanbake), with the rack just below the middle. Line a baking tray with baking paper.

2 Break the eggs into a fairly large bowl, stand it in a large bowl or sink of warm water, and beat with an electric or rotary beater until frothy. Beat in the sugar about a tablespoon at a time, and continue beating until the mixture is very thick and lemon coloured. (To judge the thickness, make a figure 8 with the mixture on the beater. The part you shaped first should not have disappeared by the time the last part is shaped.)

3 Spoon the flour into the measuring cup and level it off carefully, then sift or sieve it twice to lighten it. Then sift half of it on to the mixture in the bowl, and fold it in with a stirrer or rubber scraper. Repeat with remaining flour. Do not over-mix or you will lose some of the air beaten into the eggs. To get even shapes, drop spoonfuls of mixture from the tip of the spoon, rotating the spoon as the mixture comes off. (Allow some space between drops since they spread and flatten as they cook.) Sprinkle more caster sugar on top of each sponge drop to give a light crust.

4 Bake in batches, each for about 7 minutes, or until the sponge drops are a pale gold colour, and the centres spring back when pressed. Cool on baking tray for about 10 minutes, then transfer to rack.

5 About an hour before serving, sandwich pairs of sponge drops together with a little jam and plain or vanilla-flavoured sweetened whipped cream. (The cream softens the drops.)

NOTE: Leftover filled sponge drops may be frozen for a week or so.

Nana's Cheesecake Tarts

Alison's mother always had a pan of these little tarts on hand — they have now been enjoyed by four generations of our family. Alison was quite overwhelmed when her daughter baked and brought her a batch of them, several years after her mother's death.

67

For 24 tarts:

Pastry (see Note):

1 cup standard (plain) flour

75g cold butter, cubed

3–4 Tbsp water

Filling:

125g butter, softened

½ cup sugar

2 large eggs

1 cup standard (plain) flour

1 tsp baking powder

1 tsp vanilla essence

¼ cup raspberry jam

1 Preheat the oven to 190°C (180°C fanbake), with the rack just below the middle. Evenly coat a metal tray of patty pans with non-stick spray.

2 If using home-made pastry, make it first. Measure the flour and butter into a food processor. Process briefly while adding just enough water, a few drops at a time, to make the particles stick together. Remove from the food processor, form into a ball and chill while you mix the cake mixture.

3 Whisk or process the butter and sugar together until creamy. Add one egg and half the flour, mix until just combined, then add remaining egg, flour, baking powder and vanilla essence, and mix briefly again.

4 Roll out the bought or homemade pastry thinly, and cut circles to fit the prepared patty pans. Place a small amount (½ teaspoon) of jam on each pastry circle, then add a spoonful of the cake mixture. If you like, roll out the scraps of pastry, cut into 5 mm strips, and place a strip on top of each uncooked cake.

5 Bake for about 15 minutes, until the pastry has browned, and the centre of each little cake springs back when pressed. Remove from pans and cool on a cake rack. These are nicest eaten within a day or two of baking.

NOTE: Make your own pastry or use very thinly rolled bought flaky pastry instead.

Quark Pastry Cheesecakes

Quark, or fromage blanc, is a type of 'fresh cheese'. It has similar fat-content to cottage cheese but has a texture more like cream cheese. Quark used in these delicious little pastries gives them a very special texture.

For 16 small cakes:

Pastry:

100g cold butter

½ cup (125g) quark

1 cup standard (plain) flour

1 tsp baking powder

1–2 Tbsp cold water

Filling:

½ cup (125g) cream cheese

½ large egg

1 Tbsp sugar

few drops almond essence

apricot jam

1 Preheat the oven to 190°C (180°C fanbake), with the rack just below the middle. Evenly coat a metal tray of patty pans with non-stick spray.

2 Use a food processor, if you have one, to make the pastry. Using the pulse button, cut the butter and quark into the flour and baking powder. While still 'pulsing', add just enough liquid to dampen the mixture enough to form a dough. Keeping the dough cold, roll it on a lightly floured surface, until you can cut it into a 30cm square. Cut this into 16 (4 x 4) smaller squares, and gently ease a pastry square into each prepared patty pan.

3 To make the filling, mix together the cream cheese, egg, sugar and almond essence in the unwashed food processor. Divide the filling evenly between the pastry squares, and top with a little apricot jam. Fold the corners over the filling, towards the centre. Brush the pastry corners with some of the remaining egg.

4 Bake for about 20 minutes until pastry is an even golden brown. For a shinier glaze, heat some apricot jam in the microwave until it bubbles, and brush it over the cooked cheesecakes. While still warm, gently transfer them from the patty pans to the rack to finish cooling. These are best eaten soon after baking!

NOTES: To measure half an egg, beat the egg in a small bowl until the white and yolk are combined, then pour into two identical glasses until levels match. Expect the corners of these cheesecakes to shrink as they bake.

Tea-Trolley Tartlets

For 50 tartlet shells:

200g butter, at room temperature

½ cup icing sugar

1 tsp vanilla essence

½ tsp salt

2 cups standard (plain) flour

This recipe makes about 50 little bite-sized tart shells, which will keep for weeks at room temperature in airtight containers, ready for last minute-fillings. Try lemon honey, passionfruit honey, Christmas mincemeat, thickened berry or fruit mixtures, caramelised condensed milk with sliced bananas, etc. The fillings can be topped with plain or flavoured whipped cream (with or without a berry garnish), or a small meringue. Let your imagination run riot!

1 Preheat the oven to 150°C (140°C fanbake), with the rack just below the middle. Coat a tray of shallow patty pans well with non-stick spray.

2 Beat butter until smooth. Add the icing sugar, vanilla essence and salt, and beat until light and creamy. Add the flour, mix well and press the dough into a block. (If you find your mixture too crumbly to work with, add a small amount of milk to the dough.)

3 Cut the dough in four even-sized pieces and thinly roll out a piece at a time. Cut each piece into 12 rounds, about 6cm in diameter, using a small glass or a plain metal or serrated cutter, if you have one. You want the circles big enough to cover the bottom and sides of the patty pans, without flopping over the top. (Save scraps to re-roll at the end.) Lift the circles carefully into the prepared patty pans.

4 Bake for 10 minutes, or until the bases are straw-coloured and the edges have browned slightly. Let cases stand for a minute or two in their pans, then rotate gently to loosen them if they have stuck, then lift carefully and gently onto a rack to cool. Stack them in airtight containers and store them where they will not get bumped and broken before they are used.

NOTE: Use any broken cases in recipes that call for biscuit crumbs.

Pikelets

Pikelets are great for a quick snack, unexpected company, or a school holiday activity. Spread them with butter and jam, top the butter with hundreds and thousands for small children, or 'dress them up' with whipped cream, jam and fresh berries for a treat!

For 18–24 pikelets (depending on size):

1 rounded household Tbsp golden syrup

25g butter

1 Tbsp sugar

½ cup milk

1 large egg

1 cup self-raising flour

❶ Heat a frypan. (Use a high heat setting if frypan is electric.)

❷ Dip an ordinary (household) tablespoon in hot water, and then use it to measure the syrup. Put the syrup into a bowl with the butter. Warm (microwaving is easiest) to soften both, then mix in the sugar, milk and egg. Sprinkle or sieve the flour over the top, then mix it in briefly with a whisk or beater just until smooth.

❸ Rub surface of the hot frypan with a little butter on a paper towel. Drop dessertspoon or tablespoon lots of mixture into the pan, pouring mixture off the tip of the spoon (see Note).

❹ Turn pikelets over as soon as the bubbles begin to burst on the surface. (Turn up the heat if the cooked side of each pikelet is not brown enough OR turn heat down if they browned too much by the time the first bubbles burst.) When the centres of the second side spring back when touched with your finger, the pikelets are ready. (If pikelets are too thick and are not spreading enough, add a little extra milk to mixture.)

❺ Cook in batches until all the batter is used. Keep cooked pikelets warm by putting them between the folds of a clean tea towel, and transfer them to a plastic bag when cold.

❻ Serve soon after making, as described above.

NOTE: If you can manage to hold the spoon handle upright and turn the spoon as you let the batter run off it, you should get perfectly round pikelets.

Peg Eason's Chocolate Pikelets

These pikelets are deliciously different!

For about 20 pikelets:

1 Tbsp butter, melted

1 large egg

½ tsp vanilla essence

½ cup sugar

½ cup milk

1 cup standard (plain) flour

1–2 Tbsp cocoa

½ tsp baking soda

1 tsp cream of tartar

pinch salt

whipped cream and raspberry jam

❶ Heat a heavy frypan. (Use a high heat setting if frypan is electric.)

❷ Measure with level, standard cups and spoons. Melt the butter in a bowl big enough to mix all the ingredients. Add the egg, vanilla essence, sugar and milk, and beat with a whisk or eggbeater until well mixed.

❸ Sieve into the bowl the flour, cocoa, baking soda, cream of tartar and salt. (Extra cocoa gives more colour and flavour.) Sift these on top of the liquid mixture, then whisk or beat everything until combined. (Do not over-mix.)

❹ Cook spoonfuls of mixture on the lightly buttered, preheated frypan, turning when the first bubbles on top burst. Thin mixture with a little extra milk if pikelets seem too thick.

❺ Cool in a clean, folded tea towel. Transfer pikelets to a plastic bag when cold.

❻ To serve, split pikelets with a very sharp knife, leaving a small hinge, and fill with raspberry jam and sweetened whipped cream. (Or put jam and whipped cream on top.)

Cream Puffs & Chocolate Éclairs

Cream puffs and chocolate éclairs are made from the same mixture (called choux paste). Food processors make their preparation a breeze!

For 12 puffs or eclairs:

½ cup water

60g butter, cubed

½ cup standard (plain) flour

2 large eggs

Chocolate Glaze:

2 level Tbsp cocoa

¼ cup water

½ tsp vanilla essence

1 cup icing sugar

1 Preheat the oven to 200°C (190°C fanbake), with the rack just below the middle. Line a baking tray with baking paper.

2 Put the water and butter in a medium-sized pot and bring to the boil. As soon as it boils and the butter has melted, tip in the flour. Stir briskly with a wooden spoon, lifting the pot off the heat as soon as the dough forms a ball which does not stick to the side.

3 Break the ball of dough into three or four spoonfuls, and drop them into a food processor fitted with a metal chopping blade. Break an egg into the food processor bowl, and process the fairly hot mixture until well mixed. While the motor is going, drop another egg in through the feed tube, and process for 20–30 seconds. Lift out the blade, removing the mixture from the blade and the sides with a rubber scraper.

4 For cream puffs, put spoonfuls of mixture onto the prepared baking tray, leaving plenty of space between them to allow for rising. For chocolate éclairs, put the mixture in a forcing bag (or heavy plastic bag with one corner cut out) and pipe sausage shapes onto the prepared baking tray.

5 Bake for about 40 minutes. If puffs brown too much, lower the temperature to 190°C (180°C fanbake) after 20 minutes. The walls of the puffs must be set, and they should sound hollow when you tap them. If you are in doubt, take out a puff, leave it to cool for 2–3 minutes then cut it open. If it has uncooked mixture inside, leave the others to cook for longer.

6 When cold, fill cream puffs or éclairs with sweetened whipped cream (flavoured with vanilla essence and/or finely grated orange zest). Dust tops of cream puffs with icing sugar, and ice chocolate éclairs with Chocolate Glaze before or after you fill them.

7 To make the Chocolate Glaze, heat cocoa with water in a small frypan or pot. As soon as this thickens and starts to look dry, remove from the heat and stir in vanilla essence. Sift icing sugar. When the pan has cooled so you can touch its bottom with your hand, add half the icing sugar. Like magic, the dryish chocolate mixture becomes thin, dark brown and shiny. Add enough extra icing sugar to make the icing less runny. Tilt the pot or pan and dip the top of unfilled éclairs in it (or spoon glaze over filled éclairs). The icing should run down a little. If it runs too far, add more icing sugar. If it doesn't run, add a little water but do not heat the pan.

Raspberry & Vanilla Friands

Friands have become very popuar. We don't know whether they will ever completely replace muffins in our psyche or kitchens, but they are delicious and make a good occasional treat.

For 12 friands:

100g butter, melted

1 cup ground almonds

1 cup sugar

1 tsp vanilla essence

¼ cup milk

3 eggs

¼ tsp salt

½ cup self-raising flour

12–24 fresh or frozen raspberries (see Note)

1 Preheat the oven to 180°C (190°C fanbake), with the rack just below the middle.

2 Place the butter, almonds, sugar, vanilla essence, and milk in a medium-sized bowl and stir until well combined.

3 Separate the eggs, stirring the yolks into the almond mixture, and putting the whites into another large clean bowl (any traces of fat will prevent the whites fluffing up). Add the salt, then beat the whites with an egg beater until they form stiff peaks.

4 Sprinkle the flour over the whites, then pour or spoon in the almond mixture and gently fold everything together just enough to combine.

5 Thoroughly coat 12 friand or muffin pans with non-stick spray (it pays to do this carefully because they do have a tendency to stick) and divide the mixture between them. Place one or two raspberries on the top of each, then place in the oven and bake for 12–15 minutes until golden brown and the centres spring back when pressed.

6 Remove from the oven and leave to cool for 3–5 minutes to make them easier to remove, before turning them out of the pans to cool on a rack.

7 Dust with icing sugar and serve warm or cold at any time; particularly good with tea or coffee.

NOTE: Raspberries can be replaced with other berries or fruit: blueberries and halved strawberries work well.

Chocolate & Hazelnut Friands

Friands are traditionally made using ground almonds, but hazelnuts work really well too, especially when paired with chocolate. Try them warm from the oven so the chocolate centre is still soft.

For 12 friands:

1 cup (140g) hazelnuts

100g dark chocolate

25g butter

¾ cup sugar

1 tsp vanilla essence

¼ cup milk

3 eggs

¼ tsp salt

½ cup self-raising flour

6–12 squares (30–60g) chocolate, optional

1. Preheat the oven to 180°C (170°C fanbake), with the rack just below the middle.

2. Toast the hazelnuts by tipping them into a sponge roll pan and placing them in the oven as it heats. Keep a close watch on them, as nuts can burn quickly. Remove them from the oven as soon as they have darkened visibly. Allow to cool.

3. Place the hazelnuts in a food processor and process until they are chopped to about the consistency of fine breadcrumbs.

4. Melt the chocolate by heating in a bowl over boiling water or by microwaving at Medium (50% power) for 2–3 minutes, stirring after every minute. Add the butter and stir until it melts, then add the ground nuts, sugar, vanilla essence, and milk and mix until well combined.

5. Separate the eggs. Stir the yolks into the hazelnut mixture, and put the whites into another large clean bowl (any traces of fat will prevent the whites fluffing up). Add the salt, then beat the whites until they form stiff peaks.

6. Sprinkle the flour over the whites, then pour or spoon in the hazelnut mixture and gently fold everything together just enough to combine.

7. Thoroughly coat 12 friand or muffin pans with non-stick spray (do this carefully because they do have a tendency to stick), and divide the mixture between them.

8. Bake for 12–15 minutes until the centres spring back when pressed gently. If adding chocolate centres, bake for 4–5 minutes, then (with the tray still in the oven) gently press half to one square (or equivalent) into the top of each friand, and bake for a further 8–10 minutes.

9. Remove from the oven and leave to cool for 3–5 minutes (this makes them easier to remove), before turning them out of the pans to cool on a rack. Serve warm or reheated, with coffee.

Scones

Alison's mother Margaret (one of seven children brought up on a Canterbury farm) made truly wonderful scones — two or three batches a day, every Saturday and Sunday. Margaret used to make them 'by feel' using handfuls of flour, knobs of butter, and dashes of milk, but we like to use standard measures.

For 6 scones:

50g butter

¾ cup milk

2 cups (260g) self-raising flour

½ tsp salt

1 Tbsp sugar

1 Preheat the oven to 210°C with a rack in or just above the middle.

2 Heat the butter in a microwave-safe container, or in a pot, until just melted, then add the milk. Set aside.

3 Toss/stir the flour with a fork to make sure it is not packed, then spoon it lightly into the cup, without shaking it. Put the flour in a bowl big enough to mix all the ingredients. Add the salt and sugar and toss well to mix.

4 When the oven is up to heat, tip the slightly warm liquids into the dry ingredients all at once. Using a flat-bladed stirrer, fold the mixture together just until the dry ingredients are all dampened. Add extra milk if needed to make a soft moist ball of dough, then turn it out onto floured baking paper or a non-stick liner on an oven tray.

5 With floured hands, knead the ball of dough lightly, then pat it into a rectangle. Cut it lengthwise into two strips, then crosswise into three strips, making six scones altogether. Put the scones only 1cm apart, so the sides are soft rather than crusty, and bake for 10–15 minutes, until the tops are lightly browned.

6 Serve warm, split and buttered, or halve and top with raspberry jam and whipped cream.

VARIATIONS:

Date Scones: Simply add 1 cup of (separated) dates to the flour mixture before adding the milk.

Cheese Scones: Follow the recipe above, but omit the sugar. Stir ½ cup grated tasty cheese into the flour before adding the milk mixture. Shape as described above, then sprinkle the tops with a little additional cheese before baking, if desired.

Biscuits & Crackers

The quickest and easiest biscuits to make are those where you melt butter, stir in the remaining ingredients and drop them, in spoonfuls, or small balls quickly shaped with wet hands, onto a baking tray. This is a good type of biscuit to teach children to make (or help with) for school lunches, etc.

Soften or melt the butter using the way that suits you best:
- Put it in a microwave-safe dish, at Low or Medium power level in the microwave.
- OR put it in an oven-proof bowl in the oven as it heats to biscuit-baking temperature.
- OR put it in a bowl over a pot of boiling vegetables, etc.
- OR melt or soften it in a pot over low heat on the stove top.

Encourage children to get out all the ingredients they need before they start mixing, and always do this yourself when baking. (This way, you don't find you have a vital ingredient missing part way through mixing!)

When making several trays of biscuits one after another, put the first lot of biscuits on baking paper on top of the oven-tray. While the first lot cooks, shape the next lot on another sheet of baking paper or liner. Slide this onto the warm tray straight after you slide the first paper or liner of cooked biscuits off it.

If you replace rolled oats with finer, flourier instant oats, the mixture may seem drier than usual. Use less instant oats or add a little extra milk or water to the mixture.

To get biscuits just the way you want them, the amount of flour in the mixture must be right. Unfortunately, batches of flour sometimes vary. I use a carefully measured amount of flour (see page 7).

Before shaping and cooking the whole batch, I shape two biscuits and cook them to see how far they spread as they cook. If they spread too far, I add 1 or 2 tablespoons of extra flour to the uncooked mixture and shape and cook two more biscuits. When you have the amount of flour right, shape and cook the whole batch. I think that biscuits which spread a certain amount and finish up thin are often nicer than those which have a lot of added flour and don't spread much. Cool the cooked sample biscuits on a rack before you taste them! A good example of delicious, thin, flat, biscuits are Chocolate Chippies! Make sure you try them like this!

Sometimes biscuits need to be flattened before you cook them. Use a wet fork, your fingers, the ball of your thumb, or the bottom of a cold wet glass. You can experiment in the same way as suggested above, shaping one biscuit each way. Cook these to see which looks best, then shape the rest.

When biscuits spread as they cook, they sometimes touch the biscuit next to them and/or no longer look perfectly round. You can neaten them up easily by separating joint parts with a knife just after you take them from the oven, when they are cooked but still hot and soft. Working fast, gently push uneven edges back into shape too, again using the knife.

When you are cooking biscuits, watch the oven temperature carefully, lowering it a little if the first batch looks too dark when cooked. Well cooked biscuits are crisper, while slightly undercooked biscuits are chewy. Cook them to the stage you like best.

← Little Lava Rocks – recipe page 96

Oaty Fingers

These can be mixed in seconds, rolled out directly on the baking sheet, then baked — they couldn't be any easier!

For about 20 fingers:

100g butter

½ cup packed brown sugar

½ cup standard (plain) flour

½ cup (instant) rolled oats

½ cup oat bran

¼ cup toasted sesame seeds, optional

1 Preheat the oven to 180°C (170°C fanbake), with the rack just below the middle. Line a baking tray with baking paper.

2 Soften (but do not melt) the butter. Mix well with the sugar, then with the remaining ingredients by hand or in a food processor bowl, adding 1–2 tablespoons of water if dough will not stick together.

3 Transfer dough to the prepared baking tray and roll out, under another piece of baking paper or sheet of plastic, to a 5mm thickness. Cut through the dough, marking them into rectangles about 25 x 100mm (without moving the biscuits apart).

4 Bake for 10–15 minutes, until golden brown. While hot, mark between biscuits again with a long-bladed heavy knife. Leave to cool on the tray, then separate into individual fingers. Enjoy immediately or store in airtight containers.

Easy Oaty Cookies

We are strong believers in the goodness of rolled oats! Although we cannot always persuade our families to eat porridge, there is no problem with these biscuits which are extra-good packed for play-lunch or for after-school snacks.

For about 60 biscuits (depending on size):

200g butter

1 cup packed brown sugar

1 cup white sugar

1 large egg

¼ cup milk

½ tsp baking soda

1 tsp vanilla essence

1 cup standard (plain) flour

3 cups (instant) rolled oats

½ cup sultanas, optional

½ cup chopped walnuts, optional

½ cup sunflower seeds, optional

1. Preheat the oven to 180°C (170°C fanbake), with the rack just below the middle. Line a baking tray with baking paper.

2. Melt the butter in a large pot or microwave-safe bowl and remove from the heat as soon as it is liquid. Stir in the sugars and egg. Mix the milk, soda and vanilla essence together and add to the mixture. Sprinkle the flour, rolled oats (and any optional ingredients), over everything else and mix until well combined.

3. Drop mixture in teaspoon lots onto the prepared baking tray, leaving room for spreading. Further shaping is not necessary.

4. Bake for 10–12 minutes, or until biscuits are golden brown and feel firm. (Shape the next tray of biscuits while this one cooks.) While biscuits are warm, lift them onto a cooling rack. (Biscuits that have cooled too much are hard to lift off, so put the tray back in the oven for about a minute if this happens.)

5. When cold, store in airtight containers.

Malty Biscuits

For about 60 thin biscuits, 5–6cm across:

125g butter

½ cup malt extract

½ cup sugar

about 1½ cups standard (plain) flour

1 tsp baking soda

We love the flavour of malt, and find these crisp, flat biscuits utterly irresistible, as do our family and friends. What's more, they work out at half the price of very ordinary bought biscuits, and the electricity needed to cook them costs about 10 cents. The thinness of these simply-made malty biscuits depends on the way you shape them and the amount of flour in them. Biscuits made with more flour do not spread as much as those made with less.

1. Preheat the oven to 170°C (160°C fanbake), with the rack just below the middle. Line a baking tray with baking paper.

2. Heat the butter until liquid, then remove from the heat. Measure the malt using a quarter-cup measure (twice), which has been heated with boiling water. Tip the malt into the warm melted butter (without reheating it, since malt mixtures can be difficult to work with if they are too hot). Add the sugar and stir until no liquid butter is visible.

3. Shake 1 cup of the flour and the baking soda through a sieve into the malt mixture, then add the remaining flour, stirring until no dry flour is visible. The dough should form soft balls which flatten a little on standing.

4. Cook a few trial biscuits. Dampen your hands, and roll 4–6 balls of dough the size of large cherries or small strawberries and put them onto the prepared baking tray, leaving room for spreading. Flatten half the balls with your fingers or the heel of your hand until they are about 4cm across, and leave the rest as they are.

5. Bake for about 8 minutes, until they darken a little and are evenly golden brown. The flattened biscuits should spread to about 5–6cm across. The others will spread less and be thicker. If you think the biscuits are too thin, add more flour until you get biscuits you like. Shape the remaining dough into balls, flatten if desired, and cook in batches.

6. Leave the biscuits to cool and firm a little before lifting onto a cooling rack. To keep them crisp, store in an airtight container as soon as they are cold.

NOTE: Newly bought malt seems to require more flour to make dough of the right consistency than malt which has been sitting in your cupboard for some time. When using old malt, keep aside 2 tablespoons of the remaining flour, cook your trial biscuits and add the remaining flour only if necessary.

Hokey Pokey Biscuits

These slightly chewy biscuits make good additions to school lunches and can be mixed together very quickly in a pot. Preschoolers as well as older children usually like to help shape (and sample) the uncooked dough!

For 40–50 biscuits, 55mm across:

100g butter

1 Tbsp milk

1 rounded household Tbsp golden syrup

½ cup sugar

¼ tsp salt

about ½ cup currants or sultanas

¼–½ cup walnuts or other nuts, optional

1¾ cups standard (plain) flour

1 tsp baking soda

1. Preheat the oven to 180°C (170°C fanbake), with the rack just below the middle. Line a baking tray with baking paper.

2. Melt the butter in a medium-sized pot. As soon as it is liquid, take the pot off the heat and stir in the milk, golden syrup, sugar, salt, and dried fruit. Chop the nuts if adding them (nuts give the biscuits a definite nutty flavour).

3. Stir the flour in its container then spoon into the cup measure without packing or banging it down. Sieve the flour and baking soda into the mixture, and stir to mix everything together.

4. Roll teaspoonfuls of the mixture into balls, place on the prepared baking tray, and press down with your fingers or the heel of your hand, leaving room for spreading. Flatten with a fork dipped in water to stop sticking.

5. Bake for 15–20 minutes, taking biscuits out as soon as they are evenly, golden brown. While warm, lift them onto a cooling rack. When cold, store in an airtight container.

NOTE: If your biscuits don't spread, you have used too much flour. If they spread too far, you have not used enough flour, measure more carefully next time!

Anzac Biscuits

Anzac biscuits taste good, last well (if stored in airtight containers) and are easy to make! Let your children help you and, if you have been a good teacher, you will find that it won't take long until the children can make them all by themselves. You are unlikely to get as many cooked biscuits as you would if had no helpers, because the uncooked mixture tastes good, and you can't expect the impossible! This is the version that our family has made for years. As a matter of interest, each batch costs considerably less than half the price of the same weight of store-bought biscuits — and tastes much nicer!

For about 50 biscuits:

100g butter

¼ cup golden syrup

1 tsp vanilla essence

1 cup sugar

1 cup fairly fine rolled oats

1 cup desiccated coconut

1 cup standard (plain) flour

½ tsp baking soda

2 Tbsp warm water

1 Preheat the oven to 170°C (160°C fanbake), with the rack just below the middle. Line a baking tray with baking paper.

2 In a fairly large saucepan, melt the butter until it is liquid. Use levelled measuring cups and measuring spoons to measure everything else. Add the golden syrup, take the pot off the heat and stir until butter and syrup are blended.

3 Add the vanilla essence, sugar, rolled oats, coconut and flour to the saucepan and stir them together. Stir the baking soda and water together in a small container and tip them into the mixture in the pot and mix well. If the mixture seems too crumbly to mix easily, add 1–2 tablespoons of extra water until the mixture can be rolled into balls the size of cherry tomatoes.

4 Place the balls on the baking paper, leaving plenty of room for spreading. While they bake, shape more balls to go on the tray when the first lot are cooked.

5 Bake for about 15 minutes, until the biscuits are evenly golden brown. Lift the warm biscuits onto a cooling rack. When cold, store in an airtight container

VARIATIONS: Add a cup of chopped roasted peanuts or chopped walnuts to the mixture before adding the sugar. Replace the coconut with an extra cup of rolled oats.

Peanut Plus Cookies

Whatever age you are, we think that you'll enjoy a glass of milk and one of these peanutty cookies full of good things! Make them giant-sized for fun, or regular size if you want them to last longer.

For 24 x 10cm biscuits, or up to 60 smaller biscuits:

50g butter

¼ cup golden syrup

¾ cup peanut butter (crunchy or plain)

1 large egg

1 tsp vanilla essence

½ cup white sugar

½ cup packed brown sugar

½ cup sultanas

½ cup roasted salted peanuts, roughly chopped

½ cup chocolate chips

½ cup sunflower seeds, optional

1¾ cups standard (plain) flour

1 tsp baking soda

❶ Preheat the oven to 180°C (170°C fanbake), with the rack just below the middle. Line a baking tray with baking paper.

❷ In a large pot or microwave-safe bowl, melt the butter and the golden syrup (measured with a hot wet measuring cup) just until you can stir them together without any lumps of butter showing. Stop heating, then stir in the peanut butter until mixture is smooth.

❸ Add the egg, vanilla essence and sugars and beat with a fork or stirrer until evenly mixed.

❹ Add the sultanas, peanuts, chocolate chips and sunflower seeds (if using). Measure the flour and baking soda into a sieve over the bowl or pot, shake it in, and mix until evenly combined.

❺ With wet hands, divide the mixture into balls. For giant biscuits make 24 balls. Place six at a time on the prepared baking tray, then flatten with wet fingers until biscuits measure 9cm across. (Biscuits spread 1cm during cooking.) For smaller biscuits, make 36–60 balls, then flatten until they are about 7mm thick.

❻ Bake for 7–10 minutes, until evenly golden brown. Take from oven before biscuits brown round the edge. (Use a slightly shorter time for chewy biscuits.) While biscuits are warm, lift them onto a cooling rack. When cold, store in an airtight container.

NOTE: To cook giant biscuits more evenly, reduce heat by 10°C and cook 2–3 minutes longer.

Peanut Brownies

There may be nothing new or different about peanut brownies, but year after year they remain popular, in lunch boxes, and in cafés.

For 25–35 biscuits (depending on size):

100g butter, softened

½ cup caster or plain sugar

1 large egg

1 cup standard (plain) flour

2 tsp baking powder

2 Tbsp cocoa

1 cup roasted peanuts (see Note)

1 Preheat the oven to 180°C (170°C fanbake), with the rack just below the middle. Line a baking tray with baking paper.

2 Whisk (or process) the butter with the sugar, then add the egg and whisk (or process) again until fluffy. Using level measuring cups and spoons, measure and sift in the dry ingredients, then stir or process until mixture is smooth. (Peanut brownies should spread a certain amount as they cook — if you use more flour and cocoa than called for, they will not. On the other hand, if they spread too far, not enough flour has been added.) Add the peanuts and stir again.

3 Using two teaspoons, put spoonfuls of the mixture on the prepared baking tray. Bake for about 15–20 minutes, until the centres feel as firm as the edges.

NOTE: Lightly roasted peanuts have much more flavour than raw ones. Buy good-quality, unsalted, or lightly salted roasted peanuts for this recipe. To remove salt from salted peanuts, rinse them in a sieve, under hot water, then dry them straight away, between paper towels. To roast raw peanuts, spread out in a shallow baking pan and pop them in a hot, but turned off, oven — by the time the oven and peanuts are cool the peanuts should have changed colour slightly and lost their chewiness.

Scroggin Biscuits

'Scroggin' is a mixture of nuts, dried fruit and chocolate, which Alison took tramping in her teens. She invented this recipe when her children were at primary school, because she wanted nutritious, as well as popular, additions to the biscuits she made for lunches and after-school snacks. This recipe makes the equivalent of nearly six 200g packs of biscuits, which many mothers have told us over the years, disappear at an amazing rate!

For about 80 biscuits:

200g butter, softened

¼ cup peanut butter

½ cup sugar

1 cup packed brown sugar

2 large eggs

1 tsp vanilla or almond essence

1½ cups standard (plain) flour (see Note)

1 tsp baking soda

2 cups rolled oats

1 cup chocolate chips

1 cup sultanas

½ cup chopped walnuts

1 Preheat the oven to 180°C (170°C fanbake), with the rack just below the middle. Line baking trays with baking paper.

2 Mix or beat the softened butter, peanut butter, sugar, brown sugar, eggs and essence together in a large bowl, then sieve or sift in 1 cup of the flour and the baking soda. Mix in the remaining flour and everything else, using a wooden spoon or your hand.

3 Shape with two spoons or put flattened rounds of mixture onto prepared tray, leaving some space for spreading, baking one tray while you shape more biscuits.

4 Bake for about 12 minutes or until lightly browned. While biscuits are warm, lift them onto a cooling rack. When cold, store in an airtight container.

NOTE: Use ¼ cup less flour if using instant rolled oats.

Chocolate Chippies

These biscuits are enormously popular, and may well become family 'staples'. They are simple enough for a five-year-old to make, with a little supervision and, if hidden, will keep for weeks in airtight jars!

For 24 biscuits:

75g butter

½ cup packed brown sugar

½ cup white sugar

1 large egg

½ cup chocolate chips

½ tsp baking soda

1 cup standard (plain) flour

1 Preheat the oven to 180°C (170°C fanbake), with the rack just below the middle. Line a baking tray with baking paper.

2 Microwave the butter in a microwave-safe bowl for 1 minute or melt it in a pot until just liquid. Take off the heat, add both measures of sugar and the egg to the butter and beat with a fork until thoroughly mixed. Sprinkle the chocolate chips into the bowl. Measure the baking soda and flour into a sieve over the bowl, shake them in, and then mix everything together well.

3 Using two spoons, form half the mixture into 12 piles on the prepared baking tray, leaving room for spreading. Bake for 8–10 minutes or until golden brown, then shape and cook the rest of the mixture in the same way. (A fan oven is likely to cook the biscuits more quickly than a regular oven.)

4 While biscuits are warm, lift them onto a cooling rack. When cold, store in airtight jars.

VARIATION: To make Orange Chippies, finely grate the zest of an orange and stir into the melted butter. Proceed as above.

Almond Crisps

Flecked with toasted almonds, these buttery, crisp biscuits are irresistible.

For about 30 biscuits:

¼–½ cup toasted slivered almonds

100g butter, softened

½ cup sugar

about ½ tsp almond essence

½ cup standard (plain) flour

½ cup self-raising flour

1 Preheat the oven to 170°C (160°C fanbake), with the rack just below the middle. Line a baking tray with baking paper.

2 While the oven heats, use it to toast the slivered almonds on a shallow baking dish. Watch them carefully, and remove them as soon as they have lost their whiteness and are straw coloured.

3 Mix the butter, sugar and almond essence in a food processor then add everything else without sifting, and process briefly to mix. Alternatively, beat in the sugar and almond essence using a stirrer or wooden spoon. Stir together the flours or shake them through a sieve into the bowl. Add the almonds and stir everything together until well mixed.

4 Form dough into a cylinder on a floured board and chill in the refrigerator or freezer until it is firm enough to cut into thin slices with a sharp (serrated) knife. Place slices on the prepared baking tray.

5 Bake for about 10 minutes or until edges colour slightly. While biscuits are warm, lift them onto a cooling rack. When cold, store in an airtight container.

NOTE: If butter is too liquid, and the mixture is too crumbly to handle, add milk until dough sticks together.

VARIATIONS:

Almond and Cherry Crisps: Add 6 finely chopped, crystallised cherries to the mixture.

Walnut Crisps: Replace almonds with ½ cup chopped (untoasted) walnuts.

Almond Biscuits: Leave out slivered almonds. Roll dough into balls, flatten slightly, then top with whole almonds or halved cherries.

Chocolate Crunchies (Easy Afghans)

As a child, Alison loved the Afghan biscuits her mother made regularly. Her streamlined version takes much less time to make and seems just as popular. Sometimes we ice the biscuits, at other times we make them flatter and leave them un-iced.

For about 50 biscuits:

125g butter

1 cup sugar

3 Tbsp cocoa

1 tsp vanilla essence

1 large egg

1 cup self-raising flour

1½ cups cornflakes

50 walnut pieces or halves

1. Preheat the oven to 170°C (160°C fanbake), with the rack just below the middle. Line a baking tray with baking paper.

2. In a pot big enough to hold the whole mixture, melt the butter until it is barely liquid, then remove from the heat. Add the sugar, cocoa, vanilla essence and egg, and mix well with a fork. Measure the flour and cornflakes on top of this and stir until evenly mixed.

3. Using two teaspoons, put 50 small, compact heaps of mixture on the prepared baking tray, leaving room for spreading. The biscuits spread a certain amount as they cook, but if you want larger, flatter biscuits you should flatten the unbaked biscuits gently using several fingers or the pad of your thumb.

4. Bake for 8–12 minutes until biscuits look evenly cooked but have not darkened round the edges. While biscuits are warm, lift them onto a cooling rack.

5. When biscuits have cooled, spread with a double quantity of Chocolate Sour Cream Icing (see page 253) and top with walnut pieces or halves before the icing sets. Leave in a cool place for icing to set, then store in an airtight container.

Peanut Crisps

For maximum flavour, roast your own peanuts just before making these biscuits.

For about 75 biscuits:

200g butter, softened

1 cup packed brown sugar

1 cup white sugar

1 tsp vanilla essence

½ tsp almond essence

1 large egg

1 cup (instant) rolled oats

1 cup oat bran

1 cup self-raising flour

½ tsp salt

1–2 cups lightly chopped, roasted peanuts (see Note)

1. Preheat the oven to 180°C (170°C fanbake). Line baking trays with baking paper.

2. Tip softened butter into a large bowl with the sugars, essences and egg, and mix well. Add the rolled oats, oat bran, flour, salt and chopped peanuts, and mix until thoroughly combined.

3. Roll the mixture into balls, place them on the prepared tray, and flatten them with a fork or the heel of your hand.

4. Bake for about 10 minutes until lightly browned. If you find it hard to remove the cooked biscuits from the baking tray while hot, leave them to cool before lifting them off and storing in an airtight container.

NOTE: Raw peanuts can be roasted in a shallow baking pan at 180°C for 15–30 minutes, or until lightly browned. Cool, then chop peanuts in a food processor or with a knife.

Gingernuts

These are easy enough (and fun) for even young cooks to make because you stir everything together in a pot.

For 80 small biscuits:

100g butter

1 rounded household Tbsp golden syrup

1 cup sugar

1–2 tsp ground ginger

1 tsp vanilla essence

1 large egg

1¾ cups standard (plain) flour

1 tsp baking soda

1 Preheat the oven to 180°C (170°C fanbake). Line baking trays with baking paper.

2 Melt the butter in a medium-sized pot or microwave-safe bowl. Remove from heat when melted. Dip an ordinary tablespoon into hot water, then measure the syrup with it. Add the syrup, sugar, ginger (use more for a stronger flavour) and vanilla essence. Add the egg, then mix well with a stirrer or wooden spoon.

3 Sift in the flour and baking soda, then mix everything together again.

4 Stand pot or bowl in cold water to cool the biscuit mixture so it is firmer. With wet hands, roll teaspoonfuls of biscuit mixture into small balls. Put these on the prepared baking trays, leaving room to spread. Bake one tray at a time, for about 10 minutes, until golden brown. While biscuits are warm, lift them onto a cooling rack. When cold, store in an airtight container.

NOTE: If biscuits don't spread, you have used too much flour. If they spread too far, you have not used enough.

Colleen's Biscuits

This recipe, given to Alison by a friend many years ago, makes crisp, almost toffee-like biscuits, great for school lunches and general family snacking.

For about 100 biscuits:

250g butter

¾ cup golden syrup

1 tsp baking soda

¼ cup warm water

1½ cups sugar

2 cups standard (plain) flour

2 cups desiccated coconut

2 cups (instant) rolled oats

1 Preheat the oven to 180°C (170°C fanbake). Line baking trays with baking paper.

2 Melt the butter in a large pot and add the golden syrup. Remove from the heat as soon as the syrup is melted and liquid. Add the baking soda to the warm water.

3 Measure the sugar, flour, coconut and oats into the pot. Add the water and soda mixture and stir thoroughly.

4 Drop mixture in teaspoon lots onto the prepared baking tray, leaving room for spreading. Flatten biscuits with your hand after you have filled each tray.

5 Bake for about 12 minutes until golden. While biscuits are warm, lift them onto a cooling rack. When cold, store in an airtight container.

Kiwi Biscuits

A good old New Zealand favourite!

For 30–50 biscuits:

125g butter, softened

½ cup sugar

¼ cup sweetened condensed milk

1 tsp vanilla essence

1 large egg

1½ cups standard (plain) flour

1 tsp baking powder

½ cup chocolate chips or 100g dark chocolate, chopped

1 Preheat the oven to 170°C (160°C fanbake). Line baking trays with baking paper.

2 Place softened butter in a food processor or mixing bowl with the sugar, condensed milk, vanilla essence and egg, then mix briefly. Sift the flour and baking powder together and add, with the chocolate, to the butter mixture. Mix again until well combined.

3 Roll teaspoonfuls of the mixture into balls 25mm across and place on prepared oven trays. Press each ball with the back of a fork to flatten. (If fork sticks, dip in cold water before using.)

4 Bake for 15–20 minutes, or until very lightly coloured. While biscuits are warm, lift them onto a cooling rack. When cold, store in an airtight container.

Spicy Butter Biscuits

Deliciously aromatic, these little biscuits have delighted our friends and family for 40 years. Cut the rolled dough with interesting cutters or, when speed and ease are more important, slice cylinders of chilled dough into round biscuits.

For 20–40 biscuits (depending on size):

2 cups standard (plain) flour

1 tsp baking powder

2 Tbsp cinnamon

2 tsp mixed spice (or ½ tsp each ground cloves, coriander, nutmeg and cardamom)

225g butter, softened

1 cup packed brown sugar

1 large egg, lightly beaten

1 Preheat the oven to 180°C (170°C fanbake), with the rack just below the middle. Line a baking tray with baking paper.

2 Shake the flour, baking powder and spices through a flour sifter or sieve over a large bowl, or put in a food processor. Using your fingers or the food processor, rub the softened butter, brown sugar and egg through the dry ingredients, or process. When the mixture comes together and forms a dough, cut it into three equal parts and refrigerate them in plastic bags until firm.

3 Roll the first piece out thinly (about 3mm thick) on a well-floured surface, keeping dough as cold as possible. Cut into decorative shapes with cookie cutters of your choice, using plenty of flour to dust the dough and cutters. Lift cut shapes carefully onto the prepared baking tray using a spatula. Incorporate scraps from the first batch with the second batch of chilled dough.

4 Alternatively, roll each third of the dough into a cylinder about 7cm thick. Wrap in plastic wrap and refrigerate, or briefly freeze, while you repeat this step with the remaining pieces of dough. Cut firm dough into 3mm slices with a sharp thin-bladed knife. (If dough is too cold, the slices will break, and if not cold enough, the slices will lose their shape.) Carefully transfer slices to prepared baking tray.

5 Bake for about 15 minutes or until lightly browned. Cooking time depends on biscuit thickness, so watch carefully. Lift warm biscuits onto a cooling rack. When cold, store in an airtight container.

6 The full flavour does not develop until a few hours after baking. These crisp little biscuits are good just as they are. Or if you like, decorate round shapes with lightly beaten egg white and 1 or 2 pieces of slivered almond before cooking. Or, decorate after cooking with White Icing (see page 253).

Little Lava Rocks

For 64–80 little biscuits:

250g dark chocolate

100g butter, cubed

½ cup caster sugar

1 tsp vanilla essence

3 large eggs

1¼ cups standard (plain) flour

¼ cup self-raising flour

¼ cup cocoa

about 1 cup icing sugar

These delicious, rich little 'rocks' have a special texture and a spectacular mottled, unusual appearance. Don't worry that this recipe makes a lot because they keep well if they get the chance — but we hate to tell you how fast they disappear in our households!

1 Preheat the oven to 170°C (160°C fanbake), with the rack just below the middle. Line baking trays with baking paper.

2 Break the chocolate into even-sized squares and heat gently with the butter over low heat in a fairly large pot, stirring often, until you have a smooth mixture. Do not heat the mixture more than necessary.

3 Remove from the heat and beat in the sugar and vanilla essence, then the eggs, one at a time, using a wooden spoon or spatula. Put a sieve over the bowl and measure the flours and cocoa into it, then sift these into the chocolate mixture. Mix again, until well combined. Chill mixture for a few minutes in a freezer or longer in a refrigerator, until firm enough to roll into balls.

4 Sift the icing sugar into a large round flat-bottomed dry bowl. (Unsifted icing sugar will not coat the biscuits well). Divide the mixture into quarters and form each part into 16–20 little balls, using your hands.

5 Drop four or five balls at a time into the icing sugar and rotate the bowl until the balls are thickly coated. Without brushing off any icing sugar, place the balls on the lined baking tray, leaving at least 5cm between each one.

6 Bake for about 10 minutes, until centres feel soft and springy when you press them lightly. The 'rocks' will have spread slightly and will have a cracked surface if you used enough icing sugar. Handle and store carefully, with paper towels between layers to stop the icing sugar from smudging.

Coconut Macaroons

For 30–40 biscuits:

3 large egg whites

¼ tsp salt

1 cup caster sugar

½ tsp vanilla or almond essence

2 Tbsp standard (plain) flour

1½ cups desiccated coconut

40 blanched almonds

As a child, Alison was intrigued by the macaroons enjoyed by the characters in English storybooks. Years later, after tasting a wonderful macaroon in Spain, she talked about this on the radio and was sent this recipe by a woman who had enjoyed them as a child and had made them for 60 years!

1 Preheat the oven to 150°C (140°C fanbake), with the rack just below the middle. Line a baking tray with baking paper.

2 Beat egg whites with the salt until they form peaks that turn over, then add half the sugar and beat until the peaks stand upright when the beater is removed from the mixture. Stir in the essence. Mix together the remaining sugar, the flour, and the coconut, then fold these into the beaten egg whites.

3 Put spoonfuls of the mixture onto the prepared baking tray, using two dessertspoons frequently dipped in cold water. Keep shapes as evenly round as you can and allow enough space between each for spreading. Aim to get 8–10 macaroons from each quarter of the mixture. Top each biscuit with an almond.

4 Bake for 20–25 minutes. Biscuits should feel quite firm on the outside, but be chewy inside. The larger the biscuits, the longer they will take to cook. While biscuits are warm, lift them onto a cooling rack. When cold, store in an airtight container.

Coconut Whiskers (Haystacks)

Mix five ingredients (with no baking powder) in a food processor or bowl and you produce 30 little coconut 'mounds' (or haystacks) in a few minutes. Top each with half a cherry or an almond, if you like.

For 30 biscuits:

50g butter

½ cup sugar

½ tsp almond or vanilla essence

1 large egg

2 cups desiccated coconut

15 glace cherries or 30 almonds, optional

1 Preheat the oven to 180°C (170°C fanbake), with the rack just below the middle. Line a baking tray with baking paper or a Teflon liner.

2 Melt the butter and put it in a food processor or bowl with the sugar, essence, egg and coconut. Process briefly or mix by hand.

3 Using two spoons, drop mixture in teaspoon lots onto the prepared baking tray. Further shaping is not necessary. The mixture will flatten and increase in size only very slightly. Top mounds with a halved cherry or an almond, if desired.

4 Bake for 12–15 minutes, or until the bottom edges are golden brown, and any rough pieces on top are lightly coloured. Watch carefully towards end of cooking time as they can darken quickly. While biscuits are warm, lift them onto a cooling rack. When cold, store in an airtight container.

Shirley's Shortbread Shapes

Shortbread, with its distinctive texture and buttery flavour, makes popular gifts.

For about 20–40 biscuits (depending on size):

225g butter, softened

½ cup caster sugar

2 cups standard (plain) flour

1 cup cornflour

1 Preheat the oven to 200°C (190°C fanbake), with the rack just below the middle. Line a baking tray with baking paper.

2 Cream the softened butter, add the sugar and beat until light and fluffy. Add the sifted flour and cornflour, and mix together thoroughly. (Chill dough if necessary to make it easier to handle.)

3 Roll out about 1cm thick. Cut in rectangles, or into shapes using floured cutters to suit the occasion, e.g. star shapes for Christmas, hearts for someone special, animal shapes to please young helpers, etc. Carefully lift shapes onto the prepared baking tray and prick or mark with a fork to prevent uneven rising.

4 Bake for about 15 minutes, watching carefully towards the end of the cooking time. As soon as the edges show signs of browning slightly, take from the oven. While warm, lift carefully onto a cooling rack. When cold, store in an airtight container, or freeze if you are planning to keep the shortbread for more than two weeks before giving away as gifts.

VARIATION: Dip (or partly dip) in Chocolate Coating (see page 255), if desired.

Nutty Ginger Buttons

These small nutty biscuits keep for weeks and are perfect for nibbling after dinner or with afternoon tea or coffee. Pack them in a pretty glass jar for a special gift.

For 50 biscuits:

¾ cup sugar

150g hazelnuts or blanched almonds (or a mixture)

75g crystallised ginger, chopped

4 large egg yolks

2 Tbsp vanilla sugar or caster sugar

1 tsp ground ginger, optional

½ cup standard (plain) flour

1 tsp baking powder

pinch of salt

about 50 extra blanched almonds

1 Preheat the oven to 125°C (120°C fanbake), with the rack just below the middle. Line a baking tray with baking paper.

2 Put the sugar and nuts in a food processor and chop to a fine powder with the metal chopping blade. Add the roughly chopped ginger and process again until very fine. Remove from bowl. Process the egg yolks, sugar and ground ginger (if using) until light and fluffy. Add the ground nut mixture, flour, baking powder and salt and process well. The mixture should be quite firm.

3 Using wet hands, roll into about 50 balls, each about 1cm in diameter. Place on the prepared baking tray and push a blanched almond into the top of each ball.

4 Bake for 30 minutes. If biscuits do not harden on cooling, return them to the oven. While biscuits are warm, lift them onto a cooling rack. When cold, store in an airtight container. Flavour develops on standing.

VARIATION: Use 1½ cups ground almonds instead of the whole nuts. Leave out the flour in this case.

Almond & Cherry Biscuits

Often, when Alison travelled around the country cooking at fund-raising functions, she was given interesting recipes. This is one from Picton.

For about 36 biscuits:

175g butter, softened

½ cup sugar

¾ cup icing sugar

¼–½ cup chopped glacé cherries

¼ cup chopped blanched almonds

¼ tsp almond essence

½ tsp vanilla essence

1 cup standard (plain) flour

½ cup self-raising flour

½ cup cornflour

2 Tbsp cold water

1 Preheat the oven to 170°C (160°C fanbake), with the rack just below the middle. Line a baking tray with baking paper.

2 Mix the butter, sugar and icing sugar together in a food processor or bowl until light in colour. Add the glacé cherries, almonds and essences. Mix the sifted flours into the mixture, without breaking up the cherries too much. Add the water if the mixture seems too dry.

3 Roll the mixture into walnut-sized balls, put on the prepared baking tray and flatten slightly with a wet fork.

4 Bake for about 15 minutes, until the edges colour lightly. When cold, store in an airtight container.

Almond Rosettes

For 24–36 biscuits:

2 large egg whites

¼ cup + 2 Tbsp caster sugar

125g ground almonds

¼–½ tsp almond essence

¼ tsp salt

8–16 glacé cherries

For a present for someone special, fill a decorative glass jar, with a tight-fitting lid, with these pretty biscuits. If you don't have a forcing bag, shape them by pushing them through a thick plastic bag with the corner cut out.

1 Preheat the oven to 180°C (170°C fanbake), with the rack just below the middle. Line a baking tray with baking paper or a liner, as these biscuits stick easily.

2 Put the egg whites, caster sugar, ground almonds, almond essence and salt into a food processor. Mix until well blended and fairly smooth. If the mixture looks too soft to keep its shape, add more ground almonds. Vary the amount of almond essence, depending on its strength. The biscuits should taste definitely, but not strongly, of almonds.

3 To make these without a food processor, beat the egg whites until bubbly but not stiff, add the remaining ingredients and beat well with a wooden spoon until the mixture becomes quite stiff.

4 Pipe or otherwise shape the mixture into rosettes, making 24–36 biscuits. As the biscuits do not rise during cooking, you can put them quite close together. Cut the cherries into halves or quarters, and press them into the uncooked biscuit dough.

5 Bake for about 20 minutes, until the biscuits are golden brown all over. If they appear to be browning too soon, turn the oven down to 170°C (160°C fanbake). Cool on a rack, then store in airtight jars for up to a month.

Coffee Creams

Little biscuits sandwiched together with delicious coffee cream are irresistible to those who have tasted them once!

For 40 filled biscuits:

125g butter, softened

½ cup sugar

1 large egg, lightly beaten

1 Tbsp instant coffee

1 Tbsp hot water

about 2 cups standard (plain) flour

2 tsp baking powder

Coffee Filling:

2 tsp instant coffee

2 tsp hot water

3 Tbsp butter

about 1 cup icing sugar

1 tsp vanilla essence

1 Beat the butter with the sugar and egg in a bowl or food processor. Dissolve instant coffee in the hot water, and add, with the sifted flour and baking powder. Mix well to form a dough, adding a little extra flour if it is too sticky to handle.

2 Using your hands, roll the dough into a (thin) roll, 40cm long. Cut this into two 20cm rolls, wrap each in plastic and chill in the freezer until firm enough to cut without flattening.

3 Preheat the oven to 180°C (170°C fanbake), with the rack just below the middle. Line a baking tray with baking paper. Cut each log into about 40 slices with a very sharp (serrated) knife. Place these slices on the prepared baking tray. (Bake the first tray-full while you slice the second log.)

4 Bake for about 10 minutes or until very lightly browned. While biscuits are warm, lift them onto a cooling rack.

5 To make the filling, dissolve the instant coffee in the hot water in the (unwashed) bowl or food processor. Add remaining ingredients and mix to icing consistency. Put the filling into a plastic bag with the corner cut off, and pipe a blob onto the centre of one of each pair of biscuits (or spread filling onto biscuits with a knife). Do not 'stick' the pairs of biscuits together until you have used up all the filling as evenly as possible.

6 Leave to firm on a rack before storing in an airtight container.

VARIATIONS: Add ¼ cup of finely chopped walnuts to the dough. Reserve 2 teaspoons of beaten egg and paint a little on top of half the uncooked biscuits, then top with more finely chopped walnuts.

NOTE: Carefully wrapped rolls of uncooked biscuit dough will keep in the freezer for up to a month.

Custard Kisses

These delicious biscuits are, in fact, sweet enough to be eaten unfilled, but of course they taste even better when stuck together with vanilla icing or jam.

For about 20 filled kisses or 40 halves:

175g butter

1 cup icing sugar

1 tsp vanilla essence

1½ cups standard (plain) flour

½ cup custard powder

1 tsp baking powder

Vanilla Filling:

50g butter, softened

1 cup icing sugar

2 Tbsp custard powder

a few drops of vanilla essence

1 Preheat the oven to 180°C (170°C fanbake), with the rack just below the middle. Line a baking tray with baking paper.

2 Warm butter until very soft but not completely melted. Mix in a large bowl (or process) with the icing sugar and vanilla essence until creamy, then sift in the flour, custard powder and baking powder. Mix well, squeezing bowl-mixed dough together by hand and adding a little milk if necessary, then shape as below.

3 Roll mixture into about 40 small balls. Flatten each with your hand before putting on the prepared baking tray. Make a pattern on them with a dampened fork, a meat hammer, the bottom of a patterned glass, or your fingers.

4 Alternatively, form mixture into a cylinder and refrigerate or freeze until dough may be sliced without flattening. Cut into about 40 slices, then put on baking tray, decorate as above, or leave plain.

5 Bake for about 12 minutes, until biscuits feel firm, but have not browned at all. (Browned biscuits taste of burnt butter.) Cool on a rack, then sort into pairs of the same size. Stick together with Vanilla Filling or raspberry jam.

6 For the filling, mix softened butter with the other icing ingredients until smooth, adding a few drops of water if necessary. Put filling in a small (but tough) plastic bag, cut off the corner and squeeze a blob of icing onto one biscuit of each pair. Do not press halves together until you have used up all the filling evenly.

7 Store kisses in airtight containers when icing has set. Freeze for longer storage.

Almond Creams

As teenagers, Alison's children often complained that her cakes and biscuits were less interesting than their grandmother's. Alison didn't have time to make buttery crisp biscuits which were rolled out thinly, cut with serrated cutters, brushed with beaten egg, sprinkled with nuts, and stuck together with icing, so she streamlined some favourite recipes to keep everyone happy!

For 20–30 filled biscuits:

175g butter

¾ cup icing sugar

½ tsp vanilla essence

½ tsp almond essence

1½ cups standard (plain) flour

½ cup cornflour or custard powder

1 tsp baking powder

¼ cup flaked almonds, optional

Almond Filling:

3 Tbsp butter, softened

½ tsp almond essence

¾ cup icing sugar

few drops of water if necessary

❶ Soften (but do not melt) the butter. Beat it with the icing sugar and essences, and then stir in the sifted dry ingredients and chopped almonds (or put everything in a food processor without sifting the dry ingredients).

❷ Roll out the mixture to form a cylinder 3cm across. Roll this in plastic wrap and chill until firm in the refrigerator or freezer.

❸ Preheat the oven to 180°C (170°C fanbake), with the rack just below the middle. Line a baking tray with baking paper. Cut the chilled dough into 40–60 thin slices, depending on the thickness desired.

❹ Bake for about 12 minutes, until the edges start to brown slightly. While biscuits are warm, lift them onto a cooling rack.

❺ For the filling, mix the butter with the essence and icing sugar, adding a little water if necessary. Sandwich biscuits together with filling when biscuits are cool enough.

Rock Cakes

Once, when Alison asked her husband which of his mother's recipes he remembered most fondly, he a answered in a second, 'Rock cakes!' Don't be put off by the rather unappealing name; it refers to the shape — they aren't rock hard and they taste great!

For 30–40 cakes:

125g butter

½ cup sugar

½ tsp vanilla

1 egg

¾ cup self-raising flour

1 cup standard (plain) flour

1 cup currants, sultanas, or mixed fruit

❶ Preheat the oven to 180°C (170°C fanbake), with the rack just below the middle. Line a baking tray with baking paper.

❷ Soften but do not melt the butter. Add the sugar and vanilla, beat or food process to combine, then add the egg and a tablespoon of the measured flour, and beat or food process until light coloured.

❸ Add the remaining flours, and mix just enough to combine. Sprinkle in the dried fruit and stir or process very briefly to mix.

❹ Using two spoons, form into mounds on the baking tray, leaving a little space for spreading.

❺ Bake for 10–15 minutes, until golden at the edges, and firm in the middle. Cool on a rack, then store in an airtight container.

NOTE: For best results, sift flour with a fork before spooning it into the cup measures. Do not pack it into the cups. Rock cakes which spread a lot do not have quite enough flour, and those which stay exactly as shaped and do not flatten at all contain too much flour.

Florentines

For 16 biscuits:

50g butter

¼ cup packed brown sugar

2 Tbsp standard (plain) flour

¼ cup slivered almonds

2–3 Tbsp red glacé cherries, chopped

2–3 Tbsp green glacé cherries, chopped

2–3 Tbsp chopped peel (or chopped crystallised ginger)

about 100g dark chocolate

There is something wickedly sinful about these rich biscuits. Set in thin, brandysnap-like biscuits are slivered almonds, sliced cherries, and peel or ginger. When the biscuits are turned over, you find that their bottoms are spread with melted dark chocolate. Wonderful!

1 Preheat the oven to 180°C (170°C fanbake) with rack just below the middle. Line a baking tray with baking paper.

2 Soften (but do not melt) the butter in a small mixing bowl. Add the brown sugar and flour and stir until thoroughly mixed. (Use absolutely level tablespoons of flour since altered quantities produce biscuits that spread too far or not far enough!)

3 Stir the almonds, cherries and peel (or ginger) into the mixture. Divide mixture in quarters. Form one quarter into four small balls and arrange on the prepared tray, leaving plenty of space between them so they can spread up to 7cm across.

4 Bake for 8–10 minutes. Watch them carefully, in case they cook in a shorter time, e.g. if using a fanbake oven. Biscuits are ready when they have spread evenly and have browned evenly all over. Take from oven, and push any uneven edges back into evenly shaped circles before the biscuits cool and firm up. When cool enough to lift, transfer to a rack.

5 When cold, carefully spread the flat underside of the Florentines with melted dark chocolate. When the chocolate coating is solid, transfer biscuits to a shallow airtight container, where they can be kept for a few days. The biscuits will soften if they are allowed to stand exposed to the air.

6 For a gourmet gift, pack in an attractive airtight container and decorate with curling ribbon, etc.

NOTE: If biscuits do not spread to 6–7cm across, you used too much flour. Use 1 teaspoon less, next time!

Brandy Snaps

Home-made brandy snaps are delicate and irresistibly crunchy. With a little practice, you will find them remarkably quick and easy to mix and make.

For about 12 brandy snaps:

2 rounded household Tbsp golden syrup

100g butter

½ cup packed brown sugar

2 tsp ground ginger

½ cup standard (plain) flour

1 Preheat the oven to 180°C (170°C fanbake), with the rack just below the middle. Line baking tray with baking paper.

2 Use a household tablespoons to measure the golden syrup into a pot. Heat golden syrup with butter and brown sugar until butter melts, then remove from heat and add ginger and flour.

3 Drop one heaped teaspoonful onto each quarter of the prepared baking tray, spreading each lot flat with the back of the spoon. The brandy snaps will spread more during cooking.

4 Bake for 5–10 minutes, until mixture bubbles, spreads and darkens slightly. Cool until firm enough to roll around a wooden spoon handle, etc., reheating the flat biscuits on their baking tray briefly for easier rolling if they firm up too quickly.

5 Store in airtight containers. Fill with whipped cream (flavoured with essence, if desired), just before serving.

VARIATIONS: Leave brandy snaps flat, then layer several with whipped cream and fresh berries for dessert. Or form cone shapes, rather than tubes.

Parmesan and Sesame Crumple-Crackers

Serve these unusual crackers after dinner with cheese, dried fruit, nuts and wine.

For 80–100 crumple-crackers:

2 cups high-grade (bread) flour

2 tsp baking powder

¾ cup finely grated Parmesan

3 Tbsp toasted sesame seeds

2 Tbsp poppy seeds, optional

½ cup bath-temperature water

1½–2 tsp salt

2 tsp sugar

2 Tbsp olive or avocado oil

about ¼ cup extra hot water

1 Preheat the oven to 160°C (150°C fanbake), with the rack just below the middle.

2 Measure the flour, baking powder, Parmesan, sesame seeds and poppy seeds (if using) into a food processor or large bowl.

3 Pour the first amount of hot water into a 1-cup measure, stir in the salt and sugar until dissolved, then add the oil.

4 Process the dry ingredients in bursts (or toss them together with a fork), while you add the hot liquid mixture in a steady stream. Add as much of the remaining hot water as you need to form a ball of soft dough.

5 Cut the dough into four parts, and put three aside in a plastic bag. Roll out the other piece VERY thinly on a floured board, using extra flour to stop it sticking, making an oval shape bigger than an A4 page. Cut in half (lengthwise), then cut each half into 10–12 tall, thin (pennant shaped) triangles, with alternate narrow bases and points on the cut edge. (Perfect shapes aren't necessary and outside edges need not be trimmed.)

6 Prick crackers with a fork or skewer. Place on a metal cake rack to bake, crumpling but not folding them.

7 Bake them for 10–15 minutes, until pale gold but dry and very crisp. Lower heat and cook longer if necessary. Repeat with remaining pieces of dough.

8 When cold, store in airtight containers, reheating if crackers soften on storage. (Flavour develops fully after about 12 hours.)

Nutty Lemon Wafers

These are very crisp and lemony, and quite delicious. If you can, use a Lisbon lemon instead of a Meyer lemon, since they have more of a lime flavour, and taste particularly good.

For about 120 biscuits:

finely grated zest of 1 large or 2 small lemons

1 cup sugar

125g butter, softened

1 large egg

1¾ cups standard (plain) flour

¼ cup cornflour

1 tsp baking powder

½–1 cup pinenuts, chopped walnuts or almonds

1 Preheat the oven to 180°C (170°C fanbake), with the rack just below the middle. Line a baking tray with baking paper.

2 Place lemon zest with the sugar in the food processor. Add the softened butter and egg, and process until light and fluffy. Sift the flour, cornflour and baking powder into the butter mixture, and process until mixed. Add the nuts and pulse briefly.

3 Form the (quite soft) dough into two 20cm rolls on plastic or baking paper. Roll the plastic or baking paper around the rolls of dough. Chill in the freezer for about 30 minutes, or until firm enough to cut easily.

4 Cut each roll into about 60 x 3mm slices using a very sharp or serrated, thin-bladed knife. Put each slice on the prepared baking tray before it softens, leaving a little room for spreading.

5 Bake for about 12 minutes, until biscuits are very lightly browned. While biscuits are warm, lift onto a cooling rack. When cold, store in an airtight container.

NOTE: Refrigerate part of the dough for a day or two, if desired, or for longer storage keep the wrapped dough in the freezer, thawing it in the refrigerator before slicing and baking as above.

Cheese Crisps

Serve these buttered or plain, with tea, coffee or cocktails.

For 30–40 crackers (depending on size):

1½ cups standard (plain) flour

1½ tsp baking powder

½ tsp salt

½–1 tsp curry or mustard powder

½ tsp paprika

shake of pepper

150g cold butter

1½ cups grated tasty cheese

cold water

1 Preheat the oven to 190°C (180°C fanbake), with the rack just below the middle. Line a baking tray with baking paper.

2 Measure the flour, baking powder and seasonings into a large bowl or a food processor. Cut, grate or chop in the butter and grated cheese, keeping the mixture as cold as possible.

3 When it resembles rolled oats, add water a few drops at a time until the particles stick together to make a firm dough. Do not over-mix.

4 Lightly flour the board and dough, and roll out thinly and evenly. Cut into squares, rectangles or fingers and place on the prepared baking tray.

5 Bake for 10–15 minutes, or until golden. Transfer the warm biscuits onto a cooling rack.

6 When cold, store in an airtight container. If biscuits soften on storage, crisp them up in a warm oven.

Rachel's Crackers

In 1980, a nine-year-old girl named Rachel wrote Alison a very nice letter asking if she knew how to make plain crackers. She and her brothers and sisters ate crackers after school, and with several hungry children to feed, her mother was complaining about the cost of snacks. Since this time, many other families have made and enjoyed these crackers, judging from the letters Alison has received over the years!

For about 20–40 crackers (depending on size):

1 Tbsp golden syrup or malt

½ cup (approx) water

2 cups standard (plain) flour

1½ tsp baking powder

1 tsp salt (see Note)

50g very cold butter

Optional ingredients:

1 Tbsp poppy seeds

¼ cup toasted sesame seeds

1 Tbsp grated Parmesan

1. Preheat the oven to 190°C (180°C fanbake), with the rack just below the middle. Line a baking tray with baking paper.

2. Stir the syrup (or malt) into the water. Sift the flour, baking powder and salt into a fairly large bowl. Add one or more of the optional ingredients.

3. Cut, grate or chop the very cold butter into/through the dry ingredients as if you were making pastry. When the mixture looks like rolled oats, start adding the water and syrup mixture, a few drops at a time, tossing it as you go. (Stop adding the liquid when the dough is a little softer than pastry dough but firm enough to roll out.)

4. Roll it out thinly on a lightly floured board, then cut it into squares or rectangles, or use a biscuit cutter to make interesting shapes. Re-roll scraps until all dough is used up. Prick large shapes in several places to prevent uneven rising.

5. For extra flavour, dampen surface of rolled dough with a little water and sprinkle biscuits with one or more of the optional ingredients. Do not use a lot of water or the mixture will get too soft.

6. Bake for 10–15 minutes, or until crackers are a pale gold colour. Cool on a rack. When cold, store in an airtight container.

NOTE: Replace all or part of the salt in the recipe with celery salt, garlic salt, or any other seasoned salt, if you like, using twice as much seasoned salt as plain salt.

Slices & Squares

Belgian Bars – recipe page 135

Almond Puff Slice

This is an interesting food processor slice for anyone who enjoys making cream puffs!

For a 30cm square slice:

Base:

1 cup standard (plain) flour

75g cold butter, cubed

2–4 Tbsp cold water

Topping (Choux Paste):

½ cup water

60g butter, cubed

½ cup standard (plain) flour

2 large eggs

½ tsp almond essence

Icing:

2 Tbsp softened butter

2 cups icing sugar

½ tsp almond essence

3 Tbsp hot water

½ cup sliced almonds, lightly toasted

1 Preheat the oven to 180°C (170°C fanbake), with the rack just below the middle. While oven heats, toast almonds in one layer in a shallow baking dish.

2 For the base, put flour and cold butter (cut into nine cubes) into the food processor. Pulse to chop butter fairly finely, then add ¾ of the water, a few drops at a time, while pulsing, until the crumbly mixture can be pressed together with your fingers to form a ball of dough.

3 Roll out thinly to 30 x 30cm on a piece of baking paper, then cut into three 10 x 30cm strips. Lift the baking paper and pastry onto a baking tray.

4 For the topping, heat water and cubed butter in a pot. As soon as it boils and the butter has melted, tip in all the flour. Stir briefly off the heat until dough forms a ball. Transfer hot dough to food processor. Add one egg and almond essence and process until mixed. Beat remaining egg with a fork and add gradually, processing in bursts until mixture is smooth and glossy, and the consistency of spreadable (but not runny) icing.

5 Spread mixture evenly over the three strips of pastry. Bake for 30–45 minutes. Cool on a rack before drizzling with icing, then sprinkle with the cooled toasted almonds. Cut across the strips into slices of desired size.

6 For the icing, put the softened butter in a bowl. Add the icing sugar and almond essence. Mix with a knife, adding enough water to make icing soft enough to drizzle or spread easily over topping.

7 Serve for dessert or with tea or coffee. Best eaten on the day it is made. Store in a shallow, lidded container in a cool place.

For a 23cm square slice:

Pastry Base (see Note):

1 cup standard (plain) flour

75g cold butter about

¼ cup cold water

Filling:

½ cup raspberry jam

about ½ cup currants or sultanas

Topping:

175g butter

1½ cups sugar

1 tsp vanilla essence

3 large eggs

3 cups coconut

Coconut Slice

This has been a family favourite for 30 years. Serve warm for dessert or cut in smaller pieces when cold, for a very popular slice. It is easy to make your own pastry in a food processor, but you can use bought pastry if you like.

1 Preheat the oven to 220°C (210°C fanbake), with the rack just below the middle. Spray a 23cm square pan with non-stick spray.

2 For the pastry, put flour and cubed butter in the food processor, then process in bursts, while adding the water in a slow stream. Stop as soon as you can press the dough particles together to make a firm dough. Refrigerate dough 5–10 minutes while you mix the topping.

3 For the topping, soften but do not melt the butter. In the unwashed food processor or bowl, mix butter with the sugar, vanilla essence and eggs, then mix in the coconut.

4 Roll out the pastry, so that it is big enough to cover the base and about 1cm up the sides of the pan. Spread it with the jam and dried fruit, then drop the topping over it in blobs, spreading so most of the surface is covered. (Topping will spread during cooking.)

5 Bake for 10–15 minutes, then turn down to 180°C (170° fanbake) and cook for 15–30 minutes or until the topping has browned evenly, and the centre feels firm.

6 Serve warm for dessert with whipped cream or ice-cream, or cool completely before cutting into pieces of the desired size. Store in a shallow container (between layers of paper) in the refrigerator for 3–4 days.

NOTE: For an extra easy version, replace the homemade pastry with 200g of bought sweet short pastry, or a sheet of pre-rolled pastry. Prick the pastry all over before covering with filling.

Cherry Slice

Alison worked out this (food processor) recipe after trying a delicious but expensive store-bought slice in London.

For a 23cm square slice:

Base:

1 cup standard (plain) flour

¼ cup sugar

100g cold butter

Filling:

¼–½ cup chopped glacé cherries

½ cup raspberry jam

Topping:

1½ cups desiccated coconut

1 cup sugar

½ cup standard (plain) flour

½ cup sliced almonds, optional

50g cold butter

2 large eggs

¼–½ tsp almond essence

1 Preheat the oven to 180°C (170°C fanbake), with the rack just below the middle. Spray a 23cm square loose-bottomed pan with non-stick spray.

2 For the base, put the flour, sugar and very cold butter (in nine cubes), in the food processor bowl. Process until butter is cut into very small crumbs, then press the mixture flat in the prepared pan with the back of a spoon or a spatula.

3 Bake for 15 minutes. While it bakes, prepare the filling, chopping the cherries fairly finely. Set aside.

4 For the topping, combine coconut, sugar, flour and almonds (if using) in the unwashed food processor bowl. Add the butter, cut in nine cubes, then process until butter is cut through the mixture. Add the eggs and essence and blend until well mixed.

5 Take the partly cooked base from the oven.

6 For the filling, spread warm base with jam, then sprinkle evenly with cherries.

7 Using two teaspoons, carefully drop the topping mixture over the filling. Spread topping lightly, to cover the jam and cherries without mixing the layers.

8 Bake for 20–30 minutes longer, until lightly browned and firm when touched. Cool on a rack. When cold, cut into pieces of desired size.

9 Serve large pieces, warm, for dessert, and smaller pieces, cold, with tea, coffee, etc. Refrigerate in a covered container, between layers of baking paper, for up to one week. Freeze for longer storage.

For an 18 x 28cm (or 20cm square) slice:

Base:

125g butter, softened

½ cup sugar

1 large egg

2 cups standard (plain) flour

2 tsp baking powder

1 tsp mixed spice

1 tsp ground cinnamon

Filling:

2 Tbsp sugar

¼ cup apricot jam

¼ cup coconut

¼ cup currants

25g butter

1 large egg, beaten

zest and juice of 1 lemon

Icing, optional:

1 Tbsp butter, softened

finely grated zest of ½ lemon

1 cup icing sugar

3–4 tsp lemon juice

Spicy Fruit Slice

This slice has an irresistible combination of textures and flavours.

1 Preheat the oven to 180°C (170°C fanbake). Place rack in the middle of the oven. Line the base and sides of an 18 x 28cm pan with baking paper, or spray a 20cm square loose-bottomed pan.

2 For the base, cream butter and sugar, add the egg and mix again, then add the sifted dry ingredients (or mix in a food processor). Divide the mixture in two and press one half into the baking pan. Roll the other half out the same size, on a piece of plastic, and put aside.

3 For the filling, heat sugar, jam, coconut, currants and butter until the mixture boils. Cool the container in cold water, then beat in the egg, finely grated lemon zest and juice, with a fork. Spread this mixture over the base, cover with remaining dough, and lift away the plastic, pressing gently into the corners.

4 Bake for 25–30 minutes, until the centre springs back when lightly pressed.

5 For (optional) icing, beat together butter, lemon zest and sifted icing sugar in a small bowl. Add lemon juice one teaspoon at a time until creamy. Spread on cooled slice, making wavy patterns with a fork. Leave to set.

6 Serve cut into fingers of desired size. Store in a closed container (between layers of paper) in a cool place for up to one week.

Ginger Crunch

Ginger Crunch is another perennial family favourite; even though it seems to have been around forever, it is still popular.

For an 18 x 28cm (or 23cm square) slice:

Base:

125g butter

¼ cup sugar

1 tsp baking powder

1 cup standard (plain) flour

1 tsp ground ginger

Icing:

2 Tbsp butter

2 tsp ground ginger

2 rounded household Tbsp golden syrup

1 Tbsp water

2 cups icing sugar

1 Preheat the oven to 180°C (170°C fanbake), with the rack just below the middle. Line the base and sides of an 18 x 28cm pan with baking paper, allowing extra on the sides for lifting out the cooked slice, or spray a 23cm square loose-bottomed pan.

2 For the base, cut the cold butter into nine cubes, then process in brief bursts with remaining base ingredients, until the mixture is the texture of coarse breadcrumbs. If mixing by hand, warm butter until soft, mix it with the sugar, then stir in the sieved dry ingredients. Press the crumbly mixture into the pan firmly and evenly.

3 Bake for about 10 minutes or until evenly and lightly browned. While hot, it will still feel soft. While the base cooks, make the icing, since the base should be iced while hot.

4 For the icing, measure the butter, ginger, golden syrup and water into a small pot or microwave-safe bowl. Heat, without boiling, until melted. Take off heat, sift in the icing sugar, and beat until smooth.

5 When the base is cooked, take it from the oven, pour the warm icing onto the hot base and spread carefully so it covers the base evenly. Leave to cool and set. Do not take from the pan until it has cooled completely.

6 Serve with tea or coffee, or pack in lunches. Store in a cool place for up to one week.

VARIATION: Sprinkle partly set icing with ½–1 cup chopped nuts of your choice.

NOTE: For a really thick icing, use one-and-a-half times the icing recipe!

For a 23cm square slice:

Base:

2 cups chopped dates

½ cup chopped crystallised ginger

½ cup water

1 cup chopped walnuts

125g butter, softened

1 cup brown sugar

2 large eggs

1 tsp vanilla essence

1½ cups standard (plain) flour

½ cup (fine) rolled oats

2 tsp baking powder

Icing:

2 Tbsp butter

2–3 tsp ground ginger

2 rounded household Tbsp golden syrup

2 cups icing sugar

about 2 tsp water

Walnut, Date & Ginger Slice

This slice contains a satisfying mixture of dried fruit, nuts and crystallised ginger, topped with a delicious Ginger Crunch-like icing.

1 Preheat the oven to 180°C (170°C fanbake), with the rack just below the middle. Line the base and sides of a 23cm square loose-bottomed pan with baking paper.

2 For the base, chop each date and piece of ginger into three or four pieces. Put in a covered non-stick pan with the water. Stand over high heat until water boils rapidly. Stir fruit carefully after 2 minutes, then leave the lid off until water evaporates. Take pan off heat and stand in cold water. Stir in chopped walnuts.

3 Mix butter and sugar thoroughly in a food processor or bowl. Beat in the eggs and vanilla essence, then add the dry ingredients and mix until combined. Tip mixture from processor or bowl into the pan with the cooked mixture. Stir to mix, then pour into the prepared baking pan. Bake for about 30 minutes, until a skewer inserted in the centre comes out clean.

4 For the icing, warm the butter, ginger and golden syrup in a frypan until melted. (Do not boil.) Take off heat. Add the sifted icing sugar and beat well with a fork or wooden spoon until smooth, adding enough water to make a spreadable consistency. Ice while slice is warm (but not hot). Decorate with extra sliced ginger and walnuts if desired and, when icing is set, cut into fingers with a sharp knife.

5 Serve any time with tea or coffee, or add to packed lunches. Store in a shallow, lidded container in a cool place for three to four days.

VARIATION: Leave out ginger from slice and icing, if desired.

Walnut Cheesecake Slice

We like this slice served for dessert the day it is made or enjoy leftovers served with tea or coffee over the next few days.

For a 23cm square slice:

Base:

75g cold butter

1 cup standard (plain) flour

¼ cup brown sugar

Filling:

250g cream cheese

¼ cup sugar

2 Tbsp brown sugar

1 large egg

½ tsp vanilla essence

½–¾ cup finely chopped walnuts

1 Preheat the oven to 190°C (180°C fanbake). Place rack in the middle of the oven. Press a large piece of baking paper into a 23cm square pan or a smallish sponge roll pan, folding the paper so it covers the bottom and all sides of the pan. Do not cut the paper at the corners, or filling may run underneath.

2 For the base, rub butter into flour and sugar in a bowl using a pastry blender or fingers until mixture is crumbly (or use a food processor). Press mixture evenly into the lined baking pan. Bake for 10 minutes. While the base cooks, make the filling.

3 For the filling, soften cream cheese in a bowl with a fork, then add the sugar, brown sugar, egg and vanilla essence. Mix until smooth (or re-use unwashed food processor). Pour the cream cheese mixture over the hot, partly cooked, base and sprinkle with the walnuts.

4 Bake for 20–30 minutes, or until cream cheese mixture has set in the centre. Cool in pan on a rack. Chill for 2–3 hours before cutting into pieces of the desired size.

5 Serve larger pieces for dessert with fresh fruit, whipped cream, etc. Cut smaller pieces to serve with tea or coffee. Store in a shallow, covered container in the refrigerator for up to three days.

Orange Slice

Kirsten learned how to make this, her favourite slice, when she was young. It is now a popular addition to her children's lunch boxes.

For an 18 x 28cm slice:

Base:

100g butter

½ a 400g can sweetened condensed milk

finely grated zest of 1 orange

1 cup desiccated coconut

1 packet (250g) wine or malt biscuits

Icing:

25g (2 Tbsp) butter, softened

1 cup icing sugar

about 1 Tbsp orange juice

1 Line the base and sides of an 18 x 28cm pan with baking paper.

2 For the base, warm butter in a medium-sized pot or microwave-safe bowl until melted. Remove from heat and stir in condensed milk. Add the orange zest and coconut to the butter mixture, then stir until well combined.

3 Break biscuits into halves or quarters. Put the pieces in a big plastic bag, loosely close the bag, and bang and roll with a rolling pin until crumbed, then stir them into the pot. (If you like, crumb the biscuits in a food processor, then add the other ingredients and mix well.)

4 Press mixture firmly into the lined pan until it is the depth you like (it does not have to cover the whole pan), and level the top.

5 For the icing, put the softened butter in a clean bowl. Add icing sugar and enough juice to mix with a knife so it will spread smoothly over the base. Pattern the icing by making wiggles on top with a fork, then chill until firm. Cut into pieces of the desired size.

6 Serve at any time of day. Good for school lunches and after-school snacks. Store in a covered container in the fridge, for up to one week, or in the freezer for up to three months.

Apricot Slice

This slice has a lovely caramel and apricot flavour. Use the larger amount of dried apricots, if you can.

For an 18 x 26cm slice:

100–150g dried apricots

¼ cup orange juice or sherry

75g butter

½ a 400g can sweetened condensed milk

½ cup brown sugar

½ cup coconut

1 packet (250g) wine or malt biscuits, finely crushed (see Note)

extra coconut

❶ Line the base and sides of an 18 x 28cm pan with baking paper.

❷ Finely chop the dried apricots using kitchen scissors or a sharp knife and cook them in the orange juice or sherry in a large pot until there is no liquid left. Add the butter to the apricots and stir over low heat until melted. Add condensed milk and brown sugar, then heat gently, stirring often until the sugar is no longer grainy, and the mixture is golden brown.

❸ Remove from heat and stir in coconut and the biscuit crumbs. Stir everything together evenly.

❹ Sprinkle the lined baking pan with the extra coconut, then tip in the mixture. Press in evenly to the depth you like (it need not cover the whole pan.) Sprinkle the mixture with more coconut, then refrigerate for at least 2 hours before cutting into pieces of your desired size.

❺ Serve with tea or coffee or pack in lunches. Store in the refrigerator to keep the mixture firm.

VARIATION: For Apricot & Almond Slice, add ¼–½ cup plain or lightly toasted, slivered almonds with the crushed biscuits.

NOTE: To finely crush the biscuits without a food processor, put them in a large plastic bag, loosely closed with a rubber band, and bang and roll with a rolling pin. Sieve crushed biscuits, crushing any large remaining pieces.

Anne Ford's Churchill Squares

Sam (Simon's wife) has many happy memories of her mother making this for picnics and family gatherings.

Filling:

1 cup desiccated coconut

2 Tbsp sugar

¾ cup milk

Base:

100g butter, softened

½ cup sugar

1 large egg

1½ cups standard (plain) flour

2 Tbsp cocoa

1 tsp baking powder

1 Preheat the oven to 180°C (170°C fanbake), with the rack just below the middle. Line the base and sides of an 18 x 28cm pan with baking paper.

2 For the filling, put the coconut, sugar and milk in a non-stick pan. Heat until sugar dissolves and the milk is soaked up. Take off heat and cool in pan.

3 For the base, beat the softened butter, sugar and egg in a bowl (or use a food processor). Sift in flour, cocoa and baking powder, and mix well. Divide dough in half. Put the baking paper pan-liner on the bench for a size guide, and roll out half the dough on it. Put paper and dough back in pan. Roll remaining dough out on another piece of baking paper the same size.

4 Spread cool filling evenly on the dough in the pan. Carefully flip remaining dough on top, and lift off baking paper. Pat to neaten edges.

5 Bake for 20–30 minutes until centre feels firm. Cool on a rack. Ice when cold. Cut into squares of desired size, using a sharp serrated knife dipped in hot water.

6 Spread Chocolate Icing (see page 252) on slice.

7 Serve with tea, coffee or milk, or pack in lunches. Store in a closed container in a cool place for up to one week.

Gooey Chewy Fudge Squares

The name says it all! This square is really a cross between a square and a deliciously chewy candy. Allow time for hardening overnight.

For a 16 x 20cm slice:

Base:

75g cold butter

¼ cup sugar

¾ cup standard (plain) flour

Topping:

400g can sweetened condensed milk

1 cup dark chocolate melts or 180g chopped dark chocolate

¼ tsp rum essence or ½ tsp vanilla essence

¼–½ cup sliced almonds

❶ Preheat the oven to 170°C (160°C fanbake), with the rack just below the middle.

❷ Line the base and sides of a 16 x 20cm expanding pan (at its smallest) with baking paper, folding the lining at the corners so the topping mixture cannot run underneath during cooking.

❸ For the base, cut the cold butter into 8–12 cubes and put in a food processor (or grate into a large bowl) with the sugar and flour. Process in bursts, or rub in butter by hand, until the mixture forms small, even crumbs. Tip this into the lined baking pan and press down to cover the base evenly. Bake for 10 minutes.

❹ For the topping, heat condensed milk and chocolate in a microwave-safe bowl for 2 minutes on High (100% power), then stir until all the chocolate has melted. Add essence and stir again. Pour over base and sprinkle with sliced almonds.

❺ Bake for 30–45 minutes until you can see that the middle has risen in humps. Cool on a rack, then chill overnight, to allow the topping to firm up, before cutting into fairly small squares.

❻ Serve with coffee as an after dinner treat. Store in a shallow, lidded container, preferably one layer thick, in a cool place for up to one week.

For a 20cm square slice:

Base:

about 200g flaky pastry

Filling:

½ cup vanilla custard powder

¼ cup brown sugar

2¼ cups milk

2 large eggs

½ tsp vanilla essence

Icing:

1 cup icing sugar

2 tsp softened butter

lemon juice or passionfruit pulp
to mix

Kirsten's Custard Squares

Alison has a great weakness for custard squares, so she was delighted when her daughter Kirsten invented a custard square birthday cake for her.

1 Preheat the oven to 200°C (190°C fanbake), with the rack just below the middle. Line the base and sides of a 20cm (or 23cm) square loose-bottomed baking pan with baking paper.

2 For the base, roll the pastry out thinly to make two squares each about 2cm bigger than the pan. Prick the pastry evenly all over. Place the two pastry squares on an oven slide and bake for 7–8 minutes or until golden brown on both sides. Trim the cooked squares of pastry to fit the loose-bottomed baking pan. Place one square in it.

3 For the filling, mix the custard powder and the brown sugar together in a heavy bottomed, medium-sized pot. Add the milk and stir until well combined but not foamy. Cook gently over low heat for 2–3 minutes, until the custard thickens. Next, whisk in the beaten (but not foamy) eggs, and the vanilla essence. Again, stir constantly until the custard thickens.

4 Pour custard evenly over the pastry in the baking pan. Cover the hot custard with the other pastry layer immediately. Refrigerate until cold.

5 For the icing, put the icing sugar and butter in a bowl. Stir in small amounts of lemon juice or passionfruit pulp until you get icing of spreadable consistency. Ice the top layer of pastry and leave it to set. Cut into 16 (or nine larger) squares using a sharp knife.

6 Serve from the refrigerator, with coffee or tea, or for dessert. Store squares which are not eaten the day they are made in the refrigerator, and eat within the next two days.

Lemon Squares

This square has a delicious lemon-flavoured custardy topping and always disappears very quickly. If you don't have a food processor, you may wish to make another lemon slice instead!

For a 23cm square slice:

Base:

2 cups standard (plain) flour

½ cup icing sugar

125g cold butter, cubed

Topping:

1½ cups sugar

zest of ½ lemon

3 large eggs

¼ cup lemon juice

¼ cup self-raising flour

1 Preheat the oven to 160°C (150°C fanbake), with the rack just below the middle. Press a large piece of baking paper into a 23cm square pan or a smallish sponge roll pan, folding the paper so it covers the bottom and all sides. Do not cut the paper at the corners, or filling will run underneath.

2 For the base, measure the flour, icing sugar and butter into a food processor. Process until butter is chopped finely through dry ingredients. Tip mixture into the lined pan and press down firmly and evenly with the back of a large spoon or a spatula.

3 Bake for 15–20 minutes until firm and straw-coloured. While it cooks, prepare topping.

4 For the topping, put the sugar in the dry, unwashed food processor with the lemon zest (use a potato peeler to remove zest from lemon). Process until the zest is very finely chopped through the sugar, then add the eggs, lemon juice and flour, and process until smooth.

5 Pour over partly cooked base, then bake for about 30 minutes longer, or until top is lightly browned and centre does not wobble when pan is jiggled.

6 When quite cold, cut into squares or fingers of desired size, by pressing a heavy, lightly oiled knife straight down through the topping and base.

7 Serve large pieces for dessert, sifted with icing sugar, with Greek-style yoghurt, lightly whipped cream or mascarpone. Serve small pieces with coffee at any time of day. Store, lightly covered, for up to three or four days.

Louise Cake

A favourite café slice, this is not hard to make.

For an 18 x 28cm (or 23cm square) slice:

Base:

100g butter, softened

½ cup sugar

2 (large) egg yolks

1 tsp vanilla essence

1 cup self-raising flour

1 cup standard (plain) flour

Filling:

½ cup raspberry jam

Topping:

2 large egg whites

1 tsp vanilla essence

½ cup sugar

¾ cup shredded coconut

❶ Preheat the oven to 160°C (150°C fanbake), with the rack just below the middle. Line the base and sides of an 18 x 28cm pan with baking paper, allowing enough extra paper on the sides for lifting the cooked slice out, or spray a 23cm square loose-bottomed pan.

❷ For the base, put the softened butter and sugar in a food processor or large bowl. Separate two eggs, adding the yolks to the butter mixture (and put the whites in a very clean medium-sized bowl ready to use for the topping). Add the vanilla essence and mix, then add the two flours and mix again until evenly crumbly. Tip crumbly mixture into prepared pan and press down evenly. Bake for 15 minutes.

❸ Make the topping while base cooks. Beat the egg whites and vanilla essence until frothy, then add the sugar and beat until the tips of peaks turn over when the beater is lifted from them. Fold the coconut evenly through the meringue.

❹ For the filling, spread the jam over the hot, partly cooked shortcake.

❺ Put the meringue in spoonfuls over jam, then spread evenly with a knife. Sprinkle with 2 tablespoons of extra coconut if you like. Bake for about 15 minutes or until the meringue feels crisp and is evenly and lightly coloured. Cool completely before cutting into pieces of the desired size.

❻ Serve with tea or coffee. Store in a container, one layer deep, in a cool place with lid slightly ajar.

Margaret Payne's Neenish Squares

Alison's mother made these rich treats for special occasions! They require some skill and patience but are so good that the effort pays off.

For an 18 x 28cm slice:

Base:

100g butter, softened

1 cup icing sugar

1 cup standard (plain) flour

½ cup cornflour

milk, if necessary

Filling:

2 tsp gelatine

2 Tbsp water

100g butter, at room temperature

1 cup icing sugar

about 4 Tbsp lukewarm water

½–1 tsp rum essence

1 Preheat the oven to 170°C (160°C fanbake), with the rack just below the middle. Line the base and sides of an 18 x 28cm pan with baking paper.

2 For the base, beat butter and icing sugar in a bowl (or use a food processor). Rub (or chop) in sifted flour and cornflour until the mixture is the texture of coarse breadcrumbs. Add a little milk if too dry. Spread the crumbly mixture into the baking pan and press it down firmly and evenly. Bake for 15 minutes or until straw-coloured. Cool.

3 For the filling, soften gelatine in cold water for 2–3 minutes, then warm to dissolve. Leave to cool.

4 Cream butter and icing sugar. Beat in lukewarm water a little at a time, stopping if it shows any sign of curdling. Mix in cooled gelatine and rum essence. If necessary, refrigerate filling until firm but workable, then spread evenly over the base with a knife. Chill again.

5 Spread Chocolate Icing (see page 252) over chilled filling. Refrigerate for several hours, then cut into small squares.

6 Serve from refrigerator with coffee for a special treat. Store in a shallow, lidded container in the refrigerator for three to four days.

VARIATION: For a thinner base, use half of all ingredients.

For a 20cm square slice (16 squares):

Base:

200–250g flaky pastry

Filling:

1 cup currants

1 cup mixed fruit

½ cup brown sugar

1 cup mint leaves

½ tsp mixed spice

25g butter, softened

Minted Fruit Squares

Cut this rich slice into small squares. It has a distinctive mint flavour, which is often not recognised because it is unexpected. We imagine that it would keep for several weeks but, in our households, it is always eaten within two or three days!

1. Preheat the oven to 190°C (180°C fanbake), with the rack just below the middle. Line the base and sides of a 20cm square baking pan with baking paper.

2. For the base, roll the pastry out thinly to form two squares: one 25cm square and one 20cm square. Leave pastry to rest while you mix the filling.

3. For the filling, chop the dried fruit, brown sugar and mint leaves together, using either a large knife on a large wooden board, or a food processor. (If processing, take care not to over-mix, as you don't want to form a paste.) Stir in the spice and the butter, which has been heated until it is soft enough to be mixed evenly through the fruit mixture.

4. Put the larger sheet of pastry in the lined baking pan, so that it comes 2cm up the sides, all round, then spread the filling over the base. Cover filling with the smaller sheet of pastry. Dampen the edges of both layers of pastry, then pinch them together to seal. Tidy by trimming or folding edges decoratively. Brush top with milk, if desired. Make several small cuts in the pastry so steam can escape during baking.

5. Bake for 25–35 minutes, until the pastry is evenly brown. Press the pastry down if it has risen unevenly, then leave it to cool completely, before cutting it into 16 small squares with a sharp, serrated knife.

6. Serve at room temperature with tea or coffee. Store in a closed container in the refrigerator or a cool place, for several days (up to one week).

VARIATION: For Fruit Square, leave out the mint altogether.

Chocolate Fudge Squares

This delicious (unbaked) fudge square can be made by quite inexperienced young cooks — show them how, then let them try alone!

For an 18 x 28cm slice:

Base:

1 packet (250g) wine, or malt or digestive biscuits

½ cup brown sugar

¼ cup cocoa

3 Tbsp milk

75g butter

1 tsp vanilla essence

1 cup chopped walnuts or chopped sultanas or a mixture

Topping:

Chocolate Icing (see page 252)

1. Line the base and sides of an 18 x 28cm pan with baking paper.

2. For the base, crush biscuits in a large plastic bag, fastened loosely with a rubber band, banging and rolling with a rolling pin until quite evenly crushed (or crumb broken biscuits in a food processor without making fine crumbs).

3. Mix the sugar and cocoa in a fairly large pot, then stir in the milk and add the butter. Bring to the boil, stirring all the time. Take off the heat and stir in the vanilla essence, crushed biscuits, chopped nuts and/or sultanas.

4. Press mixture into the lined pan until it is the depth you like (it does not have to cover the whole pan). Flatten surface fairly smoothly with the back of a spoon or spatula.

5. Spread Chocolate Icing (see page 252) on base with a knife and refrigerate until set. Cut into pieces of desired size when firm, using a hot, wet knife.

6. Serve as dessert with coffee, as a mid-afternoon snack, or add to a packed lunch.

Peanut Butter Squares

These are very popular with children — and often with adults. We like these made thick and cut in small squares so they finish up as cubes.

For an 18 x 28cm slice:

Base:

100g butter

½ cup peanut butter

1 cup biscuit crumbs

1 cup icing sugar

about 6 drops almond essence

¼ tsp vanilla essence

Icing:

½ cup chocolate melts or 90g chopped dark chocolate

1 Tbsp peanut butter

1. Line the base and sides of an 18 x 28cm pan with baking paper.

2. For the base, heat the butter (cut into 4 cubes) and peanut butter (in 4–5 blobs) in a large microwave-safe bowl on High (100% power) for 2 minutes or until butter is melted. Take from the microwave and stir until the two are thoroughly blended.

3. Crumb the biscuits in a food processor, or put them in a large plastic bag, closing the top loosely with a rubber band. Using a rolling pin, bang and roll the biscuits in the bag until they are crumbed. Add the crumbs, sifted icing sugar and essences to the butter mixture. Mix well, then press into part of the lined baking pan, so that the mixture is 10–15mm high.

4. For the icing, melt the chocolate and soften the peanut butter in a small bowl in the microwave on High (100% power) for 1–2 minutes, just until the two can be mixed together smoothly. Spread over base mixture using a knife. Cool before cutting into small squares with a sharp serrated knife or sharp heavy knife.

5. Serve as after dinner treats, with tea, coffee or glasses of milk, or pack in lunches. Store in a covered container, in one layer, in the refrigerator or in a cool place, for up to one week.

Peppermint Chocolate Squares

Make these to have on hand over the holiday period, or to pack attractively in a flat box, to give away as a Christmas gift.

For an 18 x 28cm slice:

Base:

125g butter

½ a 400g can sweetened condensed milk

¼ cup sugar

¼ cup cocoa

1 tsp vanilla essence

1 packet (250g) wine biscuits

Peppermint Icing:

1 cup icing sugar

1 Tbsp softened butter

1 tsp peppermint essence

2 tsp milk

Chocolate Icing:

50g block cooking chocolate

1 tsp butter

1. Line the base and sides of an 18 x 28cm pan with baking paper.

2. For the base, place the butter, condensed milk, sugar and cocoa in a large bowl capable of holding a very hot mixture. Microwave on High (100% power) for about 4 minutes, or until mixture forms a soft ball in cold water. Stir after the first minute. Alternatively, heat in a frypan, stirring frequently, until the mixture has boiled gently for about 2 minutes and forms a soft ball.

3. Remove from heat and stir in the vanilla essence. Add crumbed biscuits (crumb biscuits in a food processor or by banging and rolling in a plastic bag with a rolling pin). Mix well. Press mixture evenly into the prepared baking pan.

4. For peppermint icing, sift or process the icing sugar to remove lumps. Add the butter and the peppermint essence. Add enough milk to mix a fairly stiff icing, using the food processor or a knife to mix. Spread this on the square.

5. For chocolate icing, cube the chocolate, and microwave with butter on Medium (50% power) for 2 minutes or until soft enough to spread over the white icing. When icing is firm, mark into small (3cm) squares.

6. Serve these little squares after dinner with coffee (they tend to disappear from the tin at other times of the day as well). Store in the refrigerator in hot weather.

VARIATIONS: Replace melted chocolate with chocolate icing, or use 1½ cups icing sugar for more peppermint icing, and leave out the chocolate layer.

Chocolate Caramel Bars

You can make a whole batch of this tasty treat for the same price as two bought pieces.

For an 18 x 28cm slice:

Base:

100g butter, softened

¼ cup caster sugar

1 cup standard (plain) flour

Filling:

100g butter

½ a 400g can sweetened condensed milk

½ cup golden syrup

¼ cup chopped walnuts, optional

Icing:

1 Tbsp cocoa

1½ Tbsp boiling water

2 tsp softened butter

¼ tsp vanilla essence

1 cup icing sugar

1 Preheat the oven to 170°C (160°C fanbake), with the rack just below the middle. Line the base and sides of an 18 x 28cm pan with baking paper.

2 For the base, cream the softened butter and caster sugar, then stir in flour. Press into prepared baking pan.

3 Bake for 6–8 minutes or until the centre is firm. Do not overcook, or your bars will be very hard to cut later.

4 For the filling, measure butter, condensed milk and golden syrup into a pot. Bring to the boil over medium heat, stirring all the time, then reduce heat and cook for 10 minutes, stirring often, until the mixture is a deep golden colour, and a drop of it forms a soft ball in cold water.

5 Take off heat, stir in chopped walnuts (if using) and pour over cooked base straight away, smoothing out if necessary. Leave to cool before icing.

6 For the icing, pour boiling water on cocoa in a small bowl. Beat in butter, vanilla essence and sifted icing sugar, adding more water if necessary, to make icing soft enough to spread easily over the caramel.

7 Leave uncovered for at least 2 hours before cutting into bars.

8 Serve with tea or coffee, or as an after dinner treat.

Chocolate Surprise Bars

This delicious slice forms a jelly-like central layer as it bakes.

For an 18 x 28cm slice:

Base:

100g cold butter, cubed

½ cup sugar

1 cup standard (plain) flour

Filling:

2 large or 3 small eggs

1 tsp vanilla essence

1½ cups brown sugar

1 cup desiccated coconut

¼ cup standard (plain) flour

2 Tbsp cocoa

½ cup dark chocolate melts or 90g chopped dark chocolate

1 tsp baking powder

¼ tsp salt

1½ cups grated, squeezed zucchini

Topping:

½ cup dark chocolate melts

1 Preheat the oven to 160°C (150°C fanbake), with the rack just below the middle. Line the base and sides of an 18 x 28cm pan with baking paper, folding it at the corners so the topping mixture cannot run underneath during cooking.

2 For the base, put the cold butter in a food processor (or grate it into a large bowl) with the sugar and flour. Process in bursts, or rub in butter by hand, forming small, even crumbs. Tip the crumbly mixture into the prepared pan and press down firmly and evenly. Bake for 10 minutes.

3 For the filling, mix eggs, vanilla essence and brown sugar well in the unwashed food processor or a bowl. Mix everything else (except zucchini) in another bowl. Toss zucchini with the other ingredients, then add to the egg mixture. Process briefly, or stir together, then pour over partly baked base.

4 For the topping, sprinkle chocolate melts over the surface.

5 Bake for 45 minutes or until the centre feels firm. Cool overnight before cutting into bars or squares of desired size.

6 Serve as a treat at any time of the day. Store (in one layer) in a shallow, lidded container in the refrigerator for up to five days.

Belgian Bars

This spicy mixture spreads an enticing smell through the house as it bakes. All age groups love it!

For 12–16 bars (depending on size):

Base:

1 cup brown sugar, packed

200g butter, softened

1 large egg

1 tsp ground cinnamon

2 tsp mixed spice

4 tsp baking powder

2 cups standard (plain) flour

Filling:

about ½ cup raspberry jam

Icing, optional:

2 cups sifted icing sugar

25g butter, softened

about 3 Tbsp lemon juice or water

red jelly crystals or coloured sugar (see Note)

❶ Preheat the oven to 160°C (150°C fanbake), with the rack just below the middle. Line the base and sides of a large sponge roll pan with baking paper.

❷ For the base, measure the brown sugar, softened butter and egg into a large bowl (or a food processor). Mix well, then add all the dry ingredients except the flour. Mix again, then add and mix in half the flour. Add remaining flour and mix well.

❸ Divide dough into two parts, and refrigerate in a plastic bag until firm enough to roll. Roll each half out to fit your baking pan. (If you like, work with the dough between sheets of floured, waxed paper or plastic to prevent sticking.)

❹ Place the first sheet in the prepared baking pan and neaten the edges. Spread it with a thin layer of jam, then cover with the second sheet of dough. Prick in a few places.

❺ Bake for 20–30 minutes until the centre is firm when gently pressed. Leave to cool before icing.

❻ For the icing (optional), mix icing sugar, butter and enough lemon juice or water to make a fairly soft icing. Spread evenly over the cooked mixture. If you like, sprinkle a few red jelly crystals or some coloured sugar on the icing. When icing is set, cut into bars.

❼ Serve with tea or coffee. Store bars in airtight jars in a cool place for about one week.

NOTE: To make coloured sugar, add a few drops of red or pink food colouring to 2 tablespoons of sugar and mix until evenly coloured. Dry before use.

Pack-A-Snack Bars

This bar makes a popular, concentrated snack food. With its many nutritious additions, it is almost a meal in itself! It carries well in a backpack, school bag or handbag.

For an 18 x 28cm slice:

Base:

1 cup standard (plain) flour

1 cup wholemeal flour

1 cup (fine) rolled oats

200g cold butter, cubed

1 cup brown sugar

Topping:

4 large eggs

½ cup brown sugar

1 tsp vanilla essence

2 cups almonds

1 cup dates, chopped

1 cup dried apricots, chopped

1 cup chocolate melts

1 cup desiccated coconut

1 Preheat the oven to 180°C (170°C fanbake), with the rack just below the middle. Line the base and sides of an 18 x 28cm pan with baking paper.

2 For the base, chop the flours, oats and cold butter together in a food processor, or grate the butter into the oats and flours in a bowl. Mix in the brown sugar and press the mixture into the prepared pan. (For a thinner base use half the base ingredients.)

3 For the topping, put eggs, brown sugar and vanilla essence in a large bowl and beat with a fork just until whites and yolks are evenly mixed. Add all the remaining ingredients and mix together with a stirrer or spatula. Spread over the uncooked base and press down fairly evenly.

4 Bake for 45 minutes, covering the top with a liner or folded baking paper if it browns too quickly. Cool in the baking pan, preferably overnight.

5 When completely cold, cut into four large pieces using a sharp serrated knife. Trim off the outer edges if necessary.

6 Store pieces in the refrigerator for up to one week, or freeze for up to six weeks in plastic bags or covered containers. Cut each piece into bars or fingers as required, just before serving.

Birdseed Bars

This sweet bar contains many healthy and flavourful additions.
Eat it with restraint — it is all too easy to keep reaching for more!

For an 18 x 28cm slice:

1 cup sesame seeds

1 cup sunflower seeds

1 cup chopped roasted peanuts

1 cup coconut or (fine) rolled oats or crushed cornflakes

1 cup sultanas

100g butter

¼ cup honey

½ cup brown sugar

1 Line the base and sides of an 18 x 28cm pan with baking paper.

2 One ingredient at a time, watching carefully to prevent over-browning, lightly toast the sesame seeds, sunflower seeds, chopped nuts, coconut, and rolled oats or crushed cornflakes, under a grill or in a large heavy-bottomed frypan on moderate heat. Stir so that the contents brown evenly and lightly. (Do not mix before heating, since they brown at different rates.)

3 Mix them in a large bowl after they are heated, and stir in the sultanas.

4 Put the butter, honey and brown sugar into the large pan and heat gently until the sugar dissolves, making a toffee-like mixture. Heat until a drop forms a soft ball when dropped in cold water, then tip the toasted ingredients back into the pan.

5 Stir well to combine, then press the mixture into the prepared pan. Leave until lukewarm, then turn out onto a board and, using a sharp serrated knife, cut into bars the size and shape you like.

6 Serve whenever a healthy snack is required. Store promptly when cold, in an airtight container (or carefully wrap pieces individually).

VARIATION: Replace peanuts with walnuts or almonds.

Super Muesli Bars

Muesli bars are really quite easy to make, and homemade bars cost a fraction of the price of bought bars.

For an 18 x 28cm (or 23cm square) slice:

1 cup (fine) rolled oats

½ cup wheatgerm

½ cup sesame seeds

½ cup sunflower seeds

¼ cup chopped dried apricots, optional

¼ cup canola or other oil

½ cup honey

¼ cup peanut butter

1 Line the base and sides of an 18 x 28cm pan with baking paper, or coat a 23cm square loose-bottomed pan with non-stick spray.

2 Mix the first four ingredients together in a sponge roll pan or heavy frypan. Lightly toast the mixture, by cooking about 10cm below a grill or on the stove-top over a medium heat, until it has coloured lightly and lost its raw taste (this should take 5–6 minutes). Stir frequently to ensure nothing burns.

3 Briefly run the dried apricots under the hot tap, then chop them finely and set aside.

4 While the oat mixture is browning, measure the oil, honey and peanut butter into a large frypan. Bring to the boil over moderate heat, stirring to blend the ingredients, then turn the heat very low and cook the mixture gently until it forms a soft ball when a little is dropped into cold water and left for about 1 minute.

5 Stir the lightly browned oat mixture and chopped apricots into the syrup until evenly mixed.

6 Carefully press the hot mixture into the prepared pan, using the back of a spoon. Leave the mixture to cool until firm but still flexible, then turn it out and cut into bars of the desired size (a sharp serrated knife works best for this).

7 Serve in school lunches and for after-school snacks for teenagers. Store in a completely airtight container, or wrap bars individually in cling wrap. (Like toffee, they soften and turn sticky if left uncovered.)

Fruit & Nut Bars

Using a food processor, you can make fruit and nut bars which taste much fresher than most bought varieties.

For an 18 x 28cm slice:

½ cup dried apricots

¼ cup orange juice

½ cup roasted peanuts

finely grated zest of ½–1 orange

½ cup sultanas

½ cup raisins

¼ cup sesame seeds, lightly toasted (see Note)

½ cup desiccated coconut, lightly toasted (see Note)

extra coconut for coating

1 Coat an 18 x 28cm baking pan with non-stick spray.

2 Cut the dried apricots in quarters and boil in the orange juice for 5 minutes or until liquid has disappeared.

3 Put roasted peanuts in the food processor (with the metal chopping blade). Pulse nuts until chopped roughly. Add orange zest, sultanas, raisins, sesame seeds and the softened apricots. Process to the consistency you like. Add coconut and process again. (If mixture is too wet to handle easily, add extra coconut.)

4 Sprinkle the baking pan with extra coconut and press in the mixture. Refrigerate, uncovered, for 24 hours. Cut into rectangular pieces of desired size and coat all surfaces in extra coconut.

5 Serve whenever a healthy snack is required! Store in a covered container in the refrigerator for up to three weeks.

Fudge Brownies

For an 18 x 28cm brownie:

½ cup canola oil + ½ tsp salt or 125g butter

1 cup sugar

2 large eggs

1 tsp vanilla essence

1 cup standard (plain) flour

¼ cup cocoa

1 tsp baking powder

½ cup chopped walnuts, optional

Brownies are traditional American favourites. With their dense, fudgy and slightly chewy texture (and, of course, their delicious chocolate flavour!), they are becoming increasingly popular in New Zealand homes and cafés.

1 Preheat the oven to 180°C (170°C fanbake), with the rack just below the middle. Line the base and sides of an 18 x 28cm pan with baking paper.

2 Measure the oil and salt into a bowl, or melt the butter in a medium-sized pot or microwave-safe bowl until it is liquid but not hot, then remove from the heat. Beat in (using a fork or stirrer) the sugar, eggs, and vanilla essence.

3 Sift in the flour, cocoa and baking powder. Add the chopped nuts (if using), and stir until just combined — avoid over-mixing.

4 Pour mixture into the lined baking pan and smooth the surface.

5 Bake for 30 minutes, or until firm in the centre. Mixture will rise up and sink again. The edges will probably be a little higher than the middle, but this does not matter. When cold, cut into pieces of the desired size.

6 Serve as is, or roll in sifted icing sugar just before serving, covering all surfaces. Brownies do not require icing. Great served as a snack with tea or coffee, or with ice-cream for dessert. Store in an airtight container in a cool place for up to five days.

Double Chocolate & Hazelnut Brownies

Everyone loves brownies! These are moist, chewy and particularly well flavoured.

For an 18 x 28cm brownie:

½ cup canola oil

½ cup white chocolate melts or 90g chopped white chocolate

1 cup brown sugar

1 tsp vanilla essence

2 large eggs

1 cup standard (plain) flour

½ tsp baking powder

½ tsp salt

½–¾ cup lightly roasted hazelnuts, roughly chopped

½ cup dark chocolate melts or 90g chopped dark chocolate

1. Preheat the oven to 180°C (170°C fanbake), with the rack just below the middle. Line the base and sides of an 18 x 28cm pan with baking paper.

2. Combine the oil and white chocolate in a medium-sized pot or microwave-safe bowl. Heat gently, stirring frequently, until the chocolate has melted. Take off heat and cool, then add the brown sugar, vanilla essence and eggs and stir until the mixture is smooth.

3. Sift in the flour, baking powder and salt, and stir gently until evenly mixed. Add the chopped nuts and dark chocolate, and stir until just combined (if the mixture is too warm, the dark chocolate will melt and 'marble' the mixture).

4. Pour into the prepared pan and bake for 25–30 minutes, or until a skewer inserted into the centre comes out clean. Cool, then remove from the pan and cut into pieces of the desired size.

5. Serve in large pieces with vanilla ice-cream for dessert, or cut into smaller bars to serve with coffee. Store in an airtight container in a cool place for up to five days.

VARIATION: Replace hazelnuts with almonds, pecans or macadamias.

Jaffa Nut Brownies

Make these as a treat for yourself, or to give away! Their rich texture makes them very popular.

For an 18 x 28cm brownie:

100g butter

75g dark cooking chocolate

2 large eggs

¾ cup sugar

1 tsp vanilla essence

zest of 1 orange

½ cup chopped walnuts

½ cup standard (plain) flour

1. Preheat the oven to 180°C (170°C fanbake), with the rack just below the middle. Line the base and sides of an 18 x 28cm pan with baking paper.

2. Cube butter and break chocolate into pieces. Put both into a microwave-safe bowl and heat for 2 minutes on Medium (50% power), or warm in a medium-sized pot over low heat, until butter has melted and the chocolate softened. Remove from heat and stir until smooth and combined.

3. Add eggs, sugar, vanilla essence, orange zest and chopped nuts and stir until well mixed. Sift in flour and fold together, but do not over-mix. Spread the mixture into the prepared pan.

4. Bake for about 15 minutes or until the centre feels firm when pressed. (Don't worry if the sides rise more than the centre.) Cool, then cut into pieces of the desired size.

5. Serve dusted lightly with sieved icing sugar, in larger pieces for dessert with whipped cream or ice-cream, or in smaller pieces with tea or coffee. Store in an airtight container in a cool place, for up to five days.

For a 23cm square shortcake:

Base & Topping:

1 cup self-raising flour

1 cup standard (plain) flour

1 cup sugar

100g cold butter

1 large egg, lightly beaten

2 Tbsp milk

Filling:

100g butter

grated zest and juice of 2 lemons

1 cup sugar

2 large eggs, lightly beaten

Marjie's Lemon Shortcake

As we devour this particularly delicious treat, we always think about the friend who was kind enough to give us her recipe. Sharing recipes with friends, over the years, is a tradition we treasure.

1 Preheat the oven to 180°C (170°C fanbake), with the rack just below the middle. Line the base and sides of a 23cm square loose-bottomed cake pan with baking paper.

2 For the base, mix the sifted flours and sugar in a bowl. Grate in the cold butter, then rub it in until it looks like rolled oats (or chop in butter cubes in a food processor). Make a well in the centre and add the beaten egg. Add just enough milk so that particles will stick together when pressed, making a dough. Press half the dough over the bottom of the pan, keeping the rest to crumble on top.

3 For the filling, melt butter in a medium-sized pot. Take off heat. Beat in the lemon zest and juice, sugar and eggs, then heat again, stirring constantly, until mixture thickens to a pouring custard. Take off heat as soon as first bubbles form. Pour it evenly over the base and crumble remaining dough mixture on top.

4 Bake for 35–45 minutes, until golden brown, with centre almost as firm as the edges. Remove from loose-bottomed pan. When cool, dust with icing sugar.

5 Serve large pieces warm for dessert, with whipped cream or ice-cream. Also delicious served cold in smaller pieces with tea or coffee. Store in a single layer in a loosely covered container, or refrigerate in an airtight container for longer.

Spiced Fruit Shortcake

This plain shortcake has an interesting spicy filling. It may be made ahead and frozen in one large piece or individual squares, if desired.

For a 23cm square shortcake:

Filling:

½ cup sultanas, raisins or currants

½ cup chopped dried apricots

½ cup brown sugar

2 tsp mixed spice

½ tsp ground cloves

½ cup orange juice

1 Tbsp balsamic or wine vinegar

3 large apples, peeled and cubed

about 1 Tbsp custard powder

Base & topping:

125g butter, softened

½ cup sugar

1 large egg

2¼ cups standard (plain) flour

2 tsp baking powder

1. Preheat the oven to 180°C (170°C fanbake), with the rack just below the middle. Line the base and sides of a 23cm square loose-bottomed baking pan with baking paper.

2. For the filling, mix the sultanas, apricots, sugar, spice and cloves together in a frypan. Add the orange juice, vinegar and the apple cubes. Cover and simmer for 2–3 minutes, then thicken with the custard powder (which you have mixed to a paste with a little cold water), until filling is thick enough to keep its shape. Remove from heat and cool to room temperature.

3. For the base and topping, beat the softened butter, sugar and egg until light and creamy, then mix in the sifted dry ingredients, making a soft dough. Cut the dough in half and chill half in refrigerator or freezer. Pat out the other piece of dough on the baking paper to fit the bottom of the pan, using enough extra flour to stop it sticking.

4. Spread the thickened, cooled filling on the base. Roll out the other half of the dough and place on top of filling, or grate coarsely over the top. (The grated topping flattens as the shortcake cooks.)

5. Bake for 30–45 minutes, until centre feels firm when pressed. Sprinkle with icing sugar.

6. Serve warm in large pieces, with whipped cream or ice-cream, or refrigerate smaller pieces to eat cold, over the next three days. If desired, freeze for up to a month.

VARIATION: Replace fresh apple with two 385g cans of diced apple.

Spicy Apple Shortcake

Plain apple is sandwiched between two layers of a deliciously spicy crust in this very popular shortcake.

For a 23cm square shortcake:

Filling:

770g can apple slices or 3 cups well-drained chunky pieces of stewed apple (see Note)

Crust:

125g butter, softened

¾ cup plain or brown sugar

1 large egg

2¼ cups standard (plain) flour

2 tsp baking powder

¼ cup cocoa

1 tsp ground cinnamon

1 tsp mixed spice

¼ tsp ground cloves, optional

1. Preheat the oven to 180°C (170°C fanbake), with the rack just below the middle. Line the base and sides of a 23cm square loose-bottomed baking pan with baking paper.

2. For the filling, open canned apple, drain, then chop into smaller, evenly sized chunks.

3. For the base and topping, beat the softened butter and sugar together in a bowl or food processor, then add the egg and beat again. Sift in the remaining ingredients and mix to make quite a soft dough. Halve the dough and chill half in the refrigerator or freezer. Pat or roll out the other half on the paper pan-lining, using extra flour to prevent sticking if you need to.

4. Spread the drained apple evenly over the base, then coarsely grate the remaining chilled dough over the apple. (The grated topping will spread and flatten as it cooks.)

5. Bake for 30–45 minutes, or until the centre feels firm. Sprinkle with icing sugar before cutting.

6. Serve warm in large pieces, with whipped cream or ice-cream, or refrigerate smaller pieces to eat cold, over the next three days. If desired, freeze for up to a month.

   NOTE: If preparing fresh apple, peel, chop and cook the apple in a small amount of water until it is barely tender, then drain in a sieve. Measure the 3 cups after cooking and draining. Cool to room temperature.

Muffins

← Glazed Passionfruit Muffins – recipe page 157

Please take a few minutes to read these pages before you make the muffin recipes, even if you already make muffins. To work really efficiently, and to make your reputation as an expert muffin maker, it helps to know all the finer points! Remember though, that these are general instructions, and that there are exceptions to every rule!

Before you start measuring and mixing, turn on the oven so it is up to heat before your muffins go into it. Try to measure dry ingredients before wet ones, since this eliminates washing and drying measuring spoons and cups part way through the measuring.

We now usually measure the liquids into a large bowl, and add the (mixed) dry ingredients to them later. We can then simply dust off the container in which the dry ingredients were combined, without washing it, saving a little extra time and effort!

Unless you are using self-raising flour as the only dry ingredient, combine the dry ingredients in a dry bowl (or other container) big enough to mix them in. Sifting or sieving them is unnecessary if you toss or whisk them with a dry whisk or fork once they are in the bowl. Mix them well, so they are light, airy, and well combined. This is important, since later mixing should be minimal.

Next, measure and mix all the liquid ingredients together. Most of the time, we mix these in a large bowl. When you use oil instead of butter, combining the liquids is easier, since you do not need to melt the butter first. If you are adding heated ingredients to liquid mixtures, try to cool them so that your final liquid mixture is not warm. If it is, your muffins may rise in the bowl rather than in the oven.

Sometimes it is easier to mix liquid ingredients in a food processor. When we do this, we tip the processed liquids into the dry ingredients in a large bowl. Follow the recipe instructions.

Nuts are a good addition to healthy muffins. You can always add ¼–½ cup of chopped nuts without altering the recipe in other ways. Add chopped walnuts to liquid ingredients so unmixed flour does not stick in their crannies!

In general, add sugar to dry ingredients, because it makes the dry ingredients easier to fold in to the wet ingredients.

The way you combine the dry and wet mixtures is vital. Always tip ALL the dry ingredients into the wet ones (or vice versa) at once. FOLD THEM TOGETHER WITH AS LITTLE MIXING AS POSSIBLE, without stirring or beating. NEVER use a whisk at this stage. A flexible straight-bladed stirrer/spreader does by far the best job. Slowly bring your stirrer, scraper, fork or spoon down the side of the bowl and under the mixture, then up through it, turning the bowl and repeating this until no pockets of flour are left. Stop while the mixture still looks rough and lumpy. NEVER give it a quick beat or stir for good measure!

Occasionally a muffin mixture may seem too dry, since ingredients sometimes vary in wetness. With experience, you can notice dryness before you finish mixing. Add 1–2 tablespoons of milk, juice or water straight away, folding it in as little as necessary, until the consistency seems right. If you do this too late, you run the risk of over-mixing, and will get peaked, tough muffins.

Muffins, especially the low-fat variety, can stick like crazy! Use pans with a non-stick finish, clean these well, but without scratching them, and always use a light, even coating of non-stick spray as well.

Spoon muffins into prepared pans, helping the mixture off with another spoon, rather than letting it drop off by itself. Try to divide the mixture evenly; put as few spoonfuls in each pan as possible. Let the mixture mound naturally; do not smooth or interfere with its surface. Add toppings to ANY muffins, for extra interest, if you like.

Bake muffins nearly always in the centre of the oven, until the centres spring back when pressed. If this is hard to judge, especially if the muffin contains 'lumpy' additions, push a skewer into the centre. When it comes out clean, the muffins are ready. Cooking times are only a guide. Ovens vary in temperature. If your muffins are too pale when they are cooked, raise the temperature 10 degrees next time. If they are too dark, lower the temperature next time.

Let cooked muffins stand in their pans for 3–4 minutes. Like magic, they stop sticking in this time! Press down gently on the edges of a muffin with several fingers of one hand, and twist slightly. As soon as the muffin will turn freely, lift it out, and let it finish cooling on a rack. Very small rubber scrapers help remove muffins from pans too.

Most muffins are best served warm, soon after baking. They will stay warm for some time, without going soggy, in a napkin-lined basket. Reheat (without overheating) in a microwave oven, or in a paper bag at about 150°C in a conventional oven.

Low-fat muffins dry out faster than richer ones. To stop them drying, put them in plastic bags as soon as they are cold. Freeze muffins you do not think you will eat within a day or two at this stage, too. When practical, warm thawed muffins before serving them. Frozen muffins in packed lunches are useful for keeping other foods cold, too.

Modifying Existing Muffin Recipes

There may be times when you want to make changes, substitutions or additions to your favourite muffin recipes. This might be to suit special dietary requirements, to fit in with your own personal eating pattern, to use the ingredients you have on hand, or to 'dress up' your muffins! We hope that the following guidelines, explanations and suggestions will help you to produce good results.

Wholemeal flour: Although white flour contains more fibre than most people realise, wholemeal flour contains even more. Research shows that most of us would benefit by eating more fibre, so using more wholemeal flour when baking is a step in the right direction. Replacing up to half the regular (white) flour in a muffin recipe with wholemeal will usually make little noticeable difference to the finished muffins. Simply substitute up to half the regular (white) flour with wholemeal flour, or half the white self-raising flour with self-raising wholemeal, adding an extra tablespoon of liquid for each cup of wholemeal used.

Low cholesterol muffins: Replace 1 large egg with the whites of 2 large eggs. Use canola or light olive oil, or an olive, avocado or canola oil-based spread in place of butter, replacing 50g butter with ¼ cup of oil. (You may want to add a little extra salt when replacing butter with oil.) In many 2-egg muffin recipes you can leave out 1 egg altogether, and add 2–4 Tbsp of extra liquid instead.

Lower fat muffins: Some 'Lite butters' (made from butter and buttermilk) are products that look and taste just like butter, but contain less fat than butter. We have successfully used these in place of regular butter in muffin recipes.

Alternatively, the butter or oil content of most muffin recipes can be reduced by half (or even more) by adding an equal volume of plain low-fat yoghurt or fruit purée in its place. The texture will not be exactly the same and the muffins should be eaten the day they are made, for best results.

For further fat reductions use low-fat milks (or non-fat dried milk and water) in place of regular milk, and other reduced fat dairy products (e.g. 98% fat-free sour cream) in place of their full-fat cousins.

Lower fat cheesy muffins: We bake cheese muffins at a high temperature to get an appetising golden-brown crust and a good flavour. Replace grated cheese with quarter to half as much Parmesan for a definite cheese flavour but less fat. Muffins that contain large amounts of cheddar cheese do not need added butter or oil as well.

Non-dairy muffins: Use soy milk instead of milk, and soy yoghurt in place of yoghurt or sour cream. Replace butter with the same amount of dairy-free margarine or with oil. When using oil, replace 50g butter with ¼ cup oil, and add a little (¼ tsp) salt.

Muffin Sizes

You can buy muffin pans of varying sizes. Whatever you buy, make sure it has a good non-stick finish, since many muffin mixtures stick badly!

We usually use regular-sized muffin pans, but sometimes it is nice to try something different. Children particularly like sweet mini muffins, while savoury mini muffins make great nibbles to serve with drinks.

Large Texan muffins can also be good if you are serving a savoury muffin as part of a meal (i.e. with soup or a salad). If you are watching your waist, we suggest that you avoid them, since they are twice the size of a regular muffin.

Regular-sized Muffins: Most widely used are muffin trays which make 12 muffins. (The 12 depressions, if filled with water, hold 4 cupfuls altogether.) Most of the recipes in this book will make 12 muffins this size. We spoon about ¼ cup of mixture into each muffin hole.

You can also buy muffin trays with 6 holes the size of those above. These fit in some bench-top ovens, and are also handy if you have a little mixture left over, and want to make a few more muffins.

We have recently also experimented with flexible silicon muffin trays. These worked well, although the bottoms and sides of the muffins don't brown in quite the same way.

Mini Muffins: Hardly anyone will refuse one of these little muffins which are a little less than half the size of those above. (A muffin tray holding 12 mini muffins, if filled with water, holds 1½ cupfuls.) A mixture making 12 medium muffins will make 24–30 mini muffins. Mini muffins usually need about 2 minutes shorter baking time than regular muffins. Mini-muffin trays usually fit in bench-top ovens.

Texan Muffins: These large muffins are made in trays of 6. Each muffin is twice the size of a regular muffin. Muffins from these trays always look extra-generous. (The tray of 6 holds 5 cups of water altogether.) These muffins usually take 2–4 minutes longer to cook than medium muffins.

Gem Irons: If you have gem irons tucked away in a bottom cupboard, by all means try cooking your muffins in them. Heat the irons in the oven as it warms up. Put the hot irons on a heat-resistant surface, spray well with non-stick spray, then drop in the mixture from the SIDE of a dessert spoon. The cooking time will be shorter than for regular muffins.

Paper Cases: Paper cases the size of regular muffin pans are sometimes used for muffins which are to be sold or handled a lot. Paper cases are helpful for microwaved muffins which otherwise stick to their plastic pans.

Toppings for Sweet and Bran Muffins

Cinnamon Sugar: Shake together in a screw-topped jar ¼ cup brown sugar, ¼ cup white sugar, and 1 Tbsp cinnamon. Sprinkle ½–1 teaspoon over each muffin before baking.

Sesame Sugar: Grind 2 Tbsp toasted sesame seeds using a pestle and mortar or a coffee grinder. Add 2 Tbsp each brown sugar and white sugar, and a pinch salt. Mix or grind briefly. Store in an airtight jar in a cool place. Sprinkle about a teaspoonful over any sweet or bran muffin before baking.

Streusel Topping: Chop until crumbly, in a food processor or bowl, 1 Tbsp each of cold butter and flour, 2 Tbsp each of sugar and chopped nuts, and ½ tsp cinnamon. Sprinkle this amount onto 12 medium sweet or bran muffins before baking them.

Rum Butter: Beat or process together 100g softened butter, 1 cup brown sugar, 1 tsp freshly grated nutmeg, and 2 Tbsp rum, until light and creamy. Serve at room temperature. (This is wonderful with any sweet or bran muffin.)

Brandy Butter: Replace the rum with brandy in the recipe above, and leave out the nutmeg.

Icing To Drizzle: Sieve ¼ cup icing sugar, add, to make a smooth, pourable cream, 1–2 tsp water, lemon or orange juice, etc. For a 'generous drizzle', double these quantities. Pour over hot or warm, not cold, muffins.

Toppings for Savoury Muffins

Horseradish Cream Cheese: Mix together ¼ cup cream cheese and 1 Tbsp grated horseradish (fresh or bottled) to taste.

Herb Butter: Food process or mix 100g softened butter and ½–1 cup chopped fresh herbs. Add ¼–½ cup finely grated Parmesan, if you like.

Best Blueberry Muffins

Blueberries make an ideal muffin ingredient because they are not sour when cooked.

For 12 regular or 24 mini muffins:

2 cups standard (plain) flour

4 tsp baking powder

1 tsp ground cinnamon

½ tsp salt

¾ cup sugar

100g butter

1 cup milk

1 large egg

1–1½ cups fresh or frozen blueberries

Cinnamon Sugar:

1 Tbsp sugar

½ tsp ground cinnamon

1. Preheat the oven to 220°C (210°C fanbake), with the rack just below the middle.

2. Sieve the first five (dry) ingredients into a fairly large bowl.

3. In another large bowl, warm the butter until just melted, then add the milk and egg, and beat to mix thoroughly.

4. Prepare fresh or partly frozen berries, then tip the dry mixture and fruit into the liquids. Fold everything together, without over-mixing. Flour should be dampened, not smooth. Berries should keep their shape.

5. Divide the muffin mixture evenly between 12 regular muffin pans that have been well coated with non-stick spray. Sprinkle lightly with the Cinnamon Sugar made by stirring together sugar and cinnamon.

6. Bake for 12–15 minutes, until muffins spring back when pressed. (Muffins made with frozen berries will take about 5 minutes longer.)

7. Always serve warm, for breakfast, with coffee, for lunch or for dessert.

'New Look' Blueberry Muffins

We're sure you will really enjoy these 'new look' muffins, which contain more fruit and fibre, and almost no saturated fat.

For 12 regular muffins:

1–1½ cups fresh or frozen blueberries

1 cup self-raising flour

¾ cup wholemeal flour

2 tsp baking powder

1 tsp ground cinnamon

½ tsp salt

½ cup apple purée

¾ cup sugar

¼ cup canola oil

1 large egg

¼ cup low-fat milk

Topping, optional:

2 tsp caster sugar

½ tsp ground cinnamon

1. Preheat the oven to 210°C (200°C fanbake), with the rack just below the middle.

2. Pick over fresh blueberries or put measured, frozen berries aside to start thawing.

3. Mix the flours, baking powder, cinnamon and salt in a medium-sized bowl and stir together thoroughly.

4. Put the next five ingredients in a large bowl and mix well. Tip in the flour mixture and fold the two mixtures together until they are fairly well combined (but do not combine completely). Add the fresh or partly thawed berries and fold through the mixture, taking care not to over-mix or to break up the berries any more than necessary.

5. Spoon the mixture into 12 regular, thoroughly non-stick sprayed muffin pans. Sprinkle lightly with a topping made by stirring together caster sugar and cinnamon, if desired.

6. Bake for about 12 minutes if using fresh berries or for about 15 minutes for frozen berries. Allow to stand in their pans for 3–5 minutes until they will lift out easily.

7. Serve as a guilt-free snack with tea or coffee, or pack in lunches.

Cinnamon & Apple Muffins

Cinnamon and apple are flavours which go wonderfully well together.

For 12 regular muffins:

2 medium apples (about 250g each)

1 cup low-fat plain yoghurt

¼ cup canola oil

1 large egg

1 cup sugar

1 cup wholemeal flour

1 cup standard (plain) flour

½ cup chopped walnuts

3 tsp baking powder

2 tsp ground cinnamon

½ tsp salt

1 Preheat the oven to 190°C (180°C fanbake), with the rack just below the middle.

2 Grate the unpeeled apples, discarding the cores. Place grated apple, yoghurt, oil and egg in a medium-sized bowl and mix well.

3 Measure all the remaining ingredients into a large bowl and stir well with a fork. Pour the liquid mixture into the dry ingredients, and gently fold together until the flour is just moistened. Do not over-mix. It doesn't matter if the mixture looks a little marbled; this looks quite good in the finished muffins.

4 Spray 12 regular muffin pans with non-stick spray, then divide the mixture evenly between them.

5 Bake for 12–15 minutes or until the muffins are golden brown on top and spring back when pressed in their centres.

6 Leave muffins to cool in their pans for 2–3 minutes, then turn out and cool on a rack. Place cool muffins in a plastic bag, freezing any you do not expect to eat within 48 hours.

7 Serve warm, any time, with tea or coffee, or include in packed lunches as a guiltless treat. Good topped with cottage cheese.

Fabulous Feijoa Muffins

Orange zest and juice, and a cinnamon topping make these muffins really interesting, without overwhelming the feijoa flavour.

For 12 regular or 24 mini muffins:

75g butter, melted

1 cup finely chopped feijoa flesh

2 large eggs

finely grated zest of 1 orange

¼ cup orange juice

¾ cup sugar

2 cups self-raising flour

1 tsp ground cinnamon

1 Tbsp sugar

1 Preheat the oven to 210°C (200°C fanbake), with the rack just below the middle.

2 Mix feijoa flesh into the melted butter with a fork. Add the unbeaten eggs, orange zest, and the juice of the orange (made up to volume with a little lemon juice if necessary). Mix until everything is combined.

3 Mix the sugar and flour in another bowl. Sprinkle it over the egg mixture, then fold it in without over-mixing. (If you have used too much firm feijoa flesh you may need to add a little extra juice or milk to reach usual muffin consistency.)

4 Divide the mixture between 12 regular or 24 mini muffin pans which have been lightly buttered or non-stick sprayed. Mix the cinnamon and second measure of sugar, and sprinkle it on the muffins.

5 Bake for 10–15 minutes, until the centres spring back when pressed.

6 Serve slightly warm for best flavour, at any time of day.

VARIATION: For Raspberry and Feijoa Muffins, add an extra ¼ cup of sugar and fold in 1 cup of frozen raspberries.

Spiced Apple Muffins

For 12 regular or 24 mini muffins:

1 cup self-raising flour

1 cup (fine) rolled oats

¾ cup brown sugar

2 tsp mixed spice

2 tsp ground cinnamon

½ tsp ground cloves

½ tsp baking soda

½ tsp salt

75g butter

1 large egg

¾–1 cup milk

1 cup raw chopped or grated apple

Make these muffins only after you know what consistency a muffin mixture should be when the dry ingredients are combined with the wet ingredients. Raw apple gives muffins a lovely fresh flavour but, when you use it, you never know exactly how much milk will be needed as well.

1 Preheat the oven to 200°C (190°C fanbake), with the rack just below the middle.

2 Measure the dry ingredients into a large mixing bowl and mix well with your fingers to ensure that the rolled oats and brown sugar are mixed evenly through the other ingredients.

3 Melt the butter in another large bowl, then add the egg and ¾ cup of the milk, and beat with a fork until mixed.

4 Next, grate or chop the apple in a food processor. Press it into the cup, removing air bubbles, then stir it into the liquids. (Work quickly to prevent the apple browning.)

5 Sprinkle the dry ingredients onto the apple-liquid mixture, then fold in to barely dampen the dry ingredients, adding as much of the extra ¼ cup of milk as you need.

6 Coat 12 regular muffin pans with non-stick spray and divide the mixture between them.

7 Bake for 12–15 minutes or until the muffins spring back when pressed. Leave for 3–4 minutes before removing from the pans and cooling on a wire rack.

8 Serve for morning tea or brunch. Nice in packed lunches and popular as after-school snacks.

Glazed Passionfruit Muffins

These muffins are a special treat for lucky people growing their own purple (or black) passionfruit, or those with a friend who grows enough passionfruit to share! (Freeze unsweetened pulp so you can make these muffins out of season, too.)

For 12 regular or 24 mini muffins:

50g butter, melted

½ cup sour cream

¼–½ cup fresh passionfruit pulp

up to ¼ cup orange juice

2 large eggs

¾ cup sugar

2 cups self-raising flour

2 Tbsp passionfruit pulp

¼ cup icing sugar

1 Preheat the oven to 210°C (200°C fanbake), with the rack just below the middle.

2 Place the melted butter in a large bowl and stir in the sour cream. Halve the passionfruit and scoop out all the pulp with a teaspoon. (Put aside two tablespoons to make the glaze.) You need at least ¼ cup to get a good flavour. Make it up to ½ cup with orange juice if necessary. Add to the bowl. Break the eggs into the bowl, add the sugar, then beat with a fork until well blended.

3 Sprinkle or sieve the flour into the mixture in the bowl, then fold it in, taking care not to over-mix.

4 Divide the mixture between 12 regular or 24 mini muffin pans which have been thoroughly coated with non-stick spray.

5 Bake for 10–15 minutes, until tops spring back when pressed.

6 While muffins cook, mix the reserved passionfruit pulp and the icing sugar to a pouring consistency. Spoon or brush it over the muffins as soon as you take them from the oven.

7 Serve preferably on the day they are made, cold or slightly warm, unbuttered, with tea or coffee.

Upside-down Nectarine Muffins

These are delicious in summer made with fresh, locally grown fruit, but try making them with Californian nectarines when you have the midwinter blues.

For 12 regular muffins:

12 tsp (about 50g) butter or oil

½ cup brown sugar

3 nectarines

2 cups self-raising flour

¾ cup sugar

1 tsp mixed spice

¾ tsp salt

2 large eggs

¾ cup plain or apricot yoghurt

¼ cup canola or other oil

1 tsp vanilla essence

1 Preheat the oven to 200°C (190°C fanbake), with the rack just below the middle.

2 Non-stick spray 12 regular muffin pans. Put a teaspoon of butter in each pan and place the pans in the oven until the butter melts, or use oil. Remove from the oven and sprinkle 2 teaspoons of brown sugar evenly over the bottom of each pan. Quarter the nectarines and cut each quarter into three slices. Arrange three slices on top of the butter-sugar mixture in each pan.

3 Measure the dry ingredients into a large bowl and stir to combine.

4 In another large bowl, lightly beat together the eggs, yoghurt, oil and vanilla essence.

5 Sprinkle the flour mixture over the liquids and fold gently together, stopping as soon as the flour is moistened. Spoon the batter into the nectarine-lined pans.

6 Bake for 12–15 minutes until golden brown. (Muffins may be flat topped — this is not a problem! Muffin pans may need soaking later.)

7 After 2 minutes standing, press down gently on each muffin and rotate about ½ a turn, then lift the muffins onto a rack. The topping usually lifts off with the muffin if you get it at the right stage — not too soon, and not too late. Reposition any fruit that stays in the pans.

8 Serve warm or reheated, within a few hours of cooking. Suitable for any meal, from breakfast to dessert.

Apricot & Walnut Muffins

Dried fruits and nuts always make good additions to muffins! If you can find New Zealand dried apricots, use them in this recipe; they break up easily after being heated in the water or juice, giving an extra-strong apricot flavour to the mixture.

For 12 regular or 24 mini muffins:

2 cups standard (plain) flour

1 tsp baking soda

1 cup brown sugar

1 tsp ground cinnamon

½ cup chopped dried apricots

¼ cup water or orange juice

100g butter, softened

2 large eggs

1 cup plain or apricot yoghurt

zest and juice of 1 large orange

½ cup chopped walnuts

❶ Preheat the oven to 190°C (180°C fanbake), with the rack just below the middle.

❷ Measure the flour, baking soda, brown sugar and cinnamon into a large bowl and mix well to ensure that the brown sugar is evenly mixed through the other ingredients.

❸ In another bowl, microwave the apricots with the water or juice until all the liquid is absorbed (about 1 minute on High).

❹ Add the softened butter, then mix in the eggs, yoghurt and grated zest. Make the juice from the orange up to ½ cup with water, if necessary, and add this and the chopped walnuts to the egg mixture.

❺ Tip the dry ingredients into the liquids, then gently fold the two mixtures together, taking care not to over-mix.

❻ Divide the mixture evenly between 12 regular muffin pans that have been well coated with non-stick spray.

❼ Bake for about 12–15 minutes or until the muffins spring back when pressed lightly.

❽ Serve for a weekend brunch, or with coffee any time. Good in packed lunches, for after-school snacks and for picnics.

Rich Raspberry Muffins

For 12 regular muffins:

2 cups self-raising flour

½ cup sugar

1 tsp ground cinnamon

¼ tsp ground cloves

100g butter, melted

1 tsp instant coffee

1 cup milk

1 large egg

zest of 1 lemon

½ cup raspberry jam (see Note)

Icing:

¼ cup icing sugar

1–2 tsp lemon juice

These muffins combine the flavours of raspberries and spices. You will find the same popular ingredients in Belgium biscuits and in Linzer Torte but it takes a long time to prepare these. Do it the easy way — enjoy the same flavours in quickly-made muffins!

1 Preheat the oven to 200°C (190°C fanbake), with the rack just below the middle.

2 Sift flour, sugar, cinnamon and ground cloves into a large bowl.

3 Dissolve the instant coffee in the milk. In a separate bowl, add coffee/milk to the melted butter along with the egg. Add the lemon zest and mix well to combine.

4 Sprinkle the dry ingredients over the liquids, then fold together without over-mixing.

5 Coat 12 regular muffin pans with non-stick spray. Half fill each pan with the muffin mixture, then make a small depression on the surface of each one with a damp teaspoon. Put 2 teaspoons of the jam in each depression, then spoon the remaining mixture over the filling, taking care to cover it completely.

6 Bake for 10–12 minutes or until the centres spring back when lightly pressed. Leave to stand in the pans for about 3 minutes before transferring to a wire rack. Before muffins cool completely, drizzle with a small amount of the icing made by combining sifted icing sugar with just enough lemon juice to mix to the consistency of thin cream.

7 Serve with tea, coffee or for dessert.

NOTE: Use homemade jam if possible, since this usually has a stronger raspberry flavour. If not available, use good-quality 'bought' jam.

Spicy Pineapple Muffins

For 12 regular muffins:

2 cups standard (plain) flour

1 Tbsp mixed spice

1 tsp baking soda

½ cup sugar

¼ tsp salt

1 cup sultanas

100g butter, melted

2 large eggs

450g can crushed pineapple

These muffins are deliciously spicy. They freeze well and can be thawed in a warm oven in 5–10 minutes. The quantity of mixed spice really is one tablespoon, but remember to use a level measure.

1 Preheat the oven to 200°C (190°C fanbake), with the rack just below the middle.

2 Sieve the flour, mixed spice, baking soda, sugar and salt into a large bowl. Add the sultanas and toss with the flour mixture to combine.

3 In a separate bowl, add the eggs to the melted butter and beat well. Drain the pineapple through a sieve, pushing with a spoon to extract as much liquid as possible. Measure the drained pineapple to ensure you have about 1 cup of fruit and ¾ cup juice. Add the measured fruit and juice to the egg mixture.

4 Tip the dry ingredients over the liquid mixture, then fold everything together until the flour has been dampened, but the mixture still looks lumpy and undermixed.

5 Spray 12 regular muffin pans with non-stick spray. Put about ¼ cup of mixture into each muffin cup.

6 Bake for 10–15 minutes, until muffins spring back when pressed in the centre.

7 Serve warm with morning or afternoon tea, in a packed lunch, or when it is your turn to 'bring a plate'.

Rum & Raisin Muffins

For 12 regular or 24 mini muffins:

1 cup dark Californian raisins

2 Tbsp rum

2 cups standard (plain) flour

1½ tsp baking soda

2 tsp ground cinnamon

2 tsp mixed spice

¼ tsp ground cloves

¾ cup sugar

½ cup chopped walnuts

1 large egg

1 cup yoghurt (any flavour)

¾ cup milk

75g butter, melted

Rum Glaze:

¼ cup icing sugar

½ tsp rum essence

1–2 tsp milk

We make these muffins for a cold weather treat. If you're going to serve them with coffee or for lunch, try drizzling them with a rum-flavoured glaze. If they are for dessert or supper, reheat them in the microwave and serve them with Rum Butter (see page 151) for a real treat!

1 Preheat the oven to 210°C (200°C fanbake), with the rack just below the middle.

2 Put the raisins and rum into a small plastic bag. Knead bag gently. Leave to stand in a warm place while you mix the other ingredients.

3 Sieve the flour, soda and spices into a large bowl. Add the sugar and chopped walnuts and stir to mix thoroughly.

4 Add the egg, yoghurt and milk to the melted butter. Add the marinated raisins with any remaining liquid and mix well. Now combine the liquid and dry mixtures without over-mixing.

5 Divide the mixture evenly between 12 regular muffin pans that have been well coated with non-stick spray.

6 Bake for about 12 minutes or until the centres spring back when pressed. Leave to stand in the pans for about 3 minutes before removing and cooling on a wire rack.

7 To glaze, mix icing sugar with rum essence and milk to make a thin icing. Drizzle, in a thin stream, over warm muffins on rack.

8 Serve for holiday season brunches, with coffee in mid-winter, or for dessert with Rum Butter on any occasion.

Carrot & Pineapple Muffins

After you've made these once, you'll find you need to keep a small can of pineapple on hand so that you can make them at any time.

For 12 regular or 24 mini muffins:

2 cups wholemeal flour

4 tsp baking powder

¾ cup brown sugar

2 tsp ground cinnamon

1 tsp mixed spice

½–1 tsp salt

½ cup chopped walnuts

150g carrot, grated (1 cup)

1 small (227g) can crushed pineapple

¼ cup orange juice

1 large egg

¼ cup canola oil or 50g butter, melted

1. Preheat the oven to 200°C (190°C fanbake), with the rack just below the middle.

2. Measure the flour, baking powder, brown sugar, cinnamon, mixed spice, salt and walnuts into a large bowl. (Use the larger amount of salt if you are going to use oil rather than butter.) Mix well using your hands, making sure that there are no large lumps of sugar in the mixture.

3. Mix the grated carrot, the contents of the can of crushed pineapple (fruit and juice), orange juice, egg and oil or melted butter together in another large bowl.

4. Tip the dry mixture into the liquid and fold everything together, until the flour is just moistened. Take care to avoid over-mixing. Add a little extra juice if the mixture seems thicker than usual.

5. Spoon the mixture into 12 regular or 24 mini muffin pans, that have been lightly buttered or non-stick sprayed.

6. Bake for 12–15 minutes, or until the muffins spring back when pressed in the middle.

7. As soon as you have taken the muffins from their pans, brush all their surfaces with Lemon Glaze (optional, see page 255).

8. These are extra good straight from the oven or reheated. Pack frozen mini muffins in children's lunch boxes.

Carrot & Walnut Muffins

If you like the flavour of hot cross buns but don't have the time to make them, try these spicy muffins instead.

For 12 regular or 24 mini muffins:

1½ cups standard (plain) flour

½ tsp salt

¾ tsp baking soda

2 tsp ground cinnamon

1 tsp ground allspice

¾ cup brown sugar

¼ cup chopped walnuts

½ cup sultanas

½ cup canola or other oil

2 large eggs

200g carrots, finely grated

1. Preheat the oven to 190°C (180°C fanbake), with the rack just below the middle.

2. Sieve the flour, salt, baking soda and spices into a large bowl. Add brown sugar, walnuts and sultanas and mix these evenly through the dry ingredients with your fingers, breaking up any lumps.

3. Beat the oil and eggs together in another bowl, then add the carrot.

4. Tip the dry mixture into the wet ingredients and fold everything together until there are no more unmixed lumps of flour. Take care not to over-mix.

5. Spray 12 regular muffin pans with non-stick spray. Put about ¼ cup of mixture into each pan.

6. Bake for about 15 minutes, or until the centres of the muffins spring back when pressed.

7. Serve warm with coffee. Nice for dessert, split in half and spread with Rum Butter (see page 151).

Raspberry & White Chocolate Muffins

These muffins have a zingy raspberry flavour which goes very nicely with the hint of vanilla provided by a little white chocolate. If you don't like the idea of chocolate in low-fat muffins, try replacing it with the same quantity of chopped macadamia nuts.

For 12 regular muffins:

1 cup (150g) frozen raspberries

1 cup (125g) 'Lite' sour cream

½ cup low-fat milk

¼ cup canola oil

1 large egg

1 tsp vanilla essence

2 cups self-raising flour

1 cup sugar

¼ cup white chocolate bits or melts

½ tsp baking soda

½ tsp salt

1 Preheat the oven to 190°C (180°C fanbake), with the rack just below the middle.

2 Measure the raspberries into a large bowl and leave to soften for a few minutes. Add the sour cream, milk, oil, egg and vanilla essence to the bowl and stir well so the raspberries break up a little. (The berries don't have to be mashed, but whole berries are quite large.)

3 Tip the flour, sugar, white chocolate, baking soda and salt into another bowl and stir them together well with a whisk or fork.

4 Sprinkle the dry ingredients into the liquid mixture, then stir until the flour is just moistened. Do not over-mix. This is quite a wet looking mixture, but this doesn't seem to matter in the end.

5 Spoon the mixture into 12 regular, non-stick sprayed muffin pans.

6 Bake for 15–18 minutes, until golden brown and a skewer comes out clean. (The frozen raspberries cool the mixture down, so these muffins do tend to take a little longer to cook.)

7 Remove the muffins from the oven and leave to cool in their pans for 2–3 minutes before cooling on a rack.

8 Enjoy warm, or cool then store in a plastic bag. The raspberry flavour actually improves with standing.

Double Chocolate Surprise Muffins

Alison invented this recipe for my little chocolate book, but it is too good to leave out of any muffin collection. Make it without the raspberry 'surprise' if you like, but it won't be quite as good.

For 12 regular muffins:

1¾ cups standard (plain) flour

4 tsp baking powder

¼ cup cocoa

½ cup sugar

½ cup (100g) chocolate chips

75g butter, melted

2 large eggs

¾ cup milk

¾–1 cup raspberry jam

extra chocolate chips

1. Preheat the oven to 200°C (190°C fanbake), with the rack just below the middle.

2. Sift the flour, baking powder and cocoa together into a medium-sized bowl. Add the sugar and chocolate chips and toss with a fork to mix.

3. Place the melted butter in a large bowl and add the eggs and milk and beat with a fork until well combined and smooth. Sprinkle the flour mixture over the liquids and fold together, mixing as little as possible. Stop as soon as there are no pockets of flour left — do not over-mix.

4. Coat 12 regular muffin pans lightly with non-stick spray or butter, then half fill each pan by spooning about a tablespoon of the mixture into the prepared pans, using two spoons.

5. Using a damp teaspoon make a small hollow in each muffin and fill it with a teaspoon of jam. Divide the remaining mixture between the muffins, ensuring that the jam is completely covered. Sprinkle each with a few extra chocolate chips, if desired.

6. Bake for about 10 minutes or until the centres spring back when pressed. Leave to stand for several minutes before twisting and removing from the pans. Leave to cool on a rack.

7. These are best enjoyed warm. For a quick dessert serve with lightly whipped cream.

Chocolate & Banana Muffins

For 12 regular or 24 mini muffins:

2 cups self-raising flour

½ cup caster sugar

½ cup chocolate chips

½ tsp salt

100g butter, melted

1 cup milk

1 large egg

1 tsp vanilla essence

1 cup (2–3) mashed bananas

Here is a recipe which is well worth trying. The banana flavour is strongest when you use over-ripe bananas. If you do not like the idea of pieces of chocolate in muffins, replace the chocolate with ¼ cup of chopped walnuts.

1 Preheat the oven to 220°C (210°C fanbake), with the rack just below the middle.

2 With a fork, stir the flour, caster sugar, chocolate chips and salt together in a large bowl.

3 Place the melted butter in another large bowl and add the milk, egg and vanilla essence. Beat well.

4 Stir the mashed banana into the liquid. Tip all the flour mixture into the bowl with the liquid mixture. Fold everything together carefully until all the flour is dampened, stopping before the mixture is smooth.

5 Spray 12 regular muffin pans with non-stick spray. Put about ¼ cup of mixture into each cup.

6 Bake for 12–15 minutes, until muffins spring back when pressed in the centre.

7 Mini muffins make very popular snacks for young children, and are good for lunch boxes and after-school snacks. Serve with tea or coffee at any time of the day.

ABC Muffins

A is for apple, B is for banana, C is for chocolate! We usually make these in mini muffin pans and freeze a good proportion of them, because they will thaw quickly in lunch boxes or spur-of-the-moment picnic packs. We find that it is not only children who enjoy mini muffins!

For 24 mini or 12 regular muffins:

1 cup (2–3) mashed ripe bananas

½ cup brown sugar

¼ tsp salt

¼ cup canola oil

1 large egg

½ cup low-fat milk

¼–½ cup chocolate chips

1 unpeeled apple, grated or finely chopped (see Note)

2 cups self-raising flour

1 Preheat the oven to 210°C (200°C fanbake), with the rack just below the middle.

2 In a large bowl, mix together the mashed banana, brown sugar, salt, oil, egg and milk until well mixed. Stir in the chocolate chips and the apple.

3 Stir the flour in its container, then spoon it into the cup measure without packing it or banging it down. Sprinkle it over the top of the other ingredients, then fold it in without over-mixing, stopping when there are no streaks or pockets of flour visible.

4 Spoon into mini muffin pans (or regular muffin pans) which have been thoroughly sprayed with non-stick spray.

5 Bake for 10–12 minutes or until golden brown, and until the tops spring back when pressed lightly. Leave to stand 2–3 minutes in their pans.

6 While muffins cool in pans, make Lemon Glaze (see page 255). Transfer muffins from pans to a rack and immediately brush with the glaze, making sure that some undissolved sugar is on each muffin.

7 Serve any time as a healthy snack. Store in plastic bags when cold, freezing muffins which will not be eaten in two days.

NOTE: Use a 'tangy' apple such as Braeburn, Cox's Orange, Sturmer or Granny Smith for best flavour.

Moist Chocolate Muffins

These muffins are so moist and delicious it's hard to believe that they're actually pretty low in fat.

For 12 regular or 24 mini muffins:

1 cup (about 200g) pitted prunes

½ cup boiling water

½ cup cold water

½ cup (125g) 'Lite' sour cream

¼ cup canola oil

1 large egg

1½ tsp lecithin, optional

1¾ cups standard (plain) flour

½ cup sugar

¼ cup cocoa powder

4 tsp baking powder

½ tsp salt

¼ cup chocolate chips, optional

❶ Preheat the oven to 190°C (180°C fanbake), with the rack just below the middle.

❷ Place the prunes in a food processor and add the boiling water. Process until the prunes are well chopped, then add the cold water, sour cream, canola oil, egg and lecithin (if using) and process until the mixture is smooth and creamy.

❸ Measure the remaining dry ingredients, including the chocolate chips (if using), into a large bowl and toss together until well mixed.

❹ Pour the liquid ingredients into the dry mixture, and fold together gently, stirring no more than is absolutely necessary.

❺ Spoon the mixture into 12 regular (or 24 mini) non-stick sprayed, muffin pans.

❻ Bake for 12–15 minutes until centres spring back when pressed lightly. Remember that mini muffins will cook more quickly than larger muffins.

❼ Remove from the oven and leave to cool in the pans for 2–3 minutes until the muffins will come out cleanly.

❽ Serve as is, or dusted lightly with icing sugar.

Double Chocolate Muffins

This recipe will delight chocolate lovers! You might think that chocolate chips on top of a chocolate muffin is 'gilding the lily', but they provide an interesting texture, and add intensity to the flavour.

For 12 regular or 24 mini muffins:

1¾ cups standard (plain) flour

1 tsp baking soda

1 cup caster sugar

¼ cup cocoa

100g butter, melted

1 large egg

1 cup plain or raspberry yoghurt

½ cup milk

½ tsp vanilla essence

¼–½ cup chocolate chips, optional

1 Preheat the oven to 200°C (190°C fanbake), with the rack just below the middle.

2 Sift the flour, baking soda, sugar and cocoa into a large mixing bowl.

3 Place the melted butter in another large bowl, then add the egg, yoghurt, milk and vanilla essence and mix until smooth.

4 Sprinkle the flour mixture over the liquids, and fold together until the flour is dampened, but not smooth.

5 Divide the mixture evenly between 12 regular muffin pans that have been well coated with non-stick spray (particularly important if using the chocolate chips). If desired, sprinkle the top of each muffin with 1–2 tsp chocolate chips before baking.

6 Bake for 10–12 minutes or until centres spring back when pressed lightly. Leave to stand in the pans for about 3 minutes before removing and cooling on a wire rack.

7 Serve with coffee for lunch. Make mini muffins for children's parties. Split muffins and serve for dessert with fresh strawberries or with raspberry jam and whipped cream.

Apricot Surprise Muffins

For 12 regular or 24 mini muffins:

1¾ cups self-raising flour

¾ cup sugar

¼ tsp baking soda

½ tsp salt

½ cup 'Lite' sour cream

½ cup milk

1 large egg

½ tsp almond essence

50g dried apricots

½ cup water

2 Tbsp ground almonds

2 Tbsp sugar

2 Tbsp wine biscuit crumbs

These muffins are one of Alison's favourites. When you bite into them, you find a delicious mixture of dried apricots and almonds hidden in the middle. Make them for special occasions or for your best friends — but make sure you keep some for yourself!

1. Preheat the oven to 200°C (190°C fanbake), with the rack just below the middle.

2. Measure the flour, sugar, baking soda and salt into a bowl and mix thoroughly.

3. Beat the sour cream, milk, egg and almond essence together in a large bowl. Tip the flour mixture into the liquids, then fold everything together, taking care not to over-mix.

4. To make the filling, chop the apricots into small pieces. Boil them with the water for 3–4 minutes, until the water has disappeared. Cool, and mix with the ground almonds, sugar and biscuit crumbs.

5. Spray 12 regular muffin pans with non-stick spray. Half fill each one with the muffin mixture. Make a small depression on the surface of each one with a damp teaspoon. Divide the apricot filling mixture between the 12 cups and place carefully in the depression. Spoon the remaining mixture over the filling, taking care to cover it completely.

6. Optional, but very nice: Sprinkle with Streusel Topping (see page 151).

7. Bake for 12–15 minutes, until muffins spring back when pressed.

8. Serve warm with coffee, or with whipped cream as a dessert.

Fruit Salad Muffins

For 12 regular or 24 mini muffins:

2 cups standard (plain) flour

4 tsp baking powder

½ cup sugar

½ tsp salt

425g can fruit salad

75g butter, melted

½ cup milk

1 large egg

Topping, optional:

1 Tbsp sugar

½ tsp ground cinnamon

When you want to brighten a winter's day and you don't have fresh fruit on hand, drain a can of fruit salad and use it, and some of the juice from it, to make these fruit salad muffins!

1 Preheat the oven to 200°C (190°C fanbake), with the rack just below the middle.

2 Sift the flour, baking powder, sugar and salt together into a large mixing bowl.

3 Drain (and reserve) the juice from the can of fruit salad. Measure ¼ cup of this juice and add to the melted butter with the milk and egg in another large bowl. Beat with a whisk or fork to combine.

4 Cut any large pieces of fruit (and the cherries) into smaller pieces. Add the fruit and the sifted dry ingredients to the liquids, then mix briefly, until just combined.

5 Coat 12 regular muffin pans with non-stick spray and spoon about ¼ cup of the mixture into each pan.

6 Make the topping by mixing together the sugar and cinnamon, and sprinkle it over the top of each of the muffins.

7 Bake for 10–12 minutes or until the centres spring back when pressed. Leave to stand in the pans for about 3 minutes before removing and cooling on a wire rack.

8 Serve warm or cold for weekend breakfast or brunch, with tea or coffee at any time of day, or for dessert.

1½ cups standard (plain) flour

1 cup sugar

3 tsp baking powder

½ tsp salt

1 cup fine desiccated coconut

½ cup cream cheese

¾ cup milk

1 large egg

1 tsp vanilla essence

¼ tsp almond essence

½–1 cup (150g) glacé cherries, halved

shredded coconut to decorate, optional

Coconut, Cherry & Cream Cheese Muffins

Coconut cakes have long been popular in our family. Perhaps the most popular was a coconut and cherry cake, and it was really only a matter of time before we applied this theme to muffins.

1 Preheat the oven to 200°C (190°C fanbake), with the rack just below the middle.

2 Sift the flour, sugar, baking powder and salt into a large bowl. Add the coconut and toss together.

3 Soften the cream cheese by warming it first, then place it in a large bowl and beat it together with the milk, egg and essences.

4 Sprinkle the dry ingredients over the liquid mixture, add the cherries, then gently fold everything together, stopping as soon as all the flour is moistened.

5 Spoon the mixture into 12 regular non-stick sprayed muffin pans. Sprinkle with some shredded coconut, if you have it.

6 Bake for 12 minutes, or until golden brown and firm when pressed in the centre.

7 These are good cold or slightly warm. Eat within two days of making.

Golden Orange Muffins

The wonderful golden colour of these food processor muffins will brighten the coldest day.

For 12 regular muffins:

1 orange (about 200g)

1 cup sugar

1 large egg

½ cup milk or orange juice

100g butter, melted

1½ cups standard (plain) flour

1 tsp baking powder

1 tsp baking soda

½ cup sultanas

½ cup chopped walnuts, optional

1 Preheat the oven to 200°C (190°C fanbake), with the rack just below the middle.

2 Cut the unpeeled orange into quarters, then each quarter into four. Put the chopped orange (skin and flesh, but no seeds) and the sugar into a food processor and process with the metal chopping blade, until the orange is very finely chopped. Add the egg, milk and melted butter and process until combined.

3 Sift the dry ingredients into the processor bowl, sprinkle in the sultanas and nuts, then process in short bursts, stopping as soon as the dry ingredients are dampened. Take great care not to over-mix.

4 Lightly butter or non-stick spray 12 regular muffin pans, then divide the mixture evenly between them.

5 Bake for 12–14 minutes, until golden brown and the centres spring back when pressed. Leave to stand in the pans for 3–4 minutes, then remove from the pans and cool on a rack.

6 These muffins are best warm. They don't need buttering.

Tutti Fruity Muffins

These low-fat muffins are always popular. They have such a good flavour they do not need buttering, as long as you eat them warm from the oven.

For 12 regular or 24 mini muffins:

2 cups standard (plain) flour

1 cup oat bran

1 tsp baking soda

1 tsp baking powder

1 cup brown sugar

2 large eggs

¾ cup apricot or orange yoghurt

½ cup milk

¼ cup concentrated orange juice

1 banana, mashed

2 Tbsp passionfruit pulp, optional

1 Preheat the oven to 200°C (190°C fanbake), with the rack just below the middle.

2 Toss the flour, oat bran, baking soda and baking powder together, thoroughly, in a large mixing bowl. Add the brown sugar and mix again.

3 In another large bowl, beat the eggs, yoghurt, milk and orange juice together, using a fork. Add the mashed banana and passionfruit (if using) and mix again.

4 Tip the dry ingredients into the liquid mixture, then fold the two together, stopping as soon as the dry ingredients are dampened. Take care not to over-mix.

5 Put spoonfuls of the mixture into 12 regular muffin pans that have been thoroughly coated with non-stick spray.

6 Bake for 10–15 minutes or until the centres spring back when pressed.

7 Serve for breakfasts, brunches, as after-school snacks, for picnics and in packed lunches. Eat within a day and a half.

Mango & Orange Muffins

These muffins have a pleasantly gentle mango-and-orange background flavour and colour.

For 12 regular muffins:

½ cup (65g) dried mango slices

½ cup orange and mango juice (or orange juice)

1 cup plain low-fat yoghurt (or orange or mango yoghurt)

¼ cup canola or other oil

1 large egg

1 tsp vanilla essence

½ tsp salt

2 cups self-raising flour

1 cup sugar

❶ Preheat the oven to 210°C (200°C fanbake), with the rack just below the middle.

❷ Cut the dried mango into thin (about 3mm) strips using a wet knife or scissors, then cut these into tiny cubes. Pour the juice over them and microwave on High (100% power) for 4 minutes, or simmer for 5 minutes. Leave to stand in the remaining juice until cool.

❸ Place the yoghurt, oil, egg, vanilla essence and salt into a large bowl. Add the cooled mango and its liquid, and stir everything together.

❹ Mix the flour and sugar together in another bowl, then tip into the liquid mixture. Fold together, stopping as soon as there are no visible streaks of flour. If the mixture looks too thick when everything is nearly mixed in, add 1–2 extra tablespoons of juice.

❺ Divide the mixture between 12 regular muffin pans which have been well coated with non-stick spray.

❻ Bake for 12–15 minutes, until muffins are golden brown and the centres spring back when pressed. Leave in pans for 3–5 minutes, then remove carefully and cool on a rack.

Mango & Macadamia Muffins

Puréed, canned mango gives these muffins a delicious fruity flavour and an attractive golden colour.

For 12 regular muffins:

425g can mango slices in light syrup or 1 cup mashed raw mango

1 cup low-fat plain or fruit-flavoured yoghurt

1 large egg

¼ cup canola or other oil

1 tsp vanilla essence

2 cups self-raising flour

1 cup sugar

½ tsp salt

about ½ cup roasted macadamia nuts (see Note)

❶ Preheat the oven to 210°C (200°C fanbake), with the rack just below the middle.

❷ Drain the canned mango slices well, then transfer the mango to a medium-sized bowl and mash it with a fork. Add the yoghurt, egg, oil and vanilla essence and mix with the fork until everything is blended.

❸ Measure the flour, sugar and salt into a larger bowl. Roughly chop the macadamia nuts, add these to the flour mixture, and toss well with a fork. Pour in the liquid ingredients and fold together until the flour is just moistened. Do not over-mix, as this toughens the muffins and causes them to rise in peaks as they bake, instead of being gently rounded.

❹ Spoon the mixture into 12 muffin pans which have been well coated with non-stick spray.

❺ Bake for 15–20 minutes until the muffins are golden brown on top and spring back when pressed in their centres. Leave to stand for 4–5 minutes in their pans, then remove carefully and cool on a rack.

Crunchy Lemon & Poppyseed Muffins

These muffins were inspired by a number of different lemon and poppyseed loaves and cakes we have tried over the years.

For 12 regular muffins:

2 cups self-raising flour

1 cup sugar

½ cup poppyseeds

finely grated zest and juice of 2 lemons

100g butter, melted

2 large eggs

1 cup milk

¼ cup sugar

1 Preheat the oven to 200°C (190°C fanbake), with the rack just below the middle.

2 Measure the flour, sugar and poppyseeds into a large bowl and add the lemon zest.

3 Place the melted butter in a separate bowl and add the eggs and milk. Beat with a fork until everything is thoroughly combined. Tip the liquid into the dry ingredients and fold together until the flour is dampened. Do not over-mix.

4 Spoon mixture into 12 regular muffin pans which have been lightly buttered or non-stick sprayed.

5 Bake for 10–15 minutes until golden brown, and until the centres spring back when pressed. While muffins cook, mix the lemon juice with the second amount of sugar. (The sugar should not be dissolved.)

6 Allow the muffins to cool in their pans for 3–4 minutes, then take them out and brush the lemon and sugar mixture over their entire surfaces. Cool on a rack.

7 Serve warm or reheated, with coffee, tea, for lunch or for dessert.

Crunchy Lemon Muffins

These get the prize for being Alison's most popular muffin ever!

For 12 regular muffins:

2 cups self-raising flour

¾ cup sugar

75g butter, melted

1 cup milk

1 large egg

grated zest of 1 large or 2 small lemons

1 Preheat the oven to 200°C (190°C fanbake), with the rack just below the middle.

2 Measure the flour and sugar into a bowl and toss to mix.

3 Place the melted butter, milk, eggs and lemon zest in a large bowl and beat well with a fork to combine.

4 Add the dry ingredients to the liquids and fold gently to combine, stopping as soon as the dry ingredients have been lightly dampened but not thoroughly mixed.

5 Divide the mixture evenly between 12 regular muffin pans that have been lightly buttered or well coated with non-stick spray.

6 Bake for 10–12 minutes or until golden brown and until the centres spring back when pressed.

7 While muffins bake, make Lemon Glaze (see page 255).

8 Allow the muffins to cool in their pans for 3–4 minutes, then take them out and brush the glaze over their entire surfaces. Cool on a rack.

9 Serve with tea or coffee for afternoon tea or as a dessert served with lightly whipped cream and fresh fruit or berries.

Lemon Yoghurt Muffins

These easy-to-mix muffins owe their moist texture to non-fat yoghurt and their lovely flavour to a generous amount of lemon zest.

For 12 regular muffins:

zest of 1 large or 2 small lemons

¾ cup sugar

¼ cup canola or other oil

1 large egg

½ tsp salt

1 cup low-fat plain yoghurt

¼ cup lemon juice

2 cups self-raising flour

1 Preheat the oven to 200°C (190°C fanbake), with the rack just below the middle.

2 Place all ingredients except the flour into a large bowl. Stir with a fork or whisk until thoroughly mixed.

3 Spoon the flour into a measuring cup and sprinkle it over the mixture in the bowl. Fold everything together until the flour is just mixed in, but do not over-mix.

4 Using two large spoons, put the mixture into 12 regular or 24 mini muffin pans which have been well sprayed with non-stick spray.

5 Bake for 10–12 minutes or until the centres spring back when pressed and the muffins are lightly browned.

6 Leave to stand for 4–5 minutes, then carefully remove from pans and finish cooling on a rack.

7 While the muffins are cooling, make Lemon Glaze (optional, see page 255). Drizzle glaze over muffins.

8 Serve warm or reheated, glazed or dusted with icing sugar. Store in a covered container when cold, if not eating straight away.

Lemonade & Cream Muffins

These light textured, very easy (and exceptionally good) muffins are based on a scone recipe which 'did the rounds' some years ago. For a summertime treat, serve them warm, split, with jam and/or fresh strawberries and whipped cream.

For 12 regular muffins:

2 cups self-raising flour

½ cup sugar

¼ tsp salt

½ cup fizzy lemonade

½ cup cream

1 large egg

1 Preheat the oven to 200°C (190°C fanbake), with the rack just below the middle.

2 Measure the flour, sugar and salt into a large bowl and toss together with a fork.

3 In another large bowl, mix the lemonade, cream and egg with the fork, until combined.

4 Tip the flour mixture into the liquid, then fold gently together until the flour is just moistened. Spoon the mixture into 12 non-stick sprayed or buttered muffin pans.

5 Bake for 10–15 minutes, until muffins are a light golden colour and firm when pressed in the centre.

6 These muffins are best when freshly made, especially with whipped cream and fresh strawberries.

Date, Lemon & Yoghurt Muffins

Puréed dates add sweetness as well as moistness to these muffins, which have a slight lemony tang as well. A food processor makes the preparation of the liquid mixture very easy.

For 12–18 regular muffins:

zest of 1 lemon

¼ cup sugar

1 cup (150g) dates, halved

½ cup boiling water

juice of 1 lemon made up to ½ cup with water

1 large egg

½ cup low-fat plain or apricot yoghurt

½ cup canola or other oil

½ cup crushed or finely chopped walnuts

½ tsp salt

1 cup self-raising flour

¾ cup wholemeal flour

2 tsp baking powder

1. Preheat the oven to 200°C (190°C fanbake), with the rack just below the middle.

2. With a potato peeler, peel the lemon into the food processor bowl. Add the sugar and process to finely chop the peel. Halve (to double check that no stones remain in them) and add the dates, then add boiling water. Process to purée dates and mix the lemon zest through them.

3. Squeeze the juice from the lemon, and make it up to ½ cup with cold water. Add it to the dates, with the egg, yoghurt and oil, and process again. Add the nuts to the food processor with the salt and process until finely ground.

4. Stir the flours and baking powder together in a large bowl. Tip in the mixture from the food processor, and fold it into the dry ingredients, stirring no more than is absolutely necessary. Do not over-mix.

5. Spoon into 12 regular muffin pans which have been well coated with non-stick spray. If you can't fit all the mixture in the pans, leave it to stand in a cool place, without stirring it, until the first batch has cooked.

6. Bake for about 15 minutes, until the centres spring back when pressed, and a skewer pushed to the bottom of the largest muffin comes out clean. Leave to stand for 2–3 minutes, or until the muffins will lift out cleanly. Top with Lemon Glaze (see page 255), if you like.

7. Serve warm or cold with tea or coffee. Store in an airtight container when cool.

Glazed Gingerbread Muffins

These muffins may not be as dark in colour as traditional gingerbread, but the combination of fresh ginger and ginger ale gives them a definite ginger flavour. They are good as is, but are particularly delicious when glazed.

For 12 regular muffins:

2 cups self-raising flour

½–¾ cup sugar

1 Tbsp grated fresh ginger

1 tsp mixed spice

1 tsp ground cinnamon

50g butter, melted

1 cup ginger ale

1 large egg

Ginger Glaze, optional:

2 tsp softened butter

1 tsp ground ginger

2 tsp golden syrup

2 tsp water

¼ cup icing sugar

1 Preheat the oven to 200°C (190°C fanbake), with the rack just below the middle.

2 Measure the flour, the desired amount of sugar, and the ginger and spices into a bowl and stir to combine evenly.

3 Place the melted butter in another large bowl, then add the ginger ale and egg. Whisk lightly to combine.

4 Tip the flour mixture into the liquids, then fold gently together until the flour is just moistened. Do not over-mix. Spoon the mixture into 12 thoroughly non-stick sprayed regular muffin pans.

5 Bake for 12–15 minutes until golden brown and the centres spring back when pressed.

6 While muffins cook, prepare the glaze by mixing together all the ingredients. Warm it to brushable consistency if necessary. As soon as the muffins are cooked, remove them from the pans and brush the glaze on their tops while they are still hot, using a pastry brush.

7 These muffins are best eaten the day they are made. Nice warm or reheated.

Fig & Honey Muffins

The ingredients in these muffins — tree-ripened figs, yoghurt, honey and nuts — remind us of warm days in the Greek Isles.

For 12 regular muffins:

150g dried figs

½ cup boiling water

½ cup honey, warmed

1 large egg

¼ cup canola or other oil

2 tsp ground cinnamon

½ tsp salt

½ cup low-fat plain yoghurt

¼–½ cup chopped almonds

1 cup self-raising flour

¾ cup wholemeal flour

½ tsp baking soda

2 Tbsp lemon juice

2 Tbsp sugar

1 Preheat the oven to 200°C (190°C fanbake), with the rack just below the middle.

2 Put the figs in a microwave-safe jug or bowl, pour in the water, cover and heat on High (100% power) for 5 minutes. Set them aside to cool without draining.

3 Place the honey, egg, oil, cinnamon, salt, yoghurt and almonds into a fairly large bowl, then beat with a fork until thoroughly mixed.

4 When the figs are cool enough to handle, cut off and discard their stems, then chop them finely. Put them in a 1-cup measure and add enough cooking liquid to fill the cup, then stir them into the liquid mixture.

5 Measure the flours and the baking soda into a separate bowl, stir or whisk to mix, then sprinkle this mixture over the cold liquids. Fold together until no streaks of flour are visible, then spoon into 12 regular muffin pans which have been thoroughly non-stick sprayed.

6 Bake for 10–12 minutes, or until the centres spring back when lightly pressed. Leave in the pans for 2–3 minutes, while you mix the lemon juice and sugar. Carefully transfer muffins from the pans to a rack. Brush with the lemon mixture, making sure that some of the undissolved sugar is on each muffin.

7 Serve warm or reheated, topped with a blob of yoghurt if desired. Freeze muffins that will not be eaten within 48 hours.

'Pumpkin & Pecan Pie' Muffins

The flavourings in these muffins are based on those used in a classic American pumpkin pie. We thought we'd add pecans too, as they're another American favourite.

For 12 regular or 24 mini muffins:

1 cup (250g) cooked pumpkin, cooled

½ cup low-fat milk

¼ cup canola or other oil

1 large egg

1 tsp vanilla essence

1 cup standard (plain) flour

1 cup wholemeal flour

4 tsp baking powder

1 cup lightly packed brown sugar

1 tsp ground cinnamon

½ tsp ground ginger

½ tsp ground cloves

½ tsp salt

½ cup chopped pecans

1. Preheat the oven to 210°C (200°C fanbake), with the rack just below the middle.

2. To cook the pumpkin, wrap it (skin-on) in baking paper and microwave on High (100% power) for about 4 minutes, or until soft when squeezed. Leave to stand until cool, then peel off the skin.

3. Put the cooled pumpkin, milk, oil, egg and vanilla essence in a food processor and process until smooth (or mash well with a fork or potato masher).

4. Measure the flours into a large bowl. Add the baking powder, brown sugar, spices and salt and stir with a whisk or fork to combine.

5. Pour the liquids into the dry ingredients, sprinkle in the chopped pecans, and gently fold together. Mix just enough to moisten the flour. Spoon the mixture into 12 regular or 24 mini muffin pans that have been thoroughly non-stick sprayed.

6. Bake for 12–15 minutes until tops begin to brown and the centres spring back when pressed (if you are unsure, test to see if a skewer inserted into the middle of a muffin comes out clean).

7. Cool in their pans for 2–3 minutes before tipping out and cooling on a rack.

8. Serve warm or cold, freezing any that will not be eaten within 24 hours of baking.

Spiced Date & Walnut Muffins

A little ground cardamom gives these muffins an interesting 'warm' flavour that's hard to put a finger on.

For 12 regular muffins:

½ cup chopped dates

½ cup boiling water

½ cup canola oil

½ cup milk or orange juice

1 large egg

1 cup standard (plain) flour

1 cup wholemeal flour

½ cup brown sugar, lightly packed

3 tsp baking powder

2 tsp ground cinnamon

1 tsp ground cardamom

½ tsp salt

½ cup chopped walnuts

1. Preheat the oven to 200°C (190°C fanbake), with the rack just below the middle.

2. Place the chopped dates in a medium-sized bowl and cover with the boiling water. Leave to stand for about 5 minutes, then add the oil, milk (or orange juice) and egg and stir to mix.

3. Measure the dry ingredients into a large bowl and toss them together until well mixed.

4. Pour the liquid mixture into the dry ingredients and fold together until just mixed. Spoon the mixture into 12 regular muffin pans which have been coated with non-stick spray.

5. Bake for 12–15 minutes, or until golden brown and the centres spring back when pressed gently and a skewer comes out clean.

6. Serve warm or reheated, great with tea or coffee.

Maple Walnut Muffins

For 12 generous regular muffins:

1½ cups wholemeal flour

1 cup All-Bran type cereal (see Note)

1 cup walnut pieces

½ cup brown sugar

½ tsp baking soda

1 tsp baking powder

¾ tsp salt

½ cup maple syrup (see Note)

½ cup canola or other oil

½ cup natural low-fat yoghurt

1 large egg or 2 egg whites

These are possibly some of our best ever muffins! This is especially pleasing considering they are low-fat and relatively high in fibre.

1 Preheat the oven to 200°C (190°C fanbake), with the rack just below the middle.

2 Measure the flour, bran cereal, walnut pieces and brown sugar into a large bowl. Sift in the baking soda, baking powder and salt, then stir until evenly combined.

3 Combine the maple syrup, oil, yoghurt and egg (or egg whites) in another bowl and whisk to combine. Pour the liquid mixture into the dry ingredients and fold everything together. Take care not to over-mix.

4 Spoon the mixture into 12 non-stick sprayed or oiled muffin pans.

5 Bake for 12 minutes or until firm when pressed in the centre.

6 Serve any time, with tea or coffee.

NOTES:

We use an extruded mixed bran cereal as our first choice, and extruded wheat bran (All-Bran) when this is not available.

Use real or 'maple-flavoured' syrup.

The maple syrup may cause these muffins to brown quickly and darken too much if they are cooked for too long or at too high a temperature. Reduce the heat during baking if necessary.

Basic Bran Muffins

These bran muffins are very easy and quick to make. Because they have no added butter or oil they stick easily, so take care to prepare the muffin pans carefully.

For 12 regular or 24 mini muffins:

2 cups baking bran (wheat bran)

½ cup standard (plain) flour

1 tsp baking powder

1 tsp baking soda

½ cup sultanas, optional

¼ cup chopped walnuts, optional

½ cup golden syrup or treacle

1 large egg

1 cup milk

1 Preheat the oven to 200°C (190°C fanbake), with the rack just below the middle.

2 Put the bran into a large mixing bowl, then sieve the flour, baking powder and baking soda on top. Add the sultanas and/or walnuts if you are using them, then mix everything together lightly using your fingers.

3 Warm the golden syrup or treacle until runny. Remove from the heat, then add the egg and milk and mix well. Pour the liquids onto the dry ingredients and fold together only until the dry ingredients are barely dampened.

4 Divide the mixture evenly between 12 regular muffin pans that have been well coated with non-stick spray.

5 Bake for about 10–15 minutes or until firm in the middle when pressed lightly.

6 Serve for brunch, with tea or coffee or at any time of the day. Excellent in packed lunches. Eat within 48 hours.

Bulk Bran Muffins

This recipe makes about three dozen regular muffins. You can refrigerate the uncooked mixture for up to two weeks, cooking them as required.

For 36 regular or 72 mini muffins:

½ cup treacle

2 cups rolled oats

1 cup baking bran (wheat bran)

1 cup boiling water

1 cup brown sugar

2 Tbsp wine vinegar

1 tsp salt

2 large eggs

2 cups milk

2 cups standard (plain) flour

1 cup oat bran

1½ tsp baking soda

1 Preheat the oven to 220°C (210°C fanbake), with the rack just below the middle.

2 Measure the treacle, rolled oats and baking bran into a large bowl. Pour over boiling water and stir until treacle and oats are mixed. Leave to cool for 5 minutes, then add the brown sugar, vinegar, salt and eggs. Beat with a fork to combine eggs.

3 Add the milk and then the flour, oat bran and baking soda, previously forked together. Stir only enough to combine.

4 Spray muffin pans with non-stick spray. Put about ¼ cup of mixture into each muffin cup.

5 Bake for about 10 minutes, until muffins spring back when pressed.

6 Alternatively, microwave in paper cases in microwave muffin moulds, for about 2 minutes on High (100% power) for five muffins. Microwave ovens vary — experiment with the first few batches you make until you know the exact time taken by your microwave oven. Always leave to stand for a few minutes before removing muffins from pans.

7 Serve warm for breakfast, brunch, with coffee, in lunches or after school. Serve microwaved muffins within 30 minutes of cooking.

Blueberry Bran Muffins

Here is our version of a classic American favourite. Keep a packet of blueberries in your freezer, so you can make a batch of these at short notice.

For 12–15 regular or 30 mini muffins:

1 cup baking bran (wheat bran)

¼ cup wheatgerm or extra bran

½ cup canola or other oil

1 cup plain or fruity yoghurt

1 large egg

¾ cup wholemeal flour

¾ cup high-grade flour

1 tsp ground cinnamon

1 tsp baking powder

¾ tsp salt

½ tsp baking soda

1 cup brown sugar

1–1½ cups (150–180g) frozen blueberries

1. Preheat the oven to 200°C (190°C fanbake), with the rack just below the middle.

2. Measure the bran, wheatgerm (or extra bran), oil, yoghurt and egg into a large bowl, mix to blend everything with a fork, then leave to stand.

3. Measure the remaining dry ingredients into a medium-sized bowl, and stir well with a fork to mix thoroughly. Do not thaw the blueberries, but separate any clumps of berries. (We use half a 350g packet and find that this is a very good amount for this recipe, although you can use less.)

4. Tip the flour mixture into the liquid mixture, then fold everything together until the dry ingredients are moistened without over-mixing.

5. Spoon the mixture into 12–15 regular or about 30 mini muffin pans which have been thoroughly non-stick sprayed.

6. Bake for about 15 minutes (longer than most other muffins, because of the frozen berries in the mixture), until centres spring back when pressed.

7. Serve warm or reheated, without any spread, at any time of the day.

Oaty Refrigerator Low-fat Muffins

Treacle gives these muffins a rich flavour, as well as enough colour to enable them to be microwaved.

For about 30 regular muffins:

½ cup treacle

1½ cups baking bran (wheat bran)

1 cup boiling water

1 cup brown sugar

2 Tbsp wine vinegar

1 tsp salt

2 large eggs

2 cups milk

2 cups standard (plain) flour

1 cup rolled oats

1 cup oat bran

½ cup wheatgerm

1½ tsp baking soda

1. Measure the treacle and bran into a large bowl. Pour over the boiling water and mix until combined. Cool for about 5 minutes. Add the sugar, vinegar, salt, eggs and milk and beat well with a fork.

2. In another bowl, toss together the flour, rolled oats, oat bran, wheatgerm and baking soda with a fork, mixing them well. Tip in the liquid ingredients and fold everything together, stirring only enough to combine. Cover and refrigerate overnight or for up to one week before baking.

3. To bake, spoon mixture (without further mixing) into lightly buttered or well sprayed muffin pans.

4. Bake at 200°C for 10–15 minutes or until the centres spring back when pressed. Refrigerate unused mixture promptly.

5. To microwave four muffins, spoon ¼ cup of mixture into Teflon lined glass ramekins, cover with plastic wrap pierced with several holes, and cook on High (100% power) for 2 minutes or until firm.

6. Serve warm, soon after cooking, for breakfast, morning coffee or brunch.

Eggless Bran Muffins

Warm from the oven, these plain, old-fashioned muffins make a very low-fat weekend breakfast or lunch. They have a lovely golden syrup flavour but each muffin contains nearly three tablespoons of bran, so is really high in fibre — and they contain no egg, butter or oil!

For 12 regular muffins:

¾ cup golden syrup

½ cup boiling water

1 cup low-fat milk

2 cups baking bran (wheat bran)

1 cup standard (plain) flour

1 tsp baking powder

1 tsp baking soda

1 tsp salt

1 Preheat the oven to 210°C (200°C fanbake), with the rack just below the middle.

2 Measure the golden syrup into a large bowl (to make measuring easier, pour hot water over a ¼ cup measure before dipping it into the tin of syrup). Add the boiling water and stir until syrup is dissolved. Add the milk and stir again.

3 Measure the remaining ingredients into another bowl (measure the baking soda into the palm of your hand and squash it with the back of the measuring spoon to ensure there are no lumps, before adding it to the bowl). Mix the dry ingredients together thoroughly.

4 Thoroughly non-stick spray 12 regular muffin pans. Tip all the dry ingredients into the cool milk mixture. Fold the dry ingredients into the wet mixture until all the bran and flour is dampened. Do not over-mix or stir until smooth. (Expect a larger, more liquid mixture than usual.) Using two spoons, divide the mixture equally between the muffin pans.

5 Bake for 12–15 minutes, until muffins are an attractive brown colour and they spring back when pressed. Because the mixture is fairly wet, the muffin tops may be flatter than usual. Leave muffins to stand in the pans for 3–4 minutes, then carefully transfer to a cooling rack. Put in plastic bags when cold.

6 Serve warm (or reheated). Cottage cheese makes a good low-fat topping. Freeze any muffins you do not expect to eat within two days.

VARIATION: Add ½ cup of small dark raisins or sultanas to the syrup mixture. And/or add ¼–½ cup chopped walnuts to the bran and flour mixture.

Kumara, Bacon & Onion Muffins

There is something memorable about these muffins! They have a mild but distinctive flavour and texture, and are a very popular addition to luncheon buffets, especially when overseas visitors are present.

For 12 regular or 24 mini muffins:

2 Tbsp canola or other oil

2 rashers (100g) lean bacon, chopped

1 small onion, peeled and finely chopped

2 cups self-raising flour

1 cup grated tasty cheese

1 tsp mild curry powder

½ tsp salt

1 cup milk

1 large egg

1 cup (200g) roughly mashed cooked kumara (see Note)

1 Preheat the oven to 200°C (190°C fanbake), with the rack just below the middle.

2 Heat the oil in a medium-sized frypan. Cook the bacon and onion in it, stirring occasionally, until bacon begins to brown.

3 Meanwhile, measure the flour, cheese, curry powder and salt into a large bowl. Toss well with a fork to mix.

4 In another bowl mix the milk and egg with the fork until blended, then stir in the roughly mashed kumara, and mix again, leaving some chunky pieces.

5 Tip the cooked bacon and onion, then the flour, into the kumara mixture. Gently fold everything together until the flour is just moistened. Do not over-mix.

6 Spoon the mixture into 12 lightly buttered or non-stick sprayed regular-sized muffin pans or 24 mini muffin pans.

7 Bake for 12–15 minutes, or until golden brown on top and firm when pressed in the centre.

8 These muffins have a good flavour when hot, warm or cold. Buttering is not necessary.

NOTE: Use golden kumara for a definite gold colour. For easy preparation, scrub about 300g of kumara, cut off any hairy protrusions, then microwave for 4–5 minutes, until the flesh in the thickest part 'gives' when gently squeezed. When cool, peel off skin and mash roughly.

Avocado & Bacon Muffins

Everybody seems to like the combination of avocados, cheese, bacon and spring onions — these are always popular.

For 12 regular or 24 mini muffins:

2 cups standard (plain) flour

4 tsp baking powder

½ tsp salt

1 Tbsp sugar

pinch of cayenne pepper

1 cup (100g) grated tasty cheese

4 spring onions, peeled and chopped

3 rashers bacon

75g butter, melted

1 large egg

1 cup milk

1 avocado

about 1 Tbsp lemon juice

1 Preheat the oven to 200°C (190°C fanbake), with the rack just below the middle.

2 Sieve the flour, baking powder, salt and sugar into a large bowl. Add the cayenne pepper, grated cheese and spring onion, and stir to combine.

3 Chop the bacon finely and cook in a frypan or under the grill until crisp. Keep the bacon drippings.

4 Place the melted butter in another large bowl, add the egg, milk and bacon drippings, and beat to combine. Halve the avocado, then scoop out the flesh with a dessert or tablespoon and cut into 7mm cubes. Sprinkle with lemon juice to stop cubes from browning. Add to the liquid mixture.

5 Add the bacon and the flour mixture to the liquid ingredients and fold together. Stir only to dampen the flour.

6 Spray 12 regular or 24 mini muffin pans with non-stick spray, then place spoonfuls of mixture into them.

7 Bake for about 10 minutes, or until the muffins spring back when pressed lightly in the centre.

8 Always serve warm, as finger food with drinks, or as the main part of lunch.

Champion Cheese Muffins

These muffins look even more inviting if you add a topping of grated cheese and a sprinkling of paprika or a pinch of chilli powder.

For 12 regular or 24 mini muffins:

2 cups (200g) grated tasty cheese

1½ cups self-raising flour

½ tsp salt

1 Tbsp sugar

pinch of cayenne pepper

1 large egg

1 cup milk

extra grated cheese for topping, optional

extra cayenne pepper or chilli powder for topping, optional

1 Preheat the oven to 210°C (200°C fanbake), with the rack just below the middle.

2 Measure the cheese, flour, salt, sugar and cayenne pepper into a large bowl. Mix lightly with your fingertips to combine.

3 In another large bowl beat the egg and milk until evenly combined. Sprinkle the flour and cheese mixture over the liquids, then fold the two mixtures together, taking care not to over-mix.

4 Spoon mixture into 12 regular muffin pans, which have been sprayed with non-stick spray.

5 Sprinkle with a little extra cheese and paprika or chilli powder before baking (optional).

6 Bake for about 12 minutes, until muffins spring back when pressed in the middle and are golden brown. Leave to stand in the pans for 3–4 minutes before transferring to a rack.

7 Serve mini muffins for cocktail snacks and afternoon tea; regular muffins for general use or if making to freeze.

Easy Cheesy Muffins

Some years ago, during a bakers' strike, an easy bread made from self-raising flour and beer 'did the rounds'. Starting with the same basic ingredients, you can make wonderful cheesy muffins!

For 12 generous regular muffins or 24 mini muffins:

2 cups self-raising flour

2 cups (200g) grated tasty cheese

1 large egg

1 cup lager or beer

about 2 Tbsp chutney, optional

1 Preheat the oven to 220°C (210°C fanbake), with the rack just below the middle.

2 Toss the flour and cheese together in a large bowl.

3 Break the egg into another large bowl and beat with a fork enough to thoroughly mix the white and yolk. Add the lager or beer (which can be flat or bubbly) and stir to mix briefly, then sprinkle in the flour and cheese mixture.

4 Fold together until most of the flour is dampened, but do not over-mix. If you like the idea, drizzle your favourite chutney over the surface, and fold it in lightly so that it stays in streaks.

5 Spoon the mixture into 12 buttered or sprayed regular muffin pans.

6 Bake for 10–15 minutes, until the muffins are nicely browned and the centres spring back when pressed.

7 Serve warm or cold, very popular for lunch. Warm mini muffins make excellent party snacks.

Chilli Cheese Mini Muffins

These little muffins, made with strongly-flavoured cheddar cheese, are quickly made, and fill the house with an irresistible aroma.

For 24 mini muffins:

2 cups (200g) grated tasty cheese

1½ cups self-raising flour

1 tsp garlic salt

2 Tbsp Thai sweet chilli sauce

1 cup milk

1 large egg

❶ Preheat the oven to 210°C (200°C fanbake), with the rack just below the middle.

❷ Measure the cheese, flour and garlic salt into a large bowl and toss gently to combine well.

❸ Measure the Thai sweet chilli sauce, milk and egg into a smaller bowl and beat with a fork until thoroughly combined. Pour the liquid mixture into the dry ingredients all at once, then fold everything together, mixing no more than necessary to dampen the flour.

❹ Thoroughly coat 24 mini muffin pans with non-stick spray. Using two dessertspoons, divide the mixture evenly between the pans.

❺ Bake for about 12 minutes, until the centres spring back when pressed and the muffins are golden brown. For easy removal from pans, leave muffins to stand 2–4 minutes before lifting out. (Some cheese may stick to the edges of the muffin pan. Remove it carefully.)

❻ Serve exactly as they come from the oven, or slash deeply from the top and insert a piece of cold-smoked salmon, salami, ham, cheese, and/or a slice of a small tomato or a piece of roasted pepper, with a fresh herb leaf.

Hawaiian Ham Muffins

'Hawaiian' is the name used for a combination of ham, pineapple and cheese!

For 12 regular or 24 mini muffins:

2 cups standard (plain) flour

4 tsp baking powder

½ tsp salt

about 100g ham or ham pieces, diced

1½ cups grated tasty cheese

2 spring onions, chopped

227–235g can crushed pineapple

about ¾ cup coconut cream or milk

1 large egg

❶ Preheat the oven to 210°C (200°C fanbake), with the rack just below the middle.

❷ Measure the flour, baking powder and salt into a large bowl. Add the ham and cheese. Add spring onion (green and white parts). Using a fork, toss everything together until evenly combined.

❸ Drain the pineapple, reserving the juice. Make the juice up to 1 cup with coconut cream or milk. Put the pineapple, liquid and egg in another large bowl and mix until well combined, again using the fork.

❹ Sprinkle the flour mixture over the liquids and fold together until the flour is just moistened, taking care to avoid over-mixing.

❺ Spoon the mixture into 12 regular or 24 mini muffin pans which have been sprayed or lightly buttered. Top with a little extra grated cheese if you like.

❻ Bake for 12–15 minutes, or until tops and sides are brown, and the centres spring back when lightly pressed. Leave to stand in their pans for 3–4 minutes before removing and cooling on a rack.

❼ Serve as party finger food; with a hot or cold drink at any time of day; or as the main part of a weekend brunch or lunch, with or without a salad.

Zucchini & Parmesan Muffins

These muffins, flecked with pale green, are light, pretty and fresh tasting, perfect for serving on a summer's day. You'll find them especially appealing if your family has seen enough zucchini from the garden on their dinner plates!

For 12 regular or 24 mini muffins:

2 cups standard (plain) flour

4 tsp baking powder

½ tsp salt

black pepper to taste

1 cup grated tasty cheese

¼ cup grated Parmesan

¾ cup milk

2 large eggs

3 zucchini, unpeeled and grated (250g altogether)

1 Preheat the oven to 210°C (200°C fanbake), with the rack just below the middle.

2 Sift or fork together the flour, baking powder and salt in a large bowl. Grind in black pepper to taste, then add the cheeses and stir to combine.

3 Break the eggs into another large bowl, add the milk and whisk together with a fork, then add the zucchini.

4 Tip the dry ingredients into the liquid mixture, then carefully fold everything together, taking care not to over-mix. As soon as all the flour is moistened, spoon the mixture into 12 lightly buttered or non-stick sprayed regular muffin pans or 24 mini muffin pans.

5 Bake for 12–15 minutes, or until the tops are golden and the muffins spring back when pressed in the centre.

6 Serve cold or warm, enjoy as they are or topped with sliced tomato and herbs. Good for picnic lunches.

NOTE: If you like freshly ground pepper, use plenty in these muffins!

Broccoli & Blue Cheese Muffins

Neither the blue cheese nor broccoli flavour in these muffins is too strong. In fact, the very pleasant savoury taste should appeal even to those who are not convinced about the merits of either.

For 12 regular or 24 mini muffins:

200g broccoli (1 small-medium head)

1½ cups low-fat plain yoghurt

¼ cup canola oil

1 large egg

50g creamy blue cheese

2 cups self-raising flour

½ tsp salt

¼ cup milk, if required

1 Preheat the oven to 200°C (190°C fanbake), with the rack just below the middle.

2 To cook the broccoli separate it into florets and place in a microwave-safe container with 1 tablespoon of water, cover, and microwave for about 3 minutes or until very tender. Alternatively, boil or steam until tender, then drain well.

3 Place the yoghurt, oil and egg in a food processor and mix well. Add the broccoli, and roughly crumble in the blue cheese. Process in short bursts until there are no large pieces of broccoli left. Try not to purée the broccoli; just chop it finely.

4 Measure the flour and salt into a large bowl and toss together with a fork. Pour in the liquid mixture and begin to fold together. If you think the mixture looks too dry, add the extra milk and fold just enough to combine.

5 Spray 12 regular or 24 mini muffin trays with non-stick spray. Divide the mixture evenly between the pans.

6 Bake for 12–15 minutes or until golden brown and centres spring back when pressed. Remove muffins from the oven and cool in their pans for 2–3 minutes before tipping out. Store cooled muffins in a plastic bag to prevent them drying out.

7 Serve warm or reheated with soup or salad for a weekend lunch, or include in packed lunches.

Spinach & Feta Muffins

It's hard to know what makes the combination of spinach and feta work so well, but it does!

For 12 regular muffins:

½ cup (100–125g) cooked spinach, chopped (see Note)

1 cup (250g) 'Lite' cottage cheese

1 cup milk

¼ cup canola oil

1 large egg

50–75g feta, cubed or crumbled

1 cup wholemeal flour

1 cup standard (plain) flour

4 tsp baking powder

½–1 tsp salt

❶ Preheat the oven to 210°C (200°C fanbake), with the rack just below the middle.

❷ Lightly squeeze the cooked spinach, reserving the liquid. Make the spinach liquid up to 1 cup with milk, then place the spinach, milk and spinach liquid, cottage cheese, oil and egg in a large bowl and mix well. Add the feta and mix lightly.

❸ Measure the flours, baking powder and salt together into another bowl and toss together with a whisk or fork.

❹ Tip the flour mixture into the liquids, then fold gently together until the flour is just moistened. The mixture does not need to be smooth.

❺ Spoon the mixture into 12 non-stick sprayed regular muffin pans.

❻ Bake for 15 minutes or until golden brown and a skewer inserted into the centre of a muffin comes out clean.

❼ Remove muffins from the oven and leave to cool in their pans for 2–3 minutes before tipping out and cooling on a rack.

❽ These muffins are delicious warm. Store cooled muffins in sealed bags to prevent drying out.

Olive, Pesto & Feta Muffins

Standard cheddar-cheesy muffins tend to be relatively high in fat so we concocted these — they still taste great and use a relatively small amount of lower-fat feta instead.

For 12 regular muffins:

2 cups self-raising flour

½ tsp salt 50–100g feta, crumbled or cubed

¼ cup chopped black olives

1 cup low-fat plain yoghurt

¼ cup olive oil

1 large egg

2 Tbsp pesto

❶ Preheat the oven to 210°C (200°C fanbake), with the rack just below the middle.

❷ Measure the flour and salt into a large bowl. Add the feta and olives, then stir until well mixed.

❸ In another bowl, mix together the yoghurt, oil, egg and pesto.

❹ Pour the liquid mixture into the dry ingredients, then stir gently until just mixed (stop as soon as all the flour has been moistened).

❺ Spoon the mixture into 12 regular muffin pans which have been well sprayed with non-stick spray.

❻ Bake for 12–15 minutes, or until the tops are golden brown and the centres are firm when pressed.

❼ Leave to stand for a couple of minutes, then remove from the pans and cool on a wire rack.

❽ Enjoy the muffins warm, or bag and freeze any you do not intend to eat within 24 hours.

Golden Cornmeal Muffins

These muffins make a good summer lunch, especially when served outdoors with salads.

For 12 regular or 24 mini muffins:

1 cup standard (plain) or wholemeal flour

½ cup yellow cornmeal

3 tsp baking powder

1 cup (100g) grated tasty cheese

¼ cup sugar

¼ tsp salt

50g butter, melted

1 large egg

½ cup creamed corn

½ cup plain yoghurt or milk

1 Preheat the oven to 210°C (200°C fanbake), with the rack just below the middle.

2 Measure the flour, cornmeal, baking powder, cheese, sugar and salt into a large mixing bowl. Toss well with a fork.

3 Place the melted butter in another large bowl. Add the egg, creamed corn and yoghurt or milk (add yoghurt in preference to milk — it makes muffins more tender), then mix with a fork.

4 Fold the liquid mixture into the dry ingredients, taking great care not to over-mix.

5 Thoroughly coat 12 regular muffin pans with non-stick spray, then put about ¼ cup of mixture in each muffin cup.

6 Bake for 10–15 minutes, until quite crusty and nicely browned. Leave to stand in the pans for about 3 minutes before removing and cooling on a wire rack.

7 Serve warm as finger food at parties, or serve for lunch, as part of a buffet, or as picnic food.

NOTE: Do not use very fine, flour-like cornmeal for this recipe.

Pizza Muffins

If your family and friends like pizza, we're sure you will find that these muffins 'go down a treat' for lunch or with coffee.

For 12 regular or 24 mini muffins:

2 cups grated tasty cheese

2 cups standard (plain) flour

3 tsp baking powder

1 Tbsp sugar

1 spring onion, chopped (white and green parts)

50g salami, finely chopped

½ tsp dried oregano

1 Tbsp tomato paste

3 Tbsp water

1 cup milk

1 large egg

Topping, optional:

½ medium tomato, deseeded and finely chopped

about ½ cup grated cheese

2–3 slices salami, chopped

1 Preheat the oven to 220°C (210°C fanbake), with the rack just below the middle.

2 Measure the cheese, flour, baking powder and sugar into a large bowl. Add the spring onion, salami and oregano, then stir lightly to combine.

3 Mix the tomato paste and water until smooth in another large bowl. Add the milk and egg, and beat with a fork until well combined.

4 Pour the flour mixture into this liquid and fold together until the flour is moistened. Take care not to over-mix.

5 Spoon the mixture into 12 regular or 24 mini muffin pans that have been thoroughly non-stick sprayed.

6 If you have the time and inclination, place a few pieces of tomato, a few shreds of grated cheese and a couple of pieces of salami on each muffin.

7 Bake for 12 minutes, or until lightly browned on top and firm when pressed in the middle.

8 These muffins are irresistible hot from the oven, but the flavour is even better when cold.

Breads & Buns

Like many other people, we get a great deal of pleasure and satisfaction from making bread by hand (or using a bread machine). Once you get into a bread-making routine, you will wonder why you ever considered it a complicated procedure — the process involves a number of steps, but few of these are very time-consuming, and can mostly be fitted in between other activities.

Using your bread-making skills, you can start with a few basic, inexpensive ingredients, and some very simple equipment, and finish up with some spectacularly good bread, literally made with your own hands.

The two most important processes are kneading and rising If you have a friend who makes bread, watch her or him kneading then try it for yourself. You can't rush these steps and get good results. (A good sturdy mixer with a dough hook does take the 'elbow grease' out of kneading.)

We give fairly specific rising times, but these may vary considerably in different or sub-optimal conditions.

We are often eager to eat our bread as soon as possible after baking but remember that it will cut much better if you leave it for an hour or so to cool down. A really sharp bread knife is well worthwhile.

Bread machine tips

Make sure you also read and reread the instructions that came with your bread machine — or whenever you have teething problems — because you are sure to learn some finer points each time. The manufacturer knows your particular machine better than we do, but these are answers we have found by trial and error.

Sunken top and/or collapsed middle?

Too much water — try 2 tablespoons less

Too much yeast — try ½ teaspoon less (the dough rises too quickly, then collapses before baking)

No salt, or too little salt (salt slows down yeast and "tightens" the dough)

The room temperature/humidity is too high — try a quick cycle

Coarse or holey texture?

Too much liquid — try 2 tablespoons less

Fermenting too quickly; try a short cycle

Room temperature too high

Too much sugar — use ½ teaspoon less

Uneven top?

Dough too stiff, not enough water — try adding 1–2 tablespoons

Small compact loaf or poor rising?

Too little yeast

No yeast. Did you forget it?

Yeast beyond expiry date

Measurement errors — not enough yeast or water, or too much salt

Dough too stiff — not enough water

Yeast has reacted with water too soon when using time delay — check the order in which ingredients should be added

If you are using the rapid cycle, try adding an extra ½ teaspoon of yeast and another teaspoon of sugar

We found that it was much easier to put ingredients in the bread machine bowl if we took the bowl out of the machine first.

One of the bonuses of bread machines is their delayed start (timer) function, but there are a few points to note about this; not all bread recipes are suitable for timer delay because of the ingredients they contain; and the bread is much nicer if removed from the machine as soon as possible at the end of the baking cycle.

Quick English Muffins – recipe page 218

Our Favourite White Bread

We find it enormously satisfying to make this delicious sweet-smelling, finely textured, nicely risen white loaf.

For 1 large loaf (8 cup pan):

3 tsp Surebake yeast

1¼ cups + 2 Tbsp warm water

2 Tbsp lecithin granules or oil

2 tsp sugar

1½ tsp salt

2 Tbsp non-fat milk powder

3 cups (420g) high-grade flour

Bread Machine Instructions:

❶ Carefully measure all the ingredients into a 750g capacity bread machine in the order specified by the manufacturer.

❷ Set to the Normal/White Bread cycle, Medium Crust and Start (or use the Dough cycle and shape and bake by hand). This is a very good timer bread.

Hand-made Bread Instructions:

❶ Measure the first six ingredients into a large bowl. Add 1½ cups of the measured flour and mix thoroughly. Cover and leave for 15 minutes or longer in a warm place.

❷ Stir in the remaining flour, adding a little extra warm water or flour if necessary, to make a dough just firm enough to knead.

❸ Knead with the dough hook of an electric mixer or by hand on a lightly floured surface for 10 minutes, adding extra flour if necessary, until the dough forms a soft ball that springs back when gently pressed.

❹ Turn the dough in 2–3 teaspoons of oil in the cleaned dry bowl, cover with plastic wrap and leave in a warm, draught-free place for about 30 minutes.

❺ Lightly knead the oiled dough in the bowl for 1 minute. Pat it into a square shape a little longer than the baking pan, then roll into a cylinder. Put into the sprayed or buttered bread pan, pressing it into the corners and levelling the top.

❻ Leave to rise in a warm, draught-free place for about 1 hour or until double its original size.

❼ If desired, brush with milk or egg glaze and sprinkle with sesame seeds, then bake at 200°C for about 30 minutes or until the sides and bottom are browned and the loaf sounds hollow when tapped.

For 1 large loaf (8 cup pan):

½ cup (85g) mixed kibbled grains (see Note)

3 tsp Surebake yeast

1¼ cups warm water

2 Tbsp olive oil

1 Tbsp sugar

1½ tsp salt

2 Tbsp lecithin granules, optional

1 cup (140g) wholemeal flour

2½ cups (350g) high-grade flour

Mixed Grain Bread

Precooking the kibbled grains may seem a bit fiddly, but it ensures a moist loaf. The large, light-textured loaf, flecked with kibbled grains, is a just reward for the extra effort.

Prepare the Kibble:

1. Place the kibble mix in a small pot with 2–3 cups (420g) of cold water. Bring to the boil, then simmer for 1–2 minutes.

2. Take from the heat and drain well in a sieve.

Bread Machine Instructions:

1. Carefully measure all the ingredients, including the prepared kibble combined with the measured water, into a 750g capacity bread machine in the order specified by the manufacturer.

2. Set to the Normal/White Bread cycle, Medium Crust and Start. This is a good timer bread.

Hand-made Bread Instructions:

1. In a large bowl, mix the prepared kibbled grains with 1¼ cups warm water. Add all the remaining ingredients except the high-grade flour. Mix thoroughly, cover and leave for 15 minutes in a warm place.

2. Stir in the high-grade flour, adding a little extra water or flour if necessary, to make a dough just firm enough to knead.

3. Knead with the dough hook of an electric mixer or by hand on a lightly floured surface for 10 minutes, adding extra flour if necessary, until the dough forms a soft ball that springs back when gently pressed.

4. Turn dough in 2–3 teaspoons of oil in the cleaned dry bowl, cover with plastic wrap and leave in a warm, draught-free place for 30 minutes.

5. Lightly knead the oiled dough in the bowl for 1 minute. Pat the dough into a square shape a little longer than the baking pan, then roll into a cylinder. Put into the sprayed or buttered bread pan, pressing it into the corners and levelling the top.

6. Leave to rise in a warm, draught-free place for about 1 hour or until double its original size. If desired, brush with milk or egg glaze and sprinkle with extra kibbled grains, then bake at 200°C for about 30 minutes until the sides and bottom are browned and the loaf sounds hollow when tapped underneath.

NOTE: Buy or make a mixture of kibbled wheat, red and/or purple wheat, and kibbled rye.

Cheese Muffin Bread

Bake this as a rich cheese loaf, top with grated cheese and cook like muffins in pans, or make novel pull-apart monkey breads if you feel like something different.

For 1 large loaf (8 cup), 12 muffin buns, or 2 x 18cm monkey bread rings:

3 tsp Surebake yeast

¾ cup warm water

2 large eggs

2 Tbsp lecithin granules or butter

2 tsp sugar

1 tsp salt

2 Tbsp non-fat milk powder

3 cups (420g) high-grade flour

¾ cup grated tasty cheese

½ tsp chilli powder, optional

melted butter

grated Parmesan or tasty cheese

milk

Bread Machine Instructions:

1. Carefully measure the first eight ingredients into a 750g capacity bread machine in the order specified by the manufacturer.

2. Set to the Normal/White Bread cycle, Medium Crust and Start (or use the dough cycle and shape and bake using the instructions given below).

Hand-made Bread Instructions:

1. Measure the first seven ingredients into a large bowl with 1½ cups of high-grade flour and mix thoroughly. Cover and leave for 15 minutes or longer in a warm place.

2. Stir in the flour, cheese and the chilli powder (if using), and a little extra flour or water if necessary, to make a dough just firm enough to knead.

3. Knead with the dough hook of an electric mixer or by hand on a lightly floured surface for 10 minutes, adding extra flour if necessary, until the dough forms a soft ball that springs back when gently pressed.

4. Turn the dough in 2–3 teaspoons of oil in the cleaned dry bowl, cover with plastic wrap and leave in a warm, draught-free place for 30–40 minutes.

5. Lightly knead the dough in the bowl for 1 minute, then shape as desired.

Shaping:

- To make a loaf: Pat the dough into a square shape a little longer than the baking pan, then roll into a cylinder. Put into the sprayed or buttered bread pan, pressing it into the corners and levelling the top. Leave to rise in a warm, draught-free place for about 1 hour or until double its original size. If desired, brush with milk or egg glaze, then bake at 200°C for about 30 minutes until the sides and bottom are browned and the loaf sounds hollow when tapped underneath.

- To make muffin buns: divide the dough into 12 pieces and roll into balls. Put into sprayed medium-sized muffin pans and leave to rise in a warm, draught-free place for 1 hour or until doubled in volume. Dampen tops with milk and sprinkle with grated tasty cheese. Bake at 220°C for 10–12 minutes until tops, sides and bottom are golden brown.

- To make monkey bread: divide the dough into four, then eight, then 16, then 32 equal-sized pieces. Roll each ball in a little melted butter, then in grated Parmesan or tasty cheese. Line the bottom of two 20cm ring pans with baking paper and oil the sides. Put 16 of the cheesy balls evenly in each pan. Cover with plastic wrap and leave to rise in a warm, draught-free place for about 1 hour or until almost double in volume. Bake at 220°C for 15–20 minutes or until golden brown. Serve warm.

For 1 large loaf (8 cup pan):

3 tsp Surebake yeast

1½ cups warm water

2 Tbsp golden syrup

2 Tbsp oil

1½ tsp salt

2 cups (280g) high-grade flour

1½ (180g) cups rye meal

2 Tbsp cocoa powder

1 tsp instant coffee granules

about 1 tsp caraway seeds

Dark Rye Bread

This large loaf has a wonderfully rich dark colour, an inviting aroma, an interesting flavour, and is very popular. You can vary the colour and flavour of the bread to suit your own taste.

Bread Machine Instructions:

1 Carefully measure all the ingredients into a 750g capacity bread machine in the order specified by the manufacturer.

2 Set to the Normal/White Bread cycle, Medium Crust and Start (or use Dough cycle and shape and bake as below). This is a good timer bread.

Hand-made Bread Instructions:

1 Measure the first five ingredients into a large bowl with 1 cup of high-grade flour and mix thoroughly. Cover and leave to stand in a warm place for 15 minutes.

2 Stir in the remaining high-grade flour, rye meal, cocoa powder, instant coffee and caraway seeds. Add a little extra flour or water to make a dough just firm enough to knead.

3 Knead with the dough hook of an electric mixer or by hand on a lightly floured surface for 10 minutes, adding extra flour if necessary, until the dough forms a soft ball that springs back when gently pressed.

4 Turn in 2–3 teaspoons of oil in the cleaned dry bowl, cover with plastic wrap and leave in a warm, draught-free place for 30 minutes.

5 Lightly knead the dough in the bowl for 1 minute before turning out onto a lightly floured surface.

6 To make a round loaf pat the dough into a ball, flatten it slightly with your hand, then pick it up and tuck and pinch all the edges underneath, so the top of the dough is smooth and stretched, forming an evenly rounded loaf when baked.

7 To help keep its shape, put the round loaf in a 23cm round pan (preferably loose-bottomed) and dust with flour. Leave in a warm, draught-free place for about 1 hour or until risen to about twice its original size.

8 Bake at 200°C for about 30 minutes or until the loaf sounds hollow when the bottom is tapped.

VARIATION: For a light rye loaf, leave out the cocoa powder and instant coffee. Vary the amount of caraway seed to suit your taste.

Bagels

Let the plane to New York leave without you! Make your own wonderfully chewy bagels for about a tenth of the price of bought ones in a surprisingly short time. Spoil yourself with traditional toppings of cream cheese and smoked salmon. Bliss!

For 8 plump bagels:

3 tsp Surebake yeast

1¼ cups warm water

2 Tbsp honey

1½ tsp salt

1 cup (140g) wholemeal flour

2 Tbsp gluten flour

2 cups (280g) high-grade flour

Bread Machine Instructions:

1. Carefully measure all the ingredients into a 750g capacity bread machine in the order specified by the manufacturer.

2. Set to the Dough cycle and Start. Stop the machine and remove the dough 40 minutes after mixing starts, even though the cycle is not complete.

3. Shape and bake by hand following the instructions below.

Hand-made Bread Instructions:

1. Measure the first five ingredients into a large bowl and mix thoroughly. Cover and leave for 15 minutes or longer in a warm place.

2. Stir in the gluten and high-grade flour, adding extra flour or water if necessary, until you have a dough just firm enough to knead.

3. Knead with the dough hook of an electric mixer or by hand on a lightly floured surface for 10 minutes until you have a soft, smooth, satiny dough that springs back when gently pressed.

4. Turn the dough in 2–3 teaspoons of oil in the cleaned dry bowl. Cover with plastic wrap and leave in a warm, draught-free place for 30 minutes.

Shaping and Baking:

1. Lightly knead the dough for 1 minute, then cut into eight equal pieces. Roll each into a 26cm long 'snake'. Working with one length at a time, dampen each end with water and press together firmly to form a ring. Place the rings on a sheet of oiled baking paper and leave for 10–15 minutes.

2. Meanwhile, bring a large pan containing 5–10cm water to the boil. Carefully lower three bagels at a time into the boiling water (slide them into the water from the paper to avoid burning your hands), lift away the paper, and cook for 30–45 seconds per side. Drain on paper towels, then put the bagels on a large baking sheet lined with baking paper, leaving space between them for rising.

3. Brush as far down the sides as you can with egg glaze and sprinkle with poppy or toasted sesame seeds.

4. Bake at 220°C for 10–12 minutes until browned top and bottom. Cool on a rack and serve warm or toasted within 24 hours of making or freeze in an airtight container as soon as they are cold.

Focaccia

We're not sure exactly what it is about this Italian-style flat bread that makes it so appealing, but this is another of our favourites. Try it plain, or with some of our favourite toppings, but really these are only a start...

For a 22 x 32cm loaf:

2 tsp Surebake yeast

1½ cups water

1 Tbsp sugar

1 tsp salt

1 Tbsp olive oil

3 cups (420g) high-grade flour

1 tsp dried oregano

1 Tbsp olive oil

coarse rock or flaky salt

Bread Machine Instructions:

1 Carefully measure the first seven ingredients into a 750g capacity bread machine in the order specified by the manufacturer.

2 Set to the Dough cycle and Start. When the cycle is complete shape and bake as below.

Hand-made Bread Instructions:

1 Measure the first five ingredients into a large bowl with 1½ cups of the high-grade flour and mix thoroughly. Cover and leave for 15 minutes or longer in a warm place.

2 Stir in the remaining flour and the oregano, adding a little extra warm water or bread flour if necessary to make a dough just firm enough to knead.

3 Knead with the dough hook of an electric mixer or by hand on a lightly floured surface for 10 minutes, adding extra flour if necessary, until the dough forms a soft dough that springs back when gently pressed.

4 Turn the dough in 2–3 teaspoons of oil in the cleaned dry bowl, cover with plastic wrap and leave in a warm, draught-free place for about 30 minutes.

5 Lightly knead the oiled dough in the bowl for about 1 minute.

Shaping and Baking:

1 Turn the dough out onto a lightly floured board and roll into a 20 x 30cm rectangle. Place on a well-oiled baking sheet or in a sponge roll pan and leave to rise in a warm, draught-free place for about 1 hour or until double its original size.

2 Pour the second measure of oil evenly over the surface, then, using your index finger, poke the dough to create a series of indentations. Sprinkle with flaky or rock salt or any of the following toppings: 2 tablespoons each pesto and olive oil mixed to a paste with ¼ cup grated Parmesan; coarsely chopped sun-dried tomatoes; anchovies; sliced or whole black olives

3 Bake at 225°C for 15 minutes or until golden brown top and bottom.

French Bread

It is hard to believe that such a basic dough can produce such delicious crusty French bread. Leaving the dough to stand overnight requires a little patience and some forethought, but it's worth the wait in the end.

For 1 large or 2 smaller baguettes:

2 tsp active dried yeast

1¼ cups warm water

2 tsp sugar

1½ tsp salt

3 cups (420g) high-grade flour

Bread Machine Instructions:

1. Carefully measure all the ingredients into a 750g capacity bread machine in the order specified by the manufacturer.

2. Set to the Dough cycle and Start. When the cycle is complete, allow to stand as described below before kneading, etc.

Hand-made Bread Instructions:

1. Measure the first four ingredients into a large bowl with 1½ cups of the flour and mix thoroughly. Cover and leave for 15 minutes in a warm place.

2. Stir in the remaining flour, and a little extra flour or water if necessary, to make a dough just firm enough to knead.

3. Knead with the dough hook of an electric mixer or by hand on a lightly floured board for 10 minutes until the dough forms a soft ball that springs back when gently pressed.

Rising, Shaping and Baking:

1. Turn the dough in 2–3 teaspoons of oil in the cleaned, dry bowl. Cover with plastic wrap and leave for at least 2 hours or preferably overnight at room temperature. It may be necessary to punch (or press) down the dough several times during this period.

2. Very lightly knead the dough in the bowl (just for a few seconds), then turn out onto a lightly floured board. Roll and shape the dough into one long characteristic French loaf (or divide the dough in half to make two smaller loaves).

3. Leave to rise at room temperature for about 1–1½ hours or until about doubled in size. Using a very sharp knife make a series of 4–5 diagonal slashes about 5mm deep on the top of the loaf or loaves.

4. Preheat the oven to 220°C. At least 5 minutes before the bread is due to go into the oven, put a roasting dish with 1cm of hot water in the bottom of the oven. To get a really chewy crust, spray the loaf with a fine mist of water before it goes in the oven, then spray again after 2 minutes.

5. Bake for 15 minutes, removing the dish of water from the oven after 10 minutes. The loaf or loaves should be golden brown and sound hollow when tapped. Eat within 12 hours of baking.

NOTE: For a loaf with a more open texture, add 2 tablespoons gluten with the flour. Add extra water as necessary; you'll probably need about ¼ cup.

Quick English Muffins

These are made from a soft yeast dough and cooked with cornmeal to stop them sticking to any surface which they touch.

For 8 muffins:

25g butter

¾ cup boiling water

½ cup milk

1 Tbsp granulated yeast

2 tsp sugar

2½–3 cups (350–420g) plain flour

1 tsp salt

about ¼ cup cornmeal

Bread Machine Instructions:

1 Measure the butter into the bread machine, pour in the boiling water then leave to stand until the butter has melted.

2 Add the milk, yeast, sugar and 2½ cups (350g) of flour, set the machine to the Dough cycle and press Start.

3 Shape and cook as described below.

Hand-made Bread Instructions:

1 Measure the butter into a large bowl. Pour the boiling water over the butter, then add the cold milk.

2 Sprinkle in the yeast and sugar then stir until yeast dissolves. Leave to stand in a warm place for 5–10 minutes, until the surface bubbles.

3 Add 2½ cups of flour and salt and beat to mix thoroughly.

4 Leave to stand in a warm place until mixture doubles in size (about 30 minutes).

Shaping and Cooking:

1 Stir the mixture back to original size, then turn it onto a well-floured board adding just enough extra flour so you can work with it without it sticking.

2 Keeping dough very soft, adding as little flour as possible, cut it into eight pieces and roll into balls using well-floured hands.

3 Roll the balls in cornmeal (to stop them sticking), then place each one on a 10cm square of sprayed or oiled lunch paper or plastic wrap and leave to rise in a warm place for 15–20 minutes, until light and puffy.

4 Carefully place muffins, paper side up and top side down, into an electric frypan or griddle which has been preheated to 150°C, then lift off the plastic or paper.

5 Cook muffins for about 2 minutes, then carefully turn. Cook second side for 5–7 minutes, turn again and cook for a further 5 minutes. (This produces muffins with even-sized cooked surfaces.)

6 Turn onto a rack to cool and store in the refrigerator.

7 Before serving, brown each side under the grill, then split and eat while hot with your favourite sweet or savoury topping. Alternatively, split the muffins, then brown in the toaster.

Irish Soda Bread

For a 20cm round (900g) loaf:

3 cups (420g) standard plain flour

1½ tsp salt

1½ tsp sugar

1 tsp baking soda

1 tsp cream of tartar

¾ cup milk

½ cup plain unsweetened yoghurt

This couldn't actually be much quicker to make, and it's so good! Not surprisingly perhaps, it is a fairly dense loaf, but served warm from the oven (less than an hour from when you start mixing) with lashings of butter, it really is delicious.

1 Preheat the oven to 180°C.

2 Sift the flour, salt, sugar, baking soda and cream of tartar into a large bowl.

3 Measure the milk and yoghurt into a small bowl and stir to combine.

4 Pour the milk mixture into the dry ingredients and gently fold the mixture together, trying to combine it evenly but without over-mixing.

5 Tip the dough onto a lightly floured board and shape it into a ball. Flatten a little until it is disc-shaped and measures just over 15cm across and place it on a lightly floured or baking-paper lined baking sheet. Using a sharp knife, cut a deep cross (about halfway down) into the dough so it opens nicely during baking.

6 Bake in the middle of the oven at 180°C for 45–50 minutes or until golden brown and hollow sounding when tapped.

Cheesy Beer Bread

For 1 medium loaf (4–6 servings):

3 cups (420g) self-raising flour

½ cup grated tasty cheese

1–2 Tbsp sugar

1 tsp salt

355ml can or bottle of beer

about 1 Tbsp oil, optional

A friend of Simon's gave him this recipe years ago. Donn's recipe breaks so many of the traditional bread-making rules, it's hard to believe it works at all. Try it — it's delicious!

As it is a quick no-knead bread, containing no baker's yeast (unless you count the yeast content in the beer), it is not surprising that its appearance and texture are so different to 'normal' bread. Having said that, as long as you're not expecting a sandwich loaf, we think you'll be delighted with the results. A slice or two, warm from the oven, with a bowl of soup makes the perfect winter warmer.

Since this mixture contains little added fat, we expected it would go stale very quickly, but much to our surprise leftovers were surprisingly good when toasted.

1. Preheat the oven to 180°C.

2. Measure the flour into a large bowl. Spoon the flour from the bag into the measuring cup, rather than scooping it straight from the bag so it is not too densely packed — this can make a big difference to the total weight of flour used, as too much will make a dry loaf.

3. Add the grated cheese, sugar (use the larger quantity if using a dryish beer, and less if using a sweeter more malty beer). Toss together the dry ingredients to combine, then add the beer.

4. Stir everything together until the mixture looks more or less uniform and will hold together.

5. Oil or non-stick spray a 6–7 cup capacity loaf pan. Tip in the dough, roughly levelling the top. Brush the top with a little oil for more even browning, if you like, then place the loaf in the oven.

6. Bake for 45–60 minutes until the top is golden brown and the loaf sounds hollow when tapped. Remove from the oven and leave to cool for 10–15 minutes before slicing.

For 1 very large pizza, 2 medium pizzas or 8 medium pita breads:

2 tsp active dried yeast

1 cup + 2 Tbsp warm water

2 tsp sugar

1 tsp salt

2 Tbsp olive oil

3 cups (420g) high-grade flour

Pizza Topping Suggestions:

- Tomato paste, sun-dried tomato paste, dried tomato pesto, sliced tomatoes, drained canned seasoned tomatoes

- Red, yellow and green peppers, roasted red and orange pepper strips and eggplant

- Onion slices, caramelised onions, chopped spring onions, roasted garlic

- Sliced mushrooms, sliced/whole olives, fresh and dried herbs, artichoke hearts

- Anchovy fillets, salmon and shrimps, salami, ham, bacon, turkey and chicken

- Mozzarella, grated tasty cheese, camembert and brie, Parmesan, feta

Pizzas and Pita Breads

One of the real joys of owning a bread machine is discovering how easy it is to make good yeasty pizza bases. Simply measure in the ingredients, set to the dough cycle and go away. The hardest part becomes selecting your toppings!

Bread Machine Instructions:

1. Carefully measure all the ingredients into a 750g capacity bread machine in the order specified by the manufacturer.

2. Set to Dough cycle and Start. When the cycle is complete, take the dough out of the machine and shape and bake as below.

Hand-made Bread Instructions:

1. Measure the first five ingredients into a large bowl with 1 cup of the measured flour and mix thoroughly. Cover and leave for 15 minutes or longer in a warm place. Stir in the remaining flour, adding extra if necessary, to make a dough just firm enough to knead.

2. Knead with the dough hook of an electric mixer or by hand on a lightly floured surface for 10 minutes, adding extra flour if necessary, until the dough forms a soft ball that springs back when gently pressed.

3. Turn the dough in 2–3 teaspoons of oil in the cleaned dry bowl, cover with plastic wrap and leave in a warm, draught-free place for about 30 minutes. Lightly knead the risen dough, then shape.

Shaping and Baking Pizzas:

1. Roll dough into thin circles, according to the number and size of pizzas you require.

2. Place on sprayed pizza pans, baking paper, or well-oiled baking sheets.

3. Add your favourite toppings (see left) and bake at 225°C until the underside is brown. For crisp, very thin pizza bake before (and after) adding desired topping.

Shaping and Baking Pita breads:

1. Cut the dough into eight equal pieces, then on a well-floured board roll out each piece into a 15–18cm circle, sprinkling with extra flour as needed. Leave to stand for at least 10 minutes.

2. Place a baking sheet on a rack in the middle of the oven. Preheat the oven to its highest temperature. Ideally, place a cast-iron pan or griddle on the rack below the middle one (it will heat up and compensate for heat loss when the oven door is opened).

3. Slide a shaped pita bread onto a piece of floured (to prevent sticking) cardboard, then, opening the oven door for as brief a time as possible, slide the bread onto the hot baking sheet. In 1–2 minutes the bread should puff up dramatically, then collapse a little.

4. Lift out the cooked bread with tongs after 2–3 minutes and put in the next one to cook. Pile the hot breads in a plastic bag so they do not dry out.

Festive Baking

← Golden Christmas Cake – recipe page 226

Golden Christmas Cake

Celebrate our summer Christmas (or a Golden Wedding) with this delicious, golden cake.

For a 20cm square or 23cm round or square (2.25kg) cake:

about 1 cup each cubed crystallised mango, papaya, pineapple and melon (see Note)

1 cup sultanas

1 cup dried cranberries or extra sultanas

1 cup chardonnay (or other white wine) or ½ cup orange juice + ½ cup water

½–1 cup quartered glacé cherries, optional

250g butter, softened

1 cup sugar

5 large eggs

1 cup ground almonds

1 tsp vanilla essence

½ tsp almond essence, optional

grated zest of 1 orange

grated zest of 1 lemon

1½ cups high-grade flour

1½ tsp baking powder

1 Add the sultanas and cranberries to the crystallised fruit. Simmer the fruit and wine in a covered frypan for 5 minutes or until nearly all liquid is absorbed, then leave to stand in the covered pan overnight or for 8 hours to soak up remaining liquid. (Fruit will have a beautiful jewel-like appearance!) Stir in the quartered cherries (if using).

2 Preheat the oven to 150°C (140°C fanbake), with rack just below middle. Line sides and base of a 20cm square, or 23cm round or square pan with baking paper.

3 In a food processor or large bowl, beat the butter and sugar until creamy. Beat in one egg at a time, adding a spoonful of the ground almonds after each one. Beat in the essences, remaining ground almonds and the orange and lemon zests, then sift in the flour and baking powder. Combine the cake mixture and the cold, prepared fruit using your hand and spread mixture evenly in the prepared pan.

4 Cakes in 23cm pans are 5–6cm high and should bake at 150°C (140°C fanbake) for 45 minutes then at 130°C (120°C fanbake) for 1½–2 hours. Cakes in 20cm pans are about 6–7cm high and should bake at 150°C (140°C fanbake) for 45 minutes then at 130°C (120°C fanbake) for 2–2½ hours. Cover top with paper if it browns too quickly. Cakes are cooked when a skewer pushed deeply into the centre comes out clean.

5 Leave for a week before eating. Serve as is, or ice with bought icing or home-made Almond Icing and Royal or Plastic Icing (see page 254). Store cake in refrigerator.

NOTE: Buy 1kg total of three or four of the crystallised fruits. Cut these into 5mm cubes with scissors or a sharp knife. (You need 3–4 cups of cubed crystallised fruit.)

Two-egg Christmas Cake

For a 15cm round or 18cm square cake:

125g butter, softened

½ cup packed brown sugar

¼ tsp baking soda

½ tsp mixed spice

½ tsp ground cinnamon

½ tsp ground ginger

1 cup standard or high-grade flour

2 large eggs

¼ tsp each vanilla, almond and lemon essence

2 cups sultanas

1 cup currants

½–1 cup dried fruit (any you like)

2 Tbsp sherry or spirits

There are many times when a small cake is all you need. This little cake has a lovely flavour and makes a good gift. It doesn't need to be made long before it is eaten, either. If you do not intend to ice the cake, decorate its top with extra cherries and almonds before you cook it.

Simple circular patterns look best, even on a square cake. For best appearance put the nuts or cherries close together, and don't arrange them alternately. After the cake is cooked, when it is cool enough to touch, put a little oil on your hand and rub it over the surface. This gives the nuts an attractive sheen.

1 Preheat the oven to 150°C (140°C fanbake), with the rack just below the middle. Line an 18cm square or 15cm round cake pan with baking paper.

2 Cream the butter and brown sugar using a food processor fitted with a plastic blade, if available. Mix or sift the baking soda, spices, and flour together and put aside. Add the eggs one at a time to the creamed mixture, with a spoonful of flour mixture with each, to prevent curdling.

3 Add half the flour and the essences and mix briefly, then add the remaining flour and all the dried fruit you are using (chop bigger pieces) and the liquid. Stir to mix well, and turn into the prepared cake pan.

4 Bake for 1½–2 hours or until a skewer comes out clean. Sprinkle or brush 2–3 tablespoons extra sherry or spirits over the hot cake, if desired.

5 If desired, top with bought icing, or make Almond and Plastic or Royal Icing (see page 254). Leave at least two days before cutting.

Easy-mix Fruit & Rum Cake

Here is a cake of modest size, which is very little trouble to put together. Its wonderful flavour comes from the dark raisins and the rum used in it — it contains no essences or spices at all.

For one 20cm square or round cake:

1kg small dark raisins

½ cup rum (or a mixture of sherry and rum)

200g butter

2 cups standard or high-grade flour

1 cup sugar

1 tsp baking soda

½ tsp salt

¼ cup golden syrup

½ cup milk

2 large eggs

1 Put the raisins in an unpunctured plastic bag with the rum and leave the fruit to stand in it for 24–48 hours, until the fruit has soaked up all the liquid (Flip bag over occasionally for most even soaking.)

2 Preheat the oven to 150°C (140°C fanbake), with the rack just below the middle. Line a 20cm square or round cake pan with baking paper.

3 Cut or rub the cold butter into the flour, sugar, baking soda and salt, using a food processor, a pastry blender, or your fingers. Measure the syrup in a measure preheated with very hot water, warm the syrup and milk just enough to combine them, beat in the eggs, then mix this liquid, the prepared fruit and the dry mixture together. If you do not intend to ice your cake, decorate the top with a pattern of blanched almonds, cherries, etc.

4 Bake for 2¼–2½ hours, until a skewer inserted in the middle (to the bottom) comes out clean.

5 If you have decorated the top of the cake with nuts, 'polish' them by rubbing a little oil on the palm of your hand, and rubbing your hand over the surface of the cake until the nuts shine.

Rich Sherried Six-egg Fruit Cake

Everybody enjoys the flavour and texture of this dense, moist, fruity, fairly light cake — you may like to try it too!

For a 23cm round cake:

4 cups sultanas

1 cup currants

1 cup sticky raisins

½–1 cup mixed red and green glacé cherries

½ cup whole blanched almonds

½ cup chopped mixed peel

½ cup chopped crystallised ginger

½ cup medium or dry sherry

½ cup rum, brandy or extra sherry

2 cups chopped dates

225g butter

¾ cup packed brown sugar

6 large eggs

2¼ cups standard or high-grade flour

1 tsp each cinnamon and mixed spice

1 tsp each vanilla, lemon and almond essence

1 Prepare first seven ingredients first. Mix in a large bowl or roasting pan, the sultanas, currants, raisins, cherries, almonds, mixed peel, and ginger. Pour very hot water over this, break up any clumps, then drain through a sieve or colander, removing all the water. Dry mixture in the pan in the oven at about 100°C (90°C fanbake), for about 20 minutes, or leave in the sun for about an hour.

2 Put the prepared mixture in a large, unpunctured plastic bag with the sherry and other liquor, and leave to stand, turning the bag occasionally, for at least an hour, but preferably overnight. Mix in the chopped dates just before mixing the rest of the cake.

3 Preheat the oven to 150°C (140°C fanbake) with the rack just below the middle. Line a 23cm round cake pan with baking paper or a Teflon liner.

4 Soften (but do not melt) the butter, and beat with the brown sugar until light and creamy. Add an egg and a tablespoon of the measured flour, and beat well. Repeat until all the eggs are added. Mix in the spices and essences. Put the prepared fruit and almond mixture and the chopped dates in any suitable large bowl or other container. Add the butter mixture and the remaining flour to the fruit using a flexible stirrer or your hands, making sure that everything is well combined.

5 Transfer the mixture to the prepared cake pan. Flatten the top and decorate with extra blanched, whole almonds if you are not going to ice the cake.

6 Bake for 1 hour, reduce the heat to 100°C and cook for a further hour or until a skewer inserted into the cake comes out clean. Leave the cake to stand in its pan until cool, and then turn onto a rack. When quite cold, wrap loosely in greaseproof paper and store in a cool place, or wrap in cling wrap or foil and refrigerate or freeze. Do not store in cling wrap or a completely airtight container at room temperature. (For Icings, see page 254.)

Pineapple Christmas Cake

Thousands of New Zealanders swear by this recipe and have used it regularly since Alison made the cake on TV more than 30 years ago!

For one 23cm, two 18cm, or 12 mini 10cm cakes:

1.5kg mixed fruit

450g can crushed pineapple

3 cups high-grade flour

1 tsp ground cinnamon

1 tsp mixed spice

½ tsp ground cloves

225g butter

1 cup sugar

½ tsp vanilla essence

½ tsp almond essence

½ tsp lemon essence

6 large eggs

For decoration, optional:

50g glacé cherries

50g blanched almonds

1 The day before mixing the cake, put the dried fruit and undrained pineapple in a large frypan. Cover pan and heat until liquid boils, then simmer until all juice is absorbed. Leave overnight, or until cold.

2 Mix flour and spices together and put aside. In a very large bowl, beat the butter, sugar and essences until light. Beat in eggs one at a time, adding 2 tablespoons of the spiced flour with each. Stir in prepared (cold) fruit and remaining spiced flour. If mixture seems too soft, add extra flour until mixture will just drop from a spoon. Put into baking paper lined cake pans, levelling the tops. Decorate with blanched almonds and cherries if you don't plan to ice the cake/s.

3 Bake the 23cm cake at 150°C for 1½ hours, then 130°C for about 2 hours longer. Bake the 18cm cakes at 140°C for 1 hour, then at 130°C for about 1 hour longer. Bake 10cm cakes at 130°C for about 1½ hours. (Use 10°C lower in all cases, if using fan-bake.) The cakes are cooked when a skewer pushed into the middle of the cake comes out clean.

4 Brush hot cake with ¼ cup brandy or sherry, if you like. Take cake/s from pan/s when cold.

Cathedral Cake

This spectacular and decorative cake (which contains no butter or oil) is mainly nuts and glace fruit! When a slice is held up to the light, it resembles a stained glass window.

**For a 20cm ring cake or
2 small loaves:**

3 cups brazil nuts

1 cup blanched almonds

1 cup cashews or pecans

1 cup red glacé cherries

½ cup green glacé cherries, optional

3–4 cups crystallised fruit, e.g.
pineapple, mango, papaya, melon

1 cup sultanas

1 cup raisins or currants

4 large eggs

1 cup packed brown sugar

1 tsp vanilla essence

1½ cups standard or high-grade flour

1 tsp baking powder

½ tsp salt

1 Preheat the oven to 130°C (120°C fanbake), with the rack just below the middle. Line a 20cm or 30cm ring pan (or 2 medium-sized loaf pans) with baking paper or Teflon liners, because this mixture sticks badly.

2 Measure out the nuts, cherries, crystallised fruit and dried fruit into a large container, putting some aside for decorating the top. Cut up large pieces of fruit, but leave some long thin pieces, if desired (especially if using melon strips, which give a wonderful colour).

3 In a large bowl, mix the eggs, sugar and vanilla essence. Mix in the sifted flour, baking powder and salt until smooth. Add nuts and fruit and mix thoroughly by hand.

4 Press evenly into the prepared cake pan/s (if pan is lined with baking paper, coat evenly with non-stick spray as well, just before use). Press the reserved cherries, fruit and nuts into the top for decoration. (If adding strips of crystallised fruit, put them in place after adding part of the cake mixture, then cover with remaining mixture.)

5 Bake for 2–3 hours, until cake feels firm when pressed in the middle. Cool, remove from pan and peel away liner/s. Brush all over with rum, brandy, or whisky. Brush the top with a light coating of oil for a shine.

6 Store at room temperature in greaseproof paper, or refrigerate in a plastic bag. This cake will keep well for several months. (If it dries out after long storage, brush it all over with spirits, sherry or port, and leave 24 hours or longer before slicing.) Cut in thin slices with a sharp serrated knife.

VARIATION: Make small individual cakes in mini-loaf pans or suitable, lined, shallow cans — these will cook more quickly so watch them carefully.

Panforte

This chewy, very firm, dark and compact festive cake is of Italian origin. It contains no baking powder or eggs. Wedges or rectangular pieces, attractively gift-wrapped, make special and unusual gifts for good friends. (When sold in specialty food stores, individual slices are wrapped and sold in a similar way.)

For about 12–15 servings:

1 cup blanched almonds

1 cup hazelnuts

1 cup pecans

¼ cup caster sugar

½ cup honey

½ cup crystallised ginger

1 cup mixed fruit

½ cup standard (plain) flour

¼ cup cocoa

2 tsp ground cinnamon

75g butter

½ cup chocolate chips

1. Preheat the oven to 150°C (140°C), with the rack just below the middle. Line the bottom and sides of a 24cm round pan or a 23cm square pan with baking paper.

2. Lightly roast all the nuts (together) in a large shallow baking dish in the oven as it heats, checking every few minutes.

3. While the nuts roast, get everything else ready. Measure the sugar and honey together in a frypan ready to heat later. Roughly chop the ginger, stir it through the mixed fruit and set aside. Sift the flour, cocoa and cinnamon together and set aside, too.

4. Melt the butter and chocolate chips together in a fairly large bowl in the microwave oven at Medium (50% power) for about 2 minutes, or over a pot of hot water. When the almonds are a light beige colour and when the other nuts are ready (in about 6–10 minutes), remove from the oven and stir them into the melted chocolate mixture.

5. Warm the sugar and honey together over low to moderate heat, stirring until the sugar dissolves. As soon as the mixture bubbles all over the surface, pour it into the chocolate and nut mixture. Now stir in the sifted flour mixture and the mixed fruit and ginger until everything is evenly blended.

6. Pour the warm mixture into the prepared pan. Pat out evenly, with a piece of plastic between the cake and your hand.

7. Bake for 30–45 minutes or until the centre looks and feels as cooked as the outer edges. Longer cooking gives a firmer, more toffee-like cake.

8. The hot cake feels much softer than a cake normally does, but it becomes much firmer on cooling, and should be left in a cool place for at least 24 hours before being cut into wedges or rectangles with a very sharp knife. If desired, dust with icing sugar before serving. If you are making it some weeks ahead, store wrapped pieces in the refrigerator or freezer.

For a 23cm cake:

100g dark chocolate

100g butter

½ cup caster sugar

½ cup ground almonds

4 large eggs, separated

½ tsp salt

1 tsp baking powder

½ cup self-raising flour

Almond Paste:

1 cup (100g) ground almonds

1 cup icing sugar

½ cup caster sugar

1 egg yolk (from above)

a few drops almond essence

1–2 Tbsp lemon juice

1–2 Tbsp apricot jam

Chocolate Simnel Cake

A traditional simnel cake is a light fruit cake, which contains a layer of almond paste. This delicious chocolate version is a bit of a departure from the traditional, retaining only the layer of almond paste in the middle, but when iced with Chocolate Cream Icing it is rather spectacular! Simnel cakes are often decorated with 11 balls of almond paste (representing each of the disciples, excluding Judas) but, sticking with a chocolate theme, why not decorate the top with 11 little chocolate eggs?

1 Preheat the oven to 150°C. Line a 23cm round cake pan with baking paper or coat with non-stick spray.

2 Melt the chocolate and butter in a medium-sized bowl over a pot of hot water. Add sugar and stir well, then add ground almonds.

3 Separate the egg whites and yolks. Stir three of the yolks into the chocolate mixture, reserving the other to use in the almond paste.

4 Place egg whites and salt in a large, clean bowl (any traces of fat will prevent the whites from foaming) and beat until they form stiff peaks. Sift the baking powder and half the flour into the beaten whites, then add half the chocolate mixture and gently fold together. Sift the remaining flour into the bowl, add the remaining chocolate mixture and repeat folding process.

5 Spoon the cake mixture into the prepared pan. Smooth the top and bake for 30–35 minutes or until firm when pressed in the centre and a skewer comes out clean. Remove from the oven and cool for 5 minutes before removing from the pan. Cool completely before slicing to make two layers.

6 Make the Almond Paste by mixing the ground almonds, icing sugar, caster sugar, egg yolk and almond essence together and adding enough lemon juice to make pliable paste. Place the paste on a sugared board and roll into a disc the same diameter as the cake. Brush paste with warmed apricot jam then sandwich it between cake layers.

7 Ice with Chocolate Cream Icing (see page 252). Leave to stand until the icing is firm (it will never set completely), then serve as is or with yoghurt or lightly whipped cream.

Christmas Mincemeat Pies

For 12–18 pies:

Pastry:

100g butter

½ cup sugar

1 egg

1 cup standard (plain) flour

1 cup self-raising flour

about 1 cup bought or home-made Christmas mincemeat (see page 251)

If you have time, turn some of your Christmas mincemeat into mince pies before you get too busy with other festive tasks, and hide them in the freezer. When time is short, make filo triangles instead.

1 Soften but do not melt butter. Beat in sugar and egg until well combined. Stir in unsifted flours and mix well to form a dough. If too dry, add a little milk. If too soft to work with, refrigerate rather than adding more flour.

2 Lightly flour a board to prevent sticking and roll out the pastry.

3 Using a glass, round lid or fluted cutter, cut out the circles for the bottom of the pies (size will depend on the muffin pans in which the pies will be baked). The circles for the tops are cut with a smaller cutter or, if available, small biscuit cutters which form hearts, stars, diamonds, etc.

4 Ease the dough into medium or mini muffin pans, then spoon in the mincemeat mixture and top with the smaller shapes or circles of pastry, pressing the edges lightly.

5 Bake at 170°–180°C for 10–15 minutes, removing from the oven as soon as the edges start to brown. Cool for 2–3 minutes before carefully lifting from the tins onto cooling racks.

6 Serve warm, dusted with icing sugar.

Filo Mincemeat Triangles

For 3–5 triangles (multiply as required):

25g butter, melted

3 sheets fresh filo pastry

about ½ cup bought or home-made mincemeat (see page 251)

Each Christmas we make some of these quickly-made triangles. Because the mincemeat has not been thickened, the mincemeat triangles shout to be eaten less than an hour after they are baked.

1 Lightly brush each of the filo sheets with melted butter then stack. Cut these crosswise into 3–5 strips. At one end of each strip put a spoonful of mincemeat.

2 Fold the filo over the filling forming a triangle. Keep folding to form triangle pastries, enclosing filling completely.

3 Brush with more melted butter.

4 Bake at 180°C for about 10 minutes or until golden brown.

5 Serve warm rather than hot, dusted with icing sugar.

Christmas Pudding Truffles

We like these truffles dressed up so that they look like mini-Christmas puddings. If you feel that this is too time-consuming, serve them as plain truffles rolled in coconut.

For 18–24 truffles:

1 cup currants

2 tsp very finely grated orange or tangelo zest

¼ cup rum, whisky, brandy or citrus juice

250g (2½ cups) crumbs from a chocolate or plain cake

125g chocolate chips

For decoration:

75g white chocolate

1 tsp oil

about 6 red cherries

about 6 green cherries

❶ Put the currants in a sieve and pour boiling water through them, then put them in a bowl with the very finely grated zest from a tangelo or orange, and the spirit of your choice or the same amount of juice from the orange or tangelo.

❷ Leave the currants to stand while you crumb the cake, and then melt the chocolate chips, heating until liquid. This will take about 4–5 minutes on Medium in a microwave oven, and a little longer in a large metal bowl standing over a pot of hot but not boiling water.

❸ When the chocolate has melted, stir the crumbs into it, then the currant mixture.

❹ Mix well together, then roll into small, walnut-sized balls, or balls which will fit nicely in small foil or fluted paper confectionery cups. (Roll in coconut if not decorating further.) Refrigerate until cold.

❺ Warm pieces of white chocolate with the oil in a clean bowl, in a microwave oven for about 3 minutes on Medium or over hot water, as before. Stir until smooth.

❻ Chop the cherries. Have red cherry pieces chunky, and the green pieces pointed like leaves.

❼ Spoon a little of the warm white mixture on top of a little pudding, helping it to look as if it is flowing, if necessary.

❽ This takes a little experience, but is mainly a matter of having the truffle cold and the melted mixture semi-liquid. Before the white chocolate sets, put about three little red berries in the middle of the icing, and a couple of green leaves around them.

Pistachio & Almond Biscotti

For about 40 pieces:

1 cup (100g) pistachio nuts

2 cups standard (plain) flour

1 cup sugar

2 tsp baking powder

75g cold butter, cubed

2 large eggs

1 tsp vanilla essence

few drops almond essence

½ cup raw almonds

These interesting little biscuits are especially good warm from the oven, when their vanilla and nut aroma makes them irresistible.

1 Preheat the oven to 180°C (170°C fanbake), with the rack just below the middle. Line a baking tray with baking paper. Shell the pistachios (to yield ½ cup).

2 Measure flour, sugar and baking powder into a food processor. Add the cold butter and pulse until mixture resembles breadcrumbs. Add eggs and essences, and pulse briefly until evenly blended, and mixture looks clumpy-crumbly and quite dry. Add almonds and pistachios and pulse twice to mix without chopping nuts.

3 Turn on to an unfloured board or bench and press together to form a dough. Halve mixture and shape into two 30cm logs. Flatten so logs are 5–6cm wide. Place on the prepared oven tray.

4 Bake for 25–30 minutes until lightly browned and firm with a little 'give'. Cool on a rack.

5 When cold, cut logs diagonally into slices 10–15mm thick. Place these on a metal cake cooling rack (for faster drying) and bake at 150°C for 5–10 minutes.

6 Eat warm, or cool before storing in airtight containers. Enjoy with tea or coffee, dip in dessert wine, or serve with ice-cream and berries for dessert.

VARIATIONS: Dip one end of cold biscotti in Chocolate Coating (see page 255). Double quantities of nuts make the biscotti even better! Add ¼ cup of extra sugar for sweeter biscotti.

Kirsten's Biscotti

Although this mixture starts as a loaf, the slices are baked again. A few slices in a small cellophane bag, tied with pretty curling ribbon, make an attractive hostess gift at any time of the year.

For about 40 biscotti:

3 large eggs

½ tsp salt

½ cup sugar

¼ tsp almond essence

½ tsp vanilla essence

finely grated zest of 1 orange

1 cup standard (plain) flour

2 cups raw almonds

1 Preheat the oven to 180°C (170°C fanbake), with the rack just below the middle. Line a 9 x 23 x 8cm loaf pan with baking paper.

2 Beat the eggs, salt, sugar and essences together until light and fluffy. Stir orange zest into the egg mixture. Stir the flour and almonds together and fold into the egg mixture. Turn the mixture into the prepared loaf pan, making sure the top is evenly flattened.

3 Bake for 45–50 minutes, or until the loaf is lightly browned and the centre springs back when pressed. When cool, remove from the loaf pan, wrap and refrigerate for at least 24 hours, then cut into about 40 thin slices with a sharp, serrated knife. Place the slices on the prepared baking tray.

4 Bake a second time at 125°C–150°C (115°C–140°C fanbake), for about 30 minutes until biscotti colours slightly. Cool on racks then store in airtight containers.

VARIATION: Add ¼ cup of extra sugar for sweeter biscotti.

Stained Glass Biscuits

These spectacular biscuits are fun to make with older children. They should be hung on a Christmas tree only if each is in an airtight wrap, since the toffee 'glass' softens, as other toffee does, if left to stand uncovered for long.

For about 30–50 biscuits (depending on size):

225g butter, softened

1¼ cups sugar

½ tsp baking soda

¼ cup water

3–4 cups standard (plain) flour

about 200g flattish, brightly coloured, hard, individually wrapped lollipops

1. Preheat the oven to 180°C (170°C fanbake), with the rack just below the middle. Line a baking tray with baking paper.

2. Put the softened butter in a food processor or bowl. Add the sugar and process, or mix thoroughly with a beater. Dissolve the baking soda in the water, and stir into the butter mixture. Mix in enough flour to make dough, which can be rolled easily.

3. Roll the dough out thinly on a floured surface, then cut heart, star or other outlines, first using a larger cutter, then using a smaller cutter to remove the centre portion, leaving a space to fill with candy. For biscuits to hang up later, also cut a small circular hole (for threading) near the top of the biscuit using a drinking straw. Place biscuits, 6–12 at a time, on the prepared baking tray.

4. Bake for about 4 minutes. While biscuits cook, crush lollipops, still in their cellophane wrapping, by hammering them gently on a board. Keep colours separate and discard sticks and papers.

5. After 4 minutes, take the partly cooked biscuits from the oven and sprinkle the crushed lollipops into the central hole in each biscuit.
(Do not mix colours in one biscuit.)

6. Bake again for 2–3 minutes, until you can see that the candy has melted, and the biscuit mixture is lightly coloured. Watch carefully during this time. After the first batch, decide whether you need more or less crushed candy for the next batch.

7. Remove from the oven and let the 'glass' centres cool and harden before lifting the biscuits carefully off the baking tray. When cold, store or wrap immediately in airtight packaging, or the candy will become soft and sticky.

VARIATION: Instead of rolling and cutting dough, roll out long 'worms' of the mixture and form these into hearts or other shapes. Flatten to an even thickness, and bake and fill as above.

Christmas Tree Biscuits

Shape and decorate these biscuits so they can be hung on a Christmas tree as ornaments, or pack them in airtight glass containers for gifts.

For about 30–50 biscuits (depending on size):

150g butter, softened

¼ tsp almond essence

1 tsp ground cardamom, optional

½ cup caster sugar

1 large egg, separated

2 Tbsp milk

about 2 cups standard (plain) flour

1 Preheat the oven to 150°C (140°C fanbake), with the rack just below the middle. Line a baking tray with baking paper.

2 Beat the softened butter, essence, cardamom and sugar together until light coloured and fluffy. Add the egg yolk and milk and beat again, then add enough flour to make a dough that is firm enough to roll out and cut into shapes.

3 Cut into festive shapes with suitable cutters. If you don't have any special cutters, cut out large circles with a glass, then cut smaller circles from the centres of these using the tops of small bottles. For biscuits to hang up later, also cut a small circular hole (for threading) near the top of the biscuit using a drinking straw. For almond wreath biscuits, beat the egg white until bubbly, brush it onto the uncooked circles of dough, and arrange flaked almonds in a pattern. Decorate other biscuits after baking.

4 Bake for about 15 minutes, or until very lightly browned. Cool on a rack.

5 Make white icing by beating the remaining egg white with sifted icing sugar until the mixture is of good spreading consistency. Spread with a small knife. Neaten up the edges by running a finger along them. Decorate iced biscuits with slices of cherries, silver cachous, etc., before the icing hardens.

6 Attach biscuits to the tree with silver or gold thread, or with tartan ribbons and fine wire. Biscuits that have been hung on trees for several days or longer are not suitable for eating later. To keep biscuits crisp, store in airtight containers.

Painted Biscuits

For about 30–50 biscuits (depending on size):

100g butter, softened

½ cup caster sugar

1 large egg

½ tsp vanilla, almond or lemon essence

1½ cups standard (plain) flour

½ tsp baking powder

These biscuits are great fun for children to make as gifts at Christmas. They are cut in shapes, and then painted before baking. They look rather like animal biscuits, but are not so sweet.

1 Preheat the oven to 180°C (170°C fanbake), with the rack just below the middle. Line a baking tray with baking paper.

2 Mix or beat the softened butter and sugar together in a food processor or bowl. Separate the egg and put the yolk aside in a small bowl or cup. Mix the egg white and essence into the butter and sugar. Sift in the flour and baking powder, and mix until everything is combined.

3 Form dough into a ball and chill for 5 minutes until cool enough to roll out thinly on a floured board. Cut biscuits from dough using a glass for circles and/or cutters for shapes. (Dip cutters in flour so they do not stick to the mixture.) Using a lightly floured spatula, carefully lift the biscuits onto the prepared baking tray so you do not distort the shapes.

4 Stir the egg yolk with a fork then divide between three saucers (or other small dishes). Colour each lot with food colouring, and then paint the biscuits using a separate brush for each colour. Simple designs look best! Try painting faces on round biscuits.

5 Bake for 5–10 minutes, depending on the thickness of the biscuit dough, until edges colour lightly. Lift warm biscuits onto a cooling rack.

6 When cold, arrange on pretty paper plates or firm card, and cover tightly with airtight plastic wrap. Or pack in cellophane bags, or other (clear) containers, and seal tightly.

Gingerbread Houses

Make fairytale gingerbread houses (or gingerbread people) to delight children at Christmas.

For 4 small houses:

50g butter, cubed

100g packed brown sugar

¼ cup golden syrup

¼ cup + 1 Tbsp treacle

2 large eggs, separated

1½ cups standard (plain) flour

1 Tbsp ground ginger

½ tsp baking soda

1 Preheat the oven to 180°C (170°C fanbake), with the rack just below the middle. Line a baking tray with baking paper.

2 Cut three shapes from cardboard. (Each piece of card will be used twice to cut the six gingerbread shapes for one cottage.) Cut an 8 x 10cm rectangle (for the roof), and a 6 x 8cm rectangle (for side walls). To make the peaked end-wall shape, draw a 10 x 6cm rectangle, then make a mark 4cm from one end on the two long sides, and another mark in the middle of the short side nearest the other two marks. Join this mark to the other two, then cut out.

3 Warm the butter, brown sugar, golden syrup and treacle together in a pot, mixing until smooth. Take off the heat and stir in the egg yolks then the sieved dry ingredients. Knead to form a smooth dough, adding a little water or extra flour if necessary. Cut the dough into four even pieces and wrap until using.

4 To make one cottage, roll one piece out about 3mm thick on the floured board. It should be just large enough to cut two each of the three cardboard shapes from it. (Re-roll dough scraps if necessary.) Place the shapes on the prepared baking tray.

5 Bake for about 7 minutes or until evenly browned. (Do not undercook.) While pieces are warm, carefully lift them onto a cooling rack. Repeat for other houses.

6 To construct and decorate houses, make White Icing for Piping (see page 253) using the two egg whites. Pipe the icing on the walls and roof making shingles, doors, windows, etc. Leave plain or decorate with sweets if desired. Using more of the icing, 'glue' the walls together on a cardboard base. When the walls are firm, position the roof on top using more icing, and leave to set.

Lebkuchen

For about 30–50 biscuits (depending on size):

50g butter

1 cup honey

¾ cup packed brown sugar

2 Tbsp lemon juice

1 Tbsp finely grated lemon zest

2 tsp ground cinnamon

1 tsp ground ginger

1 tsp ground cloves

1 tsp ground or grated nutmeg

1 tsp ground allspice

½ tsp baking soda

3½–4 cups standard (plain) flour

These biscuits are meant to be very hard, and to soften over a few weeks until they are edible. The less you heat the initial mixture, the more flour you can add to it. The more flour you can add to the mixture, the harder the biscuits will be. If less flour is added, the biscuits may be soft enough to eat straight away. Baking also affects the texture. Well-cooked biscuits are a richer brown and are harder than light coloured biscuits. This mixture is delicious raw. It should make about 50 small biscuits, allowing for some disappearance of raw dough!

1 Preheat the oven to 180°C (170°C fanbake), with the rack just below the middle. Line a baking tray with baking paper.

2 Melt butter in a medium-sized pot. Add everything except the baking soda and flour, and warm only as little as needed to soften and blend the honey into everything else. Remove the pot from the heat, and stir in the soda sifted with one cup of the flour. Add the rest of the flour gradually to make a stiff dough. If necessary, add a little water, then extra flour (see Note below).

3 Roll mixture out about 5mm thick on a lightly floured board, and then cut into shapes with whatever interesting cutters you have. Pierce a hole in each biscuit so you can thread ribbon through it later. If desired, make patterns in raw dough with skewers (if biscuits are not being iced later).

4 Bake for about 10 minutes or until lightly browned. (Longer baking makes harder biscuits.) Cool on a rack. For optional icing, make White Icing for Piping (see page 253).

NOTE: If you want very hard biscuits, follow the instructions, then roll out and cook two or three biscuits. If these are soft enough to eat when cold, add about ½ cup of extra flour to the remaining uncooked biscuit mixture, and add water in small amounts until you get a workable dough. Different flours produce different results, so some experimenting may be necessary.

Lindsay's Christmas Mincemeat Squares

These are far quicker to make than Christmas Mincemeat Pies, and they are just as popular.

For an 18 x 28cm slice:

Base:

100g chilled butter

½ cup (packed) brown sugar

1 cup standard (plain) flour

Topping:

1 cup (packed) brown sugar

¼ cup standard (plain) flour

½ tsp baking powder

½ tsp salt

1 cup desiccated coconut

2 large eggs

1 tsp vanilla essence

1 cup (280–300g) fruit mince

1. Preheat the oven to 160°C (150°C fanbake), with the rack just below the middle. Line the base and sides of an 18 x 28cm pan with baking paper.

2. For the base, cut the cold butter into 8–12 cubes and put in a food processor (or grate it into a large bowl) with the brown sugar and flour. Process in bursts, or rub in butter by hand, until it is evenly through the flour, and mixture is crumbly. Tip this mixture into the prepared pan and press it down so it covers the base evenly. Bake for 10 minutes.

3. For the topping, measure all the dry ingredients into the unwashed food processor or large bowl and mix well. Add the eggs, vanilla essence and fruit mince and process or beat until everything is well blended. Pour on top of the cold, warm or hot base and bake for about 30 minutes, until centre of topping feels firm and has browned evenly.

4. Cool thoroughly before cutting into small squares or bars.

5. Serve squares at any festive occasion, with wine, cocktails or coffee, or warm them and serve for dessert, cut in larger pieces, with vanilla ice-cream or lightly whipped cream and a fresh berry garnish. Store in a shallow container, one layer deep, in a cool place with lid slightly ajar.

Christmas Mincemeat Muffins

Although mincemeat pies are nice, making their crust is quite time consuming. Why not put spoonfuls of the mixture in muffins instead?

For 12 regular muffins:

1¾ cups self-raising flour

¾ cup caster sugar

½ tsp salt

2 large eggs

½ cup sour cream

½ cup milk

½ tsp rum, whisky or brandy essence

½ cup Christmas (fruit) mincemeat

1. Preheat the oven to 200°C (190°C fanbake), with the rack just below the middle.

2. Measure the flour, sugar and salt into a bowl and mix together with a fork or whisk. In another large bowl, whisk the eggs, sour cream, milk and essence together until smooth. Add the dry ingredients to the liquids and, without over-mixing, stir gently to combine.

3. Coat 12 regular muffin pans with non-stick spray and half fill the pans with the mixture. Using a dampened teaspoon, make a small indentation on the top of each, and into it put 1–2 teaspoons of the mincemeat. Cover each with a spoonful of the remaining mixture, trying to cover the 'enclosed' mincemeat.

4. Bake for about 12–15 minutes or until golden brown. The centres should spring back when pressed. Cool in the pans for 3–4 minutes before transferring to a rack.

5. These are best warm, ideal for Christmas Day breakfast or brunch, or with coffee at any time of the day over the holiday period. Serve hot for dessert between Christmas and New Year, with fresh berries and ice-cream or whipped cream, or Rum Butter (see page 151).

Macadamia & White Chocolate Muffins

These 'All White' or 'White Christmas' muffins are rich and 'cakey' with a delicious vanilla flavour. They may look plain on the outside, but inside they are full of chunky pieces of white chocolate and macadamia.

For 12 regular or 24 mini muffins:

2 cups standard (plain) flour

3 tsp baking powder

1 cup sugar

½ cup (75g) chopped macadamia nuts

¾ cup (100g) chopped white chocolate

100g butter, melted

1 cup milk

1 large egg

2 tsp vanilla essence

1 Preheat the oven to 200°C (190°C fanbake), with the rack just below the middle.

2 Measure the flour, baking powder and sugar into a large bowl. Add the macadamia nuts and white chocolate, then mix well with a fork to combine.

3 Place the melted butter in another large bowl, then add the milk, egg and vanilla essence and beat with the fork until thoroughly blended.

4 Tip the flour mixture into the liquid and gently fold together until the flour is moistened. Do not over-mix.

5 Spoon the batter into non-stick sprayed or lightly buttered, regular muffin pans, or mini muffin pans.

6 Bake for about 12 minutes until golden brown, and firm when pressed in the centre.

7 Serve only slightly warm or cold (definitely unbuttered), with coffee or for dessert. Great for gifts.

NOTE: We used roasted, salted macadamia nuts (which we had bought for nibbling) when we made these. They were excellent for both purposes!

Cranberry & Apple Muffins

By adding fruit purée to uncooked muffin mixture, you can produce tender, moist muffins using the minimum amount of oil or butter. We have added dried cranberries as well, for their tartness, but you can replace them with sultanas or raisins if you prefer.

For 12 regular-sized muffins:

½ cup boiling water

½ cup (60g) dried cranberries

½ cup apple purée

½ cup canola or other oil

1 large egg

¼–½ cup chopped walnuts, optional

1 cup self-raising flour

¾ cup wholemeal flour

¾ cup sugar

2 tsp baking powder

½ tsp salt

1 Preheat the oven to 210°C (200°C fanbake), with the rack just below the middle.

2 Pour the boiling water over the dried cranberries and leave them to stand for about 5 minutes. Without draining, add the apple purée, oil and egg, and mix well with a fork. Stir in the chopped nuts (if using).

3 Measure the flours into another bowl. Add the remaining dry ingredients, and mix with a fork or whisk.

4 Sprinkle this mixture over the liquid ingredients and fold them together, stopping as soon as there are no pockets or streaks of flour. Do not over-mix.

5 Spoon the mixture into 12 regular, thoroughly non-stick sprayed muffin pans.

6 Bake for 10–12 minutes, until lightly browned, and until the centres spring back when pressed. Stand in their pans for 2–4 minutes, or until the muffins may be lifted out without breaking them.

7 Serve plain or dusted with icing sugar, at any time of day with tea or coffee.

VARIATION: For Sultana and Apple Muffins, replace the cranberries with sultanas. Pour boiling water over them and proceed in the same way.

Herbed Chicken & Cranberry Muffins

Make these unusual, savoury muffins with the last of a festive chicken (or turkey) or a smoked chicken breast.

For 10 regular or 24 mini muffins:

2 cups standard (plain) flour

3 tsp baking powder

½ tsp salt

¼ cup chopped fresh herbs (half parsley, half thyme or marjoram, etc.)

freshly ground black pepper

1 cup (150g) chopped cooked chicken

75g butter

½ medium onion, peeled and diced

275g cranberry sauce

1 large egg

½ cup milk

❶ Preheat the oven to 200°C (190°C fanbake), with the rack just below the middle.

❷ Sift the flour, baking powder and salt into a large bowl. Add the herbs, black pepper to taste and the cooked (plain or smoked) chicken. Toss together until evenly mixed.

❸ Melt the butter in a medium-sized frypan, add the diced onion and cook for 2–3 minutes until the onion is soft. Reduce the heat and spoon in the cranberry sauce. Heat, stirring gently, until the sauce has just melted.

❹ Whisk the egg and milk together in another large bowl, stir in the warm cranberry mixture, then sprinkle in the dry ingredients.

❺ Gently fold everything together until the flour is just dampened. Take care not to over-mix. Spoon the mixture into 10 regular or 24 mini muffin pans which have been non-stick sprayed or lightly buttered.

❻ Bake for 12 minutes or until lightly browned and firm when pressed in the centre.

❼ Serve warm, with a salad, for lunch. If made without the chicken, serve warm with roast poultry. Good at a buffet meal.

VARIATION: Add ¼–½ cup of dried cranberries.

Hot Cross Buns

A wonderful treat for Easter (or any time for that matter!), home-made hot cross buns are well worth the effort. When time is short, make Easter buns (i.e. buns without crosses).

For 16–20 buns:

½ cup each warm milk and water

½ cup brown sugar

4 tsp active dried yeast

4 cups (560g) high-grade flour

75g butter, barely melted

1 large egg

1 tsp salt

1 Tbsp each mixed spice and cinnamon

1 tsp ground cloves

1 tsp vanilla essence

1 cup mixed fruit or currants

Bread Machine Instructions:

1 Carefully measure all the ingredients into a 750g capacity bread machine in the order specified by the manufacturer.

2 Set to the Dough cycle and Start. (Add the mixed fruit at the beep if your machine offers this option.)

3 When the cycle is complete, shape and bake as below.

Hand-made Bread Instructions:

1 Measure the warm milk, water and 1 tablespoon of the brown sugar into a large bowl, warm or cool the mixture to body temperature, then sprinkle in the yeast granules.

2 Stir after 2 minutes to ensure yeast has dissolved before adding 2 cups of the measured high-grade flour. Cover and leave in a warm place for about 30 minutes.

3 In another bowl, mix together the melted butter and remaining brown sugar, then beat in the egg, salt, spices, vanilla essence and dried fruit.

4 Add the risen yeast mixture and the remaining high-grade flour and mix to make a dough just firm enough to knead, adding a little extra flour if necessary.

5 Knead with the dough hook of an electric mixer or by hand on a lightly floured surface for 10 minutes.

Shaping and Baking:

1 Divide the dough evenly into four pieces, then again into four or five so you have 16 or 20 pieces in total.

2 Shape each piece into a round ball and arrange in non-stick sprayed baking pans or in a rectangular roasting dish, leaving about 1cm between each bun.

3 Cover with plastic wrap and leave in a warm place until doubled in size.

4 If you want to add pastry crosses, rub 60g cold butter into 1 cup high-grade flour, then add about 3 tablespoons cold water to form a stiff dough. Roll out very thinly then cut into strips, brush with beaten egg and place carefully on the risen buns, egg side down.

5 Bake at 225°C for 10–12 minutes or until lightly browned. Glaze immediately with a syrup made by bringing to the boil 1 tablespoon each golden syrup, honey and water.

Chocolate Hot Cross Buns

We like traditional, fruit and spice-flavoured hot cross buns but, for some reason, Simon's children have gone off them, and now prefer this chocolate version.

Bread Machine Instructions:

1 Measure all the ingredients into a 750g capacity bread machine in the order specified by the manufacturer.

2 Set to the Dough cycle and start. (Add the chocolate chips at the beep if your machine offers this option).

3 When the cycle is complete, shape and bake as below.

Hand-made Bread Instructions:

1 Measure the yeast, milk, hot water, 1 tablespoon of the brown sugar and the salt into a large bowl. Stir after 2 minutes to ensure the yeast has dissolved before adding 2 cups of the measured high-grade flour.

2 Cover and leave in a warm place for about 30 minutes.

3 In another bowl, mix together the melted butter and remaining brown sugar, then beat in the egg. Add the risen yeast mixture and the cocoa powder and remaining flour and mix to make a dough just firm enough to knead, adding a little extra flour if necessary.

4 Knead with the dough hook of an electric mixer or by hand on a lightly floured surface for 10 minutes.

5 Add the chocolate chips and knead for 1 minute longer.

6 Shape and bake as below.

Shaping and Baking:

1 Divide the dough evenly into four pieces, then again into four quarters so you have 16 pieces in total.

2 Shape each one into a round ball and arrange in non-stick sprayed (and/ or baking paper-lined) baking pans or in a rectangular roasting dish, leaving about 1cm between each bun.

3 Cover with plastic wrap and leave in a warm place until doubled in size.

4 If you want to add pastry crosses, use the method in the previous recipe. Alternatively, bake the buns first and decorate when cooled with crosses made with vanilla or chocolate icing or melted white or dark chocolate.

5 Bake at 200°C for 12–15 minutes or until lightly browned.

6 Glaze immediately with a syrup made by bringing to the boil 1 tablespoon each golden syrup, honey and water.

Traditional Christmas Mincemeat

For 3–4 cups:

zest of 1 lemon

zest of 1 orange

½ cup sugar

½ cup brown sugar

2 large Granny Smith apples

juice of 1 lemon

2 cups sultanas

2 cups mixed fruit

1 tsp each cinnamon, mixed spice, grated nutmeg and salt

½ tsp ground cloves

¼ cup brandy, whisky, rum, sherry or port

❶ Peel the zest from the lemon and orange with a potato peeler. Place it in a food processor fitted with the metal chopping blade, add the white sugar and process until the zest is very finely chopped.

❷ Add the brown sugar, the unpeeled apples cut into chunks, lemon juice, half the sultanas and half the mixed fruit. Process until the apple is finely chopped.

❸ Add the remaining fruit and the flavourings, and process briefly.

❹ You can use this immediately or transfer it to clean airtight containers and refrigerate until required (2–3 weeks). Freeze for longer storage.

Chocolate Icing

2 Tbsp butter

1 Tbsp cocoa

2 Tbsp water

1½ cups icing sugar

1. Warm the butter, cocoa and water together until butter melts.
2. Take off the heat, sift in icing sugar and mix until smooth.
3. Spread on the cake.

Chocolate Cream Icing

250g chocolate dark or milk chocolate

1 cup cream

1 tsp instant coffee, optional

1. Break the chocolate into the marked squares.
2. Heat the cream in a small pot until just boiling, then take it off the heat and stir in the chocolate and coffee (if using). Keep stirring until mixture is smooth, then pour into a cold dry bowl.
3. Beat mixture with a whisk or electric beater until cool to touch (about 10 minutes).
4. Cover and refrigerate for at least an hour or overnight.
5. Use as desired, warming slightly for easier spreading. Make larger quantities and spread between cake layers if desired.

Chocolate Sour Cream Icing

50g dark chocolate or ¼ cup chocolate chips

2 Tbsp sour cream

1 Break up chocolate if necessary, and heat with sour cream over boiling water or in a microwave until the chocolate has melted.

2 Stir until well combined.

3 Cool to a spreadable consistency if necessary.

Lemon or Orange Icing

25g (2 Tbsp) butter

about 1½ cups icing sugar

1–2 Tbsp lemon or orange juice

finely grated lemon or orange rind, optional

1 Put the soft (but not melted) butter in a clean bowl.

2 Add the sieved icing sugar and enough juice to mix it to a spreadable consistency. (Use more juice if you want to drizzle the icing rather than spread it.)

3 If you want a stronger citrus flavour and have lemon or orange rind available, add some finely grated rind too.

VARIATION: To make Passionfruit Icing, follow the instructions for Lemon or Orange Icing, replacing the citrus juice with the same quantity of passionfruit pulp. Omit orange or lemon rind.

Cream Cheese Icing

2 Tbsp cream cheese

2 Tbsp room temperature butter

½ tsp vanilla essence

2 cups icing sugar

1 Beat the cream cheese, the soft (but not melted) butter, vanilla and icing sugar together until creamy.

2 Spread over the cooled cake.

White Icing for Piping

1 egg white

icing sugar, sifted

1 Whisk egg white until foamy.

2 Beat in about ½ cup of sifted icing sugar at a time, until the icing holds its shape when piped from an icing bag (or a tough plastic bag with a small hole in one corner).

NOTE: This icing sets hard and can be quite brittle if not stuck firmly to (or supported by) the biscuit base.

Almond Icing

100g ground almonds

1 cup icing sugar

½ cup caster sugar

1 large egg yolk

2 Tbsp lemon juice, strained

¼ tsp almond essence, optional

Almond icing is easy to make. This is enough for a medium sized cake. Double the quantity if you want enough for a very thick layer, for icing down the sides, or for marzipan fruit.

1. Combine the ground almonds and sugars in a food processor or mixing bowl.
2. Mix the egg yolk with half of the lemon juice and add to the almond mixture with a little almond essence if desired.
3. Add remaining lemon juice, a little at a time, until you have a paste that is easy to roll out.
4. Warm a little apricot jam, strain it, and brush it over the cake.
5. Roll out the almond paste on a dry board sprinkled with icing sugar.
6. Place over the cake smoothly, using a rolling pin.

Plastic Icing

1 Tbsp gelatine

3 Tbsp cold water

3 Tbsp liquid glucose

2 tsp glycerine

1 kg icing sugar

Plastic icing is not really difficult to make yourself, but is best not attempted by an inexperienced cook.

1. Mix the gelatine and cold water, stand for 3–4 minutes, then warm it in a microwave or over low heat until the gelatine has just dissolved.
2. Warm the liquid glucose if it is too stiff to deal with, then add the measured amount to the warm gelatine, with the glycerine.
3. Sift the icing sugar into a large bowl, pour the lukewarm gelatine mixture into the centre of it, then mix it with a dough hook or a wooden spoon. As soon as reasonably firm, mix with your hands until you have a smooth, workable dough (you may need to add a little hot water).
4. Roll out on a board dusted with icing sugar, and place over moistened almond icing.
5. Prick any air bubbles with a needle, and put a smooth surface on the icing by polishing it with a square of smooth, shiny card. As you rub the card around and around, you will find that a lovely, smooth, shiny surface forms.

Royal Icing

1 large egg white

1 tsp lemon juice, strained

½ tsp glycerine, optional

2 cups sifted icing sugar

The top coat of icing on a fruit cake is often made of royal icing, rather than plastic icing. It is very white, sets hard and is easy to pipe into rosettes, lines, dots, etc.

1 In a food processor or bowl, mix the egg white and lemon juice only until frothy.

2 Add the icing sugar a few tablespoons at a time, mixing well between additions. Stop when the icing is the consistency you want. Mix in glycerine.

3 Use the icing immediately, or store it in an airtight bag for up to two or three days. For piping, thin down with a little water if necessary.

NOTE: If you want to pipe royal icing into elaborate shapes such as leaves and roses, buy icing sugar that does not contain cornflour. (Read ingredient list on bag.) Glycerine is supposed to keep royal icing softer than it would be otherwise, but it is not essential.

Chocolate Coating

For dipped biscuits, strawberries, etc.

80g dark, milk or white chocolate

2 Tbsp (25g) vegetable shortening (e.g. Kremelta)

1 Melt the chocolate and Kremelta together in a bowl over a simmering pot of hot water.

2 Remove the pot from the heat when ready, but leave the bowl standing over the hot water so it does not cool and thicken too much while you are dipping.

3 Dip cold biscuits, strawberries, etc, into the warm chocolate, partially coating each one.

4 Place carefully on a plastic sheet to set. Peel off when chocolate is hard.

Lemon Glaze

½ cup icing sugar

1 Tbsp lemon juice

1 Mix icing sugar and lemon juice to pouring consistency.

2 Drizzle it over the partly cooled cake.

Mock Cream

50g butter, at room temperature

½ tsp vanilla or other essence

½ cup icing sugar without lumps

about 2 Tbsp water

1 Put the butter, vanilla and icing sugar in a food processor or bowl.

2 Add 1 measuring tablespoon of hot water and process or beat until smooth.

3 Add about 1 tablespoon of cold water, gradually. You should finish up with a light-coloured fluffy cream.

Gluten-free Baking

Gluten is a protein (or rather a set of proteins) found in wheat (including kamut and spelt) and barley, rye and triticale. While it actually makes up a relatively small proportion (usually 8–14%) of wheat flour it has some almost unique properties. When gluten proteins are mixed with water (as in a dough or batter), the molecules interact with one another to form a matrix which has both fluid and elastic characteristics, this allows the matrix to trap little bubbles of gas (released by yeast or baking powder) which expand during cooking and create a light texture.

The trick, then, to creating gluten-free baked products is to somehow create an elastic mixture. There are two major ways of doing this (which are often used in combination). Eggs, or particularly egg whites, can be beaten to a foam that will, to some extent, hold gas a bit like gluten. The other way is to use vegetable gums such as guar or xanthan gums. The powdered gums mix with cold water to form thick, sticky gels that again convey a slight elasticity to batters or doughs.

The starchy component of wheat flour can be replaced with maize cornflour, rice flour and/or tapioca flour all of which are gluten free. In theory, any one could be used in place of wheat starch, but they all have slightly different properties and we find we get the best results when they are used in combination.

While wheat starch (cornflour) it is being removed from more and more mainstream baking ingredients, there are still some products that you should be careful about if on a strict gluten-free diet. Make sure you select a gluten-free baking powder, likewise icing sugar contains a small amount of added starch, make sure you buy one that is gluten free. Custard powder is also largely starch based; check the label before you buy.

← Fruit & Nut Loaf – recipe page 281

Cheese Scones

These aren't as solid as a traditional scone, but they're quick and simple to make (like the traditional version), and they taste delicious — a winning combination.

For 10–12 scones:

1 cup rice flour

1 cup tapioca flour

4 tsp gluten-free baking powder

1 tsp guar gum

½ tsp salt

75g cold butter, cubed

1 cup grated cheese

1 cup milk

a little extra grated cheese to decorate, optional

1 Preheat the oven to 200°C.

2 Sift the flours, baking powder, guar gum and salt into a food processor. Add the cold butter and process in short bursts until the mixture looks like fine crumbs.

3 Add the cheese and process briefly, then, with the processor running, gradually add enough of the milk to make a soft dough.

4 Tip the mixture out onto a sheet of baking paper that has been lightly dusted with rice or tapioca flour. Sprinkle a little more of the flour over the dough, then pat it out to make a roughly rectangular shape about 25cm long by 12cm wide and about 2cm thick.

5 Cut the dough into 10–12 evenly sized portions, then arrange these a few centimetres apart on a baking paper-lined baking sheet. Sprinkle the tops with a little extra grated cheese, if desired.

6 Bake at 200°C for 12–14 minutes or until golden brown.

7 Serve warm or cold.

Pikelets

These aren't quite the same as regular pikelets but, if anything, they're lighter and fluffier, which we think is a good thing!

For about 20 pikelets:

½ cup rice flour

½ cup tapioca flour

2 tsp gluten-free baking powder

½ tsp guar gum

25g butter, melted

1 large (size 7) egg

1 rounded household Tbsp golden syrup

½ cup milk

1. Sift the dry ingredients into a medium-sized bowl and stir to combine thoroughly.

2. Whisk the melted butter, egg, golden syrup, and milk together in a small bowl.

3. Pour the wet mixture into the dry ingredients, then stir well until smooth. The mixture will be runny at first but should thicken if left to stand for a few minutes. If the mixture is too thick to flow when dropped off a spoon, thin with a little extra milk.

4. Heat a large, preferably non-stick, frypan over a medium to low heat. Wipe the pan with a thin film of oil, then drop dessertspoonfuls of the mixture into the pan. Cook until bubbles begin to break on the upper surface, then turn and cook until golden brown on the second side too. (If the first side is too dark, reduce the heat a little.) Repeat with the remaining batter.

5. Serve with jam and cream.

Gingerbread

Gingerbread is a good, all-purpose stand by! We like this version because it is really quick and easy to mix, it cooks in 25–30 minutes, and it's easy to have all the ingredients on hand in the pantry.

For a 25 x 11cm loaf:

50g butter

1 household Tbsp golden syrup

½ cup (packed) brown sugar

1 egg

½ cup rice flour

½ cup tapioca flour

1 tsp guar gum

2 tsp ground ginger

1 tsp ground cinnamon

1 tsp baking soda

½ cup milk

1 Preheat the oven to 180°C.

2 Melt the butter and golden syrup together in a medium-sized pot. Once they are combined, remove from the heat and beat in the sugar and egg.

3 Sift in all the dry ingredients except the baking soda. Dissolve the baking soda in the milk, then add this to the pot and stir until just combined.

4 Line the bottom and sides of a small loaf pan with baking paper, then pour in the fairly thin mixture.

5 Bake at 180°C for 25–30 minutes or until the centre springs back when pressed, and until a toothpick comes out clean.

6 Turn out onto a cooling rack after 5 minutes.

7 Serve warm or cool — it always seems particularly good with butter!

Blueberry Muffins

Somewhere along the line, blueberry muffins seem to have become the 'standard' sweet muffin, so we decided they really ought to be the ideal candidate for a gluten free make over. These are best served warm from the oven or reheated.

For 12 medium-sized muffins:

1 cup brown sugar

½ cup canola oil

2 eggs

1¼ cups plain or fruit-flavoured yoghurt or unsweetened yoghurt

1 tsp vanilla essence

¼ tsp salt

1 cup fine cornmeal

1 cup rice flour

3 tsp gluten-free baking powder

1 tsp ground cinnamon

1 cup frozen blueberries

1. Preheat the oven to 200°C (190°C fanbake), with the rack just below the middle.

2. Measure the sugar and oil into a food processor, and process until smooth. Add the eggs and process again until the mixture is light and creamy looking.

3. Pour in the yoghurt and vanilla essence, then sprinkle in the salt. Process until mixed.

4. Measure in the cornmeal, rice flour, baking powder and cinnamon, then process in short bursts until there are no lumps. Remove the processor blade, then add the blueberries and stir by hand just enough to mix them evenly through.

5. Thoroughly non-stick spray 12 regular muffin pans, then divide the mixture evenly between them using two large spoons.

6. Bake for 12–15 minutes or until golden brown. Remove from the oven and leave to stand for 3–4 minutes before removing from the pans.

7. Best enjoyed warm from the oven or reheated.

Double Chocolate Muffins

These wheat-free muffins make a treat for anybody who cannot eat a chocolate cake made with flour, and will be enjoyed by everyone in the family. They can be 'dressed up' for a party, too.

For 12 medium-sized muffins:

1 cup rice flour

¼ cup cocoa powder

½ tsp baking soda

½ tsp salt

1 cup caster sugar

2 eggs, separated

1 cup plain or fruit-flavoured yoghurt

½ cup chocolate chips

1 Preheat the oven to 200°C (190°C fanbake), with the rack just below the middle.

2 Sift the rice flour, cocoa powder, baking soda and salt and half of the sugar into a large bowl.

3 Separate the eggs, putting the whites into a large clean glass or metal bowl, and mixing the yolks with the yoghurt in another container.

4 Using an electric (or hand) beater, beat the egg whites until their peaks turn over when the beater is lifted from them, then add the remaining sugar and continue to beat until they will again form peaks that turn over.

5 Stir the egg yolk and yoghurt mixture into the dry ingredients then fold in a third of the beaten egg whites. Gently fold in the remaining egg whites and the chocolate chips. This should make a very soft, light batter.

6 Spoon the batter into 12 well-sprayed or oiled muffin pans and bake at 200°C for 12–15 minutes, until firm when pressed in the centre.

7 Serve warm or cold. Cut out centres, fill with whipped cream for 'fairy cakes', if desired.

Jalapeno, Coriander & Corn Muffins

These muffins, made without wheat flour, have a slightly different texture to 'regular' muffins, but are interesting and well-flavoured. They disappear remarkably fast — often before cooling so the difference is obviously not a worry.

For 12 medium-sized muffins:

2 cups grated tasty cheese

2 cups fine yellow cornmeal (see Note)

1 tsp baking soda

2 tsp cream of tartar

¾ tsp salt

1 tsp ground cumin

2 Tbsp chopped fresh coriander leaves

1–2 Tbsp chopped (bottled) jalapeno peppers, optional

2 large eggs

¾ cup milk

1 Preheat the oven to 200°C (190°C fanbake), with the rack just below the middle.

2 Measure the cheese and cornmeal into a large bowl. Sift in the baking soda, cream of tartar, salt and ground cumin. Toss well to combine, then add coriander leaves and jalapeno peppers, using the larger amount for spicier muffins.

3 Whisk the eggs and milk together until lightly coloured and frothy on top. Add this immediately to the dry ingredients and mix until evenly combined.

4 Spoon into 12 non-stick sprayed muffin pans then sprinkle with a little paprika and bake at 200°C for about 12 minutes (until firm when pressed in the centre and lightly browned).

5 Serve warm or reheated.

NOTE: Use cornmeal which is as finely ground as flour, and which is a soft golden colour.

Pistachio Macaroons

Macaroons are fashionable at the moment — and by happy chance they're also gluten free!

For 30–40 'halves':

2 large or 3 small egg whites

pinch of cream of tartar

¼ cup caster sugar

100g shelled pistachios, ground finely

1 cup lightly packed icing sugar

Ganache:

125g white chocolate

2 Tbsp cream

1 Tbsp orange blossom water, optional

1. Place the egg whites in a large clean bowl. Add a pinch of cream of tartar, then beat until they form soft peaks. Sprinkle in the caster sugar, then beat again until the mixture forms stiff peaks.

2. While the whites beat, grind the pistachios very finely in a blender or food processor. Sift the ground nuts and icing sugar together into a bowl.

3. Sift the dry mixture (again!) into the egg whites, then fold the mixture together. Getting the texture of the mixture right at this stage will determine the final shape of the biscuits — the more you fold, the more liquid the mixture will become; fold until it just begins to flow.

4. Drop 3–4cm wide spoonfuls of the mixture onto baking paper-lined baking sheets (leave 2–3cm between each 'blob' to allow for spreading).

5. Bake at 150°C for 20–25 minutes. Leave to cool on the trays for a few minutes, then lift off onto racks to cool completely.

6. To make the ganache, place the chocolate in a small bowl with the cream (and orange blossom water, if using). Heat by microwaving at 50% (Medium) power for 60–90 seconds stirring every 30 seconds, or by placing the bowl over a pot of simmering water. Stir until smooth then cool until thick enough to spread.

7. Sandwich the biscuit halves together with about a teaspoon of the ganache, then store in an airtight container.

Chocolate Chip Cookies

These delicious cookies look big and chunky, but actually have a surprisingly light texture.

For 24–36 cookies:

200g butter, softened

1 cup brown sugar

2 large eggs

2 tsp vanilla essence

1 cup rice flour

1 cup tapioca flour

3 tsp gluten-free baking powder

1 tsp guar gum

1 cup chocolate chips

½ cup chopped walnuts, optional

1 Preheat the oven to 180°C.

2 Beat the butter and sugar with an electric mixer until light and fluffy. Add the eggs and vanilla essence and beat briefly to combine.

3 Sift in the flours, baking powder and guar gum, then beat to combine — the mixture may look very dry initially, but should come together to form a soft dough after a minute or so. Add the chocolate chips and chopped walnuts (if using) and stir these through the mixture.

4 Line two baking sheets with baking paper. Drop heaped tablespoonfuls of the mixture onto the baking sheets, leaving at least 5cm for spreading between each.

5 Place one tray at a time in the middle of the oven. Bake at 180°C for 10–12 minutes or until the cookies just begin to darken around the edges.

6 Allow to cool on the trays for a few minutes before removing and cooling completely on a rack. Transfer to an airtight container for storage.

Double Chocolate & Raspberry Cookies

These large cookies make a perfect decadent treat!

For about 20 cookies:

125g butter, softened

1 cup brown sugar

1 large (size 7) egg

¾ cup tapioca flour

½ cup rice flour

1 tsp gluten-free baking powder

¼ cup cocoa powder

90–100g dark chocolate, roughly chopped

½ cup (about 75g) frozen raspberries

1 Preheat the oven to 180°C.

2 Measure the softened butter and sugar into a large bowl. Add the egg, then beat the mixture until pale and creamy.

3 Sift in the dry ingredients, then stir to combine. Add the chocolate and raspberries. Stir again until evenly combined.

4 Using dessertspoons or an ice-cream scoop, drop spoonfuls of the mixture onto baking paper-lined baking trays leaving at least 5cm between them for spreading.

5 Place one tray in the middle of the oven and bake for 12–15 minutes at 180°C until the cookies are just beginning to change colour around the edge.

6 Remove from the oven and allow to cool on the tray for a few minutes before transferring to a rack to cool completely.

Belgian Biscuits

The texture of these biscuits isn't quite the same as their 'regular' cousins, but they have the same spicy flavour and spread a deliciously enticing smell through the house as they bake.

For about 30 biscuits (60 halves):

1 cup brown sugar, packed

200g butter, softened

1 large egg

1 tsp ground cinnamon

2 tsp mixed spice

4 tsp gluten-free baking powder

1 cup rice flour

1 cup tapioca flour

¼–½ cup raspberry jam to fill

Icing:

1 cup sifted icing sugar

1 Tbsp butter, softened

about 1½ Tbsp lemon juice or water

red jelly crystals (or coloured sugar)

❶ Measure the brown sugar, softened butter and egg into a food processor. Process until creamy, then sift in all the dry ingredients. Process again (scrape down the sides if required) until the mixture begins to come together in clumps.

❷ Divide the dough in half. Transfer the first half to a square of plastic wrap and pat it out to form a cylinder about 4cm thick, then roll it in the plastic wrap. Repeat with the second half of the dough. Refrigerate the cylinders until firm (about 2 hours).

❸ Preheat the oven to 180°C.

❹ Working one at a time, unwrap the cylinders, then cut the dough into 5mm slices. Arrange the slices a few centimetres apart on baking paper-lined baking sheets.

❺ Bake one tray at time for 8–9 minutes or until the edges of the biscuits just begin to colour. Remove the tray from the oven and cool for a few minutes before lifting onto a rack to cool completely.

❻ Sandwich the halves together, using ½–1 teaspoon of jam for each pair.

❼ To ice, mix icing sugar, butter and enough lemon juice or water to make a fairly soft icing. Spread a little onto the top of each sandwiched biscuit. Sprinkle a few red jelly crystals on the icing, if desired.

Louise Cake

This is a long-time family favourite — Simon fondly remembers his grandmother always seeming to have some stashed away. Here's our gluten-free version which we think stacks up very favourably and it's not hard to make.

For an 18 x 28cm slice:

Base:

100g butter, softened

½ cup sugar

2 (large) egg yolks

1 tsp vanilla essence

1 cup rice flour

½ cup tapioca flour

½ cup maize cornflour

2 tsp gluten-free baking powder

2 Tbsp water

Filling:

½ cup good-quality raspberry jam

Topping:

2 large egg whites

1 tsp vanilla essence

½ cup sugar

¾ cup shredded coconut

1 Preheat the oven to 160°C (150°C if using fan bake), with the rack just below the middle. Line the bottom and sides of an 18 x 28cm pan with baking paper.

2 For the base, put the softened butter and sugar in a food processor or large bowl. Separate two eggs, adding the yolks to this mixture (and put the whites in a clean medium-sized bowl ready to use for the topping). Add the vanilla essence, and mix to combine, then add the flours and mix again. Sprinkle in the water and process again until evenly crumbly.

3 Tip crumbly mixture into prepared pan and press down evenly. Bake for 15 minutes.

4 For the topping, beat the egg whites and vanilla essence until frothy, then add the sugar and beat until the tips of peaks turn over when the beater is lifted from them. Then fold ½ cup of the coconut evenly through the meringue.

5 For the filling, spread the jam over the warm base.

6 Put the meringue in spoonfuls on top, then spread evenly with a knife. Sprinkle with the remaining coconut. Bake for about 15 minutes or until the meringue feels crisp and is evenly and lightly coloured.

7 Cool completely before cutting into pieces of the desired size.

8 Serve with tea or coffee. Store in a container, preferably one layer deep, in a cool place, with lid slightly ajar.

Chocolate Caramel Bars

This is the perfect sweet treat to enjoy with a cup of tea or coffee, or perhaps to include as a little something special in a lunchbox.

Base:

125g cold butter, cubed

¼ cup caster sugar

½ cup rice flour

½ cup tapioca flour

¼ cup cocoa powder

1 Tbsp water

Filling:

100g butter

½ a 400g can sweetened condensed milk

½ cup golden syrup

Icing:

1 Tbsp cocoa

1½ Tbsp boiling water

2 tsp butter, softened

¼ tsp vanilla essence

1 cup icing sugar

1. Preheat the oven to 170°C (160°C fanbake), with the rack just below the middle. Line an 18 x 28cm pan with baking paper.

2. For the base, measure the butter and sugar into a food processor, then sift in the flours and cocoa powder and process well. Drizzle in the water and process until the mixture looks like fine crumbs.

3. Press the crumbs into the prepared pan. Bake for 8–10 minutes or until the centre is firm.

4. For the filling, measure butter, condensed milk and golden syrup into a pot. Bring to the boil over medium heat, stirring all the time, then reduce heat and cook for 10 minutes, stirring often, until the mixture is a deep golden colour, and a drop of it forms a soft ball in cold water.

5. Remove from heat and pour over cooked base straight away, smoothing it out if necessary. Leave to cool before icing.

6. For the icing, pour boiling water on cocoa in a small bowl. Beat in butter, vanilla essence and sifted icing sugar, adding more water if necessary, to make icing soft enough to spread easily over the caramel.

7. Leave uncovered for at least 2 hours before cutting into bars.

8. Serve with tea or coffee, or as an after-dinner treat.

Chocolate Brownie

This brownie is dense and moist, but still has a fine cakey texture.

For an 18 x 28cm brownie:

100g butter

90–100g dark chocolate, chopped

1 cup sugar

3 large (size 7) eggs

2 tsp vanilla essence

½ cup tapioca flour

½ cup rice flour

¼ cup cocoa powder

1 tsp guar gum

½ tsp baking soda

¼ tsp salt

½ cup chopped walnuts, optional

1 Preheat the oven to 180°C.

2 Cut the butter into 3–4 pieces and place in a medium-sized pot along with the chopped chocolate. Heat over a low-medium heat, stirring frequently, until the chocolate has just melted.

3 Remove the pot from the heat and stir in the sugar, then break in the eggs and add the vanilla essence and stir until smooth and evenly combined. Sift in flours, cocoa powder, guar gum, baking soda and salt then stir until well combined. Fold in the walnuts (if using).

4 Line an 18 x 28cm brownie pan with baking paper, then pour in the brownie mixture.

5 Bake in the middle of the oven for 25–30 minutes or until a skewer inserted in the centre comes out clean.

6 Remove from the oven and allow to cool in the pan for about 5 minutes before removing from the pan and cooling on a rack.

7 Cut as desired, then dust with icing sugar before serving.

Ginger Crunch

This is another perennial family favourite.

For an 18 x 28cm slice:

Base:

125g butter

¼ cup sugar

1 tsp gluten-free baking powder

½ cup rice flour

½ cup tapioca flour

1 tsp ground ginger

1 Tbsp cold water

Icing:

3 Tbsp butter

3 tsp ground ginger

3 rounded household Tbsp golden syrup

4 tsp water

3 cups icing sugar

1 Preheat the oven to 180°C (170°C fanbake), with the rack just below the middle.

2 Line the base and sides of an 18 x 28cm pan with baking paper, allowing extra on the sides for lifting out the cooked slice, or spray a 23cm square loose-bottomed pan.

3 For the base, cut the cold butter into nine cubes, then process in brief bursts with remaining base ingredients, until the mixture is the texture of coarse breadcrumbs. If mixing by hand, warm butter until soft, mix it with the sugar, and then stir in the sieved dry ingredients.

4 Spread the crumbly mixture into the pan and press it down firmly and evenly. Bake for about 10 minutes or until evenly and lightly browned. It will still feel soft while it is hot. While the base cooks make the icing, since the base should be iced while hot.

5 For the icing, measure the butter, ginger, golden syrup and water into a small pot or microwave-safe bowl. Heat, without boiling, until melted. Remove from the heat, sift in the icing sugar, and beat until smooth.

6 As soon as the base is cooked, remove it from the oven. Pour the warm icing onto the hot base and spread carefully so it covers the base evenly. Sprinkle with chopped nuts, if desired, then leave to cool and set, marking it into pieces while still warm. Do not remove from the pan until it has cooled completely.

Lemon Square

This square has a delicious lemon-flavoured custard topping and always disappears very quickly.

For an 18 x 28cm slice:

Base:

1 cup tapioca flour

1 cup rice flour

½ cup icing sugar

125g cold butter

2 Tbsp water

Topping:

1½ cups sugar

zest of ½ lemon

3 large eggs

¼ cup lemon juice

¼ cup custard powder flour

½ tsp gluten-free baking powder

1 Preheat the oven to 160°C (150°C fanbake), with the rack just below the middle. Press a large piece of baking paper into an 18 x 28cm pan, folding the paper so it covers the bottom and all sides. Do not cut the paper at the corners, or filling will run underneath.

2 For the base, measure the flours, icing sugar and cubed butter into a food processor. Process until butter is chopped finely through dry ingredients. With the processor running, drizzle in the water.

3 Tip mixture into the lined pan and press down firmly and evenly. Bake for 15–20 minutes until firm and just beginning to brown lightly.

4 For the topping, put the sugar in the dry, unwashed food processor with the lemon zest. Process until the zest is very finely chopped through the sugar, then add the eggs, lemon juice and custard powder, and process until smooth.

5 Pour over partly cooked base, then bake for about 30 minutes longer, or until top is lightly browned and centre does not wobble when pan is jiggled.

6 When quite cold, cut into squares or fingers of desired size, by pressing a heavy, lightly oiled knife straight down through the topping and base.

7 Serve small pieces with tea or coffee at any time of day. Dust with icing sugar, then serve larger pieces for dessert, with Greek-style yoghurt or lightly whipped cream. Store lightly covered, up to three or four days.

Chocolate Cake

For a 23cm cake:

3 large (size 7) eggs, separated

¼ tsp cream of tartar

½ cup oil

1 cup plain unsweetened yoghurt

2 tsp vanilla essence

1½ cups sugar

1 cup rice flour

1 cup tapioca flour

½ cup cocoa powder

1 tsp guar gum

1 tsp baking soda

½ tsp salt

This makes a large cake, perfect for a party or special occasion, or for when you just feel like a delicious moist chocolate cake! If you want something particularly decadent, ice it with Chocolate Sour Cream Icing (see page 253) or use your favourite icing.

1 Preheat the oven to 180°C, with the rack just below the middle

2 Separate the eggs and place the whites in a large clean bowl. Add the cream of tartar then beat the egg whites until they form stiff peaks.

3 Place the yolks in another bowl or jug, then add the oil, yoghurt, vanilla essence and sugar then whisk to combine.

4 Sift the dry ingredients into the egg whites, pour the yoghurt-yolk mixture over the dry ingredients, then gently fold everything together until just uniformly mixed.

5 Non-stick spray and/or line a 23cm round pan with baking paper. Pour the batter into the prepared pan and level the top if required.

6 Bake at 180°C for 40–50 minutes or until a skewer inserted in the middle comes out clean. Remove from the oven and allow to cool for 5–10 minutes before removing from the pan and cooling completely on a rack.

7 Spread with Chocolate Sour Cream Icing (see page 253).

8 Leave the cake to stand until the icing is firm, then serve as is or with yoghurt or lightly whipped cream.

Carrot Cake

A good carrot cake is hard to go past and this one is no exception. We don't think you'd know it was gluten free unless you were told.

For a 21cm ring cake:

½ cup canola or other oil

2 large eggs

1 cup brown sugar

½ cup tapioca flour

½ cup potato starch

1 tsp guar gum

1 tsp baking soda

2 tsp gluten-free baking powder

2 tsp ground cinnamon

1 tsp ground mixed spice

½ tsp salt

¼ cup milk

1–1½ cups (about 180g) grated carrot

½ cup chopped walnuts, optional

1 Preheat the oven to 180°C.

2 Measure the oil into a large bowl, add the eggs and sugar then beat until pale and creamy.

3 Sift in the flours, guar gum, baking soda and powder, spices and salt. Add the milk, then stir until evenly mixed. Add the grated carrot and nuts (if using) and stir until evenly mixed.

4 Non-stick spray a round 21cm ring pan. Pour the batter into the pan, then bake at 180°C for 30–40 minutes or until a skewer inserted in the centre comes out clean.

5 Remove the cake from the oven, allow to cool in the pan for a few minutes before turning it out and cooling completely on a rack.

6 Ice with Cream Cheese Icing (see page 253).

Chocolate & Raspberry Roll

The 'conventional' version of this sponge roll has been a standby in our house for decades, celebrating many birthdays and special occasions.

For a 22 x 30cm sponge roll:

3 large eggs

½ cup sugar

¼ tsp salt

¼ cup tapioca flour

¼ cup maize cornflour

½ tsp guar gum

2 Tbsp cocoa powder

1 tsp baking powder

1 Tbsp boiling water

Rum Cream:

1 cup cream

¼ cup icing sugar

1–2 Tbsp rum

1 Preheat the oven to 230°C (220°C if using fanbake), with the rack just below the middle.

2 Beat the eggs, sugar and salt together in a fairly large bowl, until mixture is thick, creamy and pale. (Use room temperature eggs and don't hurry the beating.) Meantime, line the sides and base of a 22 x 30cm sponge roll pan with baking paper. Spray with non-stick spray.

3 Sift the dry ingredients into a clean bowl, return mixture to the sieve, and sift it again onto the thick egg mixture. Fold in carefully but thoroughly. Add the boiling water and fold it in too, then spread the thick mixture evenly in the lined pan.

4 Bake for 7–10 minutes or until the centre springs back when pressed lightly. (Take care not to cook longer than necessary or the sponge will shrink.)

5 Moisten (wet it lightly, then wring well) a clean tea towel and lay it on a large board or the bench. When the roll is cooked turn it out of the pan onto the tea towel. Carefully lift off the baking paper, then, using the tea towel to help get started, roll the sponge up (in the tea towel) and leave to cool on a rack.

6 To make Rum Cream, beat cream with icing sugar and rum until thick.

7 When sponge is cooled to room temperature, carefully unroll, spread with raspberry jam, then whipped Rum Cream. Roll up, starting from a short end, lifting the tea towel to help you.

8 Serve join-side down, as is, or dusted with icing sugar, with chocolate or white chocolate curls for extra decoration, if you like.

VARIATION: If preferred, cool the sponge flat, then cut it into two or three pieces and layer these, instead of forming a roll.

Cornflour Sponge

A sponge may seem a little old fashioned, but it is actually a rather useful recipe to master. Aside from looking impressive and tasting delicious it actually cooks remarkably quickly and can be used for the base of other desserts such as trifle.

For 8–10 servings:

4 large (size 7) eggs

¼ tsp salt

¾ cup (170g) caster sugar

1 tsp vanilla essence

1 cup (150g) maize cornflour

3 tsp gluten-free baking powder

2 Tbsp boiling water

❶ Preheat the oven to 180°C (160°C fan bake), with the rack just below the middle. Line the bottom of two 20cm round baking pans with baking paper and coat the sides thoroughly with non-stick spray.

❷ Separate the eggs, placing the whites in a large clean bowl with the salt, and the yolks in another small bowl.

❸ Beat the whites until they form soft peaks, then gradually add the sugar, beating until the mixture forms a glossy meringue that forms stiff peaks. Fold in the yolks and vanilla essence.

❹ Sift the cornflour and baking powder onto a sheet of paper (or into a small bowl) then sift again into the egg white mixture. Add the boiling water and fold the mixture together.

❺ Divide the mixture evenly between the pans, levelling the tops as much as possible. Bake for about 20 minutes or until the cakes just begin to come away from the edges of the pans.

❻ Remove the cakes from the oven, leave to cool for a few minutes in the pans, then tip onto a rack covered with a clean tea towel to cool completely.

Butterfly Cakes

Alison's mother always used to include butterfly cakes as part of her tea parties. As a result we think of them served on finest china with an array of other delicate sweet treats alongside.

For 12 cakes in large paper cups:

1 cup (140g) rice flour

1 cup (130g) tapioca flour

2 tsp gluten-free baking powder

1 tsp guar gum

100g butter, softened

¾ cup (170g) caster sugar

2 tsp vanilla essence

2 large (size 7) eggs

½ cup (125ml) milk

To decorate:

whipped cream

raspberry or strawberry jam

fresh strawberries or raspberries, optional

icing sugar

1. Preheat the oven to 170°C (160°C fanbake), with the rack just below the middle. Put pleated paper muffin baking cups in 12 medium-sized muffin pans.

2. Sift the dry ingredients together into a small bowl.

3. Mix the softened (but not melted) butter and the sugar together in the food processor, until cream coloured, then add the vanilla essence and process again.

4. Add one of the eggs and a tablespoon of flour mixture and process until the batter is smooth. Repeat with the second egg and another tablespoon of flour mixture. Tip the remaining flour mixture into the food processor and pour the milk over everything. Process in bursts until the flour is incorporated.

5. Using two dessertspoons, spoon the mixture into the paper cases, using one spoon to help the mixture off the other. Each case should be about three-quarters full.

6. Bake for 15–20 minutes until cakes are golden brown, spring back when gently pressed, and a skewer in the middle comes out clean.

7. When cool, cut the top off each cake carefully so the under-side of the part removed is cone-shaped, leaving a depression to fill with jam and vanilla-flavoured whipped cream. Carefully cut each removed top in half and arrange the two pieces, with the just-cut edges facing down, in the cream, rather like butterfly wings. Add a small piece of strawberry or a raspberry if you like, and dust with icing sugar.

Chocolate Truffle Cake

We've tried various flourless chocolate cakes, with similar ingredients to this, but the method makes this one a little different. Beating the egg whites separately lightens the texture a little, but the cake is still fudgy and moist.

For 8–10 servings:

200g chocolate (about 60% cocoa solids)

200g butter, cubed

¾ cup (170g) sugar

4 large (size 7) eggs

❶ Preheat the oven to 180°C. Line a round 23cm pan with baking paper and coat it thoroughly with non-stick spray.

❷ Break the chocolate into small pieces and place in a microwave-safe bowl with the butter. Microwave on Medium (50% power) for 2 minutes, stirring every 30 seconds, or until the butter and chocolate have melted and are evenly combined. Add half of the sugar and stir again.

❸ Separate the eggs, placing the whites in a large clean bowl and add the yolks to the chocolate mixture. Beat the whites until they look foamy, then add the remaining sugar and beat until they form stiff peaks.

❹ Add the chocolate mixture to the beaten whites, then fold everything together. Spoon the batter into the prepared pan.

❺ Bake for 30–40 minutes or until a skewer comes out clean.

Sponge Fingers

Italian-style sponge fingers are really best suited to use in desserts like the classic tiramisu, but can at a pinch be eaten as a biscuit or served alongside a dessert like chocolate mousse or chocolate pots. If you make tiramisu often, consider making a double batch and storing the extra sponge fingers in an airtight container for use at a later date.

For about 20 sponge fingers:

2 large (size 7) eggs

pinch of salt

6 Tbsp (85g) caster sugar

1 tsp vanilla essence

½ cup (75g) maize cornflour

1½ tsp gluten-free baking powder

❶ Preheat the oven to 180°C (160°C fan bake). Cover two baking sheets with baking paper and lightly coat with non-stick spray.

❷ Separate the eggs, placing the whites in a large clean bowl with the salt, and the yolks in another small bowl. Beat the whites until they form soft peaks, then gradually add the sugar, beating until the mixture forms a glossy meringue that forms stiff peaks. Fold in the yolks and vanilla essence.

❸ Sift the cornflour and baking powder onto a sheet of paper (or into a small bowl) the sift them again into the egg white mixture.

❹ Transfer the mixture to a sturdy plastic bag (with 1cm snipped off the corner) or forcing bag fitted with a 1cm nozzle. Pipe the mixture into thick lines about 10cm long and 4–5cm apart on the prepared trays.

❺ Bake for 15–20 minutes or until golden brown and firm to touch. Remove from the oven and cool on a rack. Store in an airtight container if making in advance.

Panforte

This Italian-style Christmas cake is flavoured with chocolate, nuts and fruit. It contains no flour, baking powder or eggs so it's firm, dark and rather compact with a fairly chewy texture.

For a 23–24cm cake (about 12–15 servings):

1 cup (160g) blanched or raw almonds

1 cup (150g) hazelnuts

75g butter

½ cup (90g) chocolate chips

1 cup (180g) dried apricots, halved

1 cup (170g) dried figs, quartered

¼ cup (55g) caster sugar

½ cup (125ml) honey

finely grated zest of 1 orange

½ cup (75g) cornflour

¼ cup (25g) cocoa

2 tsp ground cinnamon

1 tsp ground ginger

¼ tsp ground cloves, optional

1 Preheat the oven to 150°C (140°C), with the rack just below the middle. Line the bottom and sides of a 23cm round pan with baking paper.

2 Lightly roast the nuts in the heating oven. Check the nuts every few minutes — they should turn a light beige colour, probably in 6–10 minutes.

3 Melt the butter and chocolate chips together in a large bowl in the microwave oven at Medium (50% power) for about 2 minutes, or over a pot of hot water. Tip the hot nuts and prepared fruit into the chocolate mixture, then stir together.

4 Heat the sugar and honey together over low to moderate heat, stirring until the sugar has dissolved. As soon as the mixture bubbles all over the surface, pour the hot syrup into the nut mixture and stir again.

5 Add the orange zest, then sift the cornflour, cocoa and spices into the bowl and stir together until blended. Pour the warm mixture into the prepared pan and pat out evenly (with a piece of plastic between the cake and your hand, if necessary).

6 Bake for 35–45 minutes or until the centre looks as cooked as the edges. The mixture may still be bubbling over the surface (longer cooking gives a firmer, more toffee-like cake). The mixture feels much softer than a cake normally does, but it becomes much firmer on cooling, and should be left for 24 hours in a cool place before it is cut into wedges or rectangles.

7 Dust with icing sugar before serving, if desired, or leave plain. Store wrapped pieces in the refrigerator or freezer if you are making it some weeks before it is needed.

White Bread

Although this isn't exactly like a wheat-based bread, we think it's pretty close. The flavour and texture are good and it can be used for sandwiches and/or toast just as you would regular bread.

For a 750g loaf:

2 tsp instant active yeast

1 cup + 2 Tbsp warm water

3 tsp sugar

1½ tsp salt

3 tsp guar gum

1 large egg + 1 large egg white

¼ cup skim milk powder

3 Tbsp canola oil

½ cup (65g) chickpea flour

½ cup (65g) tapioca flour

1 cup (140g) rice flour

1 cup (150g) maize cornflour

Bread Machine Instructions:

1 Carefully measure all the ingredients into a 750g capacity bread machine. For the most effective mixing, it is best to add the liquids first.

2 Set to the Gluten Free Bread cycle, Medium Crust and Start.

Hand-made Bread Instructions:

1 Measure the yeast, water, sugar and salt into the bowl of a heavy-duty mixer and leave to stand for 5 minutes.

2 Sprinkle in the guar gum (do this gradually to avoid it forming lumps), then add the egg and egg white and the milk powder. Beat on a medium-high speed for 2 minutes until the mixture looks foamy.

3 Add the oil and flours, then mix again at medium speed for 2 minutes, stopping and scraping down the sides of the bowl after about 1 minute.

4 Thoroughly coat the inside of a large loaf pan with non-stick spray, then pour/spoon the batter into it. Spread the batter evenly in the pan and smooth the top with an oiled spatula.

5 Put the pan in a warm place to rise for 50–60 minutes or until the mixture has reached to the top of the pan.

6 Bake at 200°C for 15–20 minutes until golden brown and hollow sounding when tapped. Remove from the oven and cool in the pan for a few minutes before tipping onto a rack to cool completely.

Fruit & Nut Loaf

Nothing beats the smell of a spicy bread baking (well, maybe the smell of it being toasted) — and this is no exception.

For a 1kg loaf:

2 tsp instant active yeast

1 cup + 2 Tbsp warm water

2 Tbsp sugar

1½ tsp salt

50g butter, softened

3 tsp guar gum

2 large eggs

¼ cup skim milk powder

½ cup (55g) chickpea flour

1½ cups (190g) tapioca flour

1 cup (150g) maize cornflour

¼ cup brown sugar

2 tsp ground cinnamon

½ tsp ground mixed spice

½ cup sultanas

½ cup walnut pieces

Bread Machine Instructions:

❶ Carefully measure all the ingredients into a 750g capacity bread machine. For the most effective mixing, it is best to add the liquids first.

❷ Set to the Gluten Free Bread cycle, Medium Crust and Start.

Hand-made Bread Instructions:

❶ Measure the yeast, water, first measure of sugar, the salt and butter into the bowl of a heavy-duty mixer and leave to stand for 5 minutes.

❷ Sprinkle in the guar gum (do this gradually to avoid it forming lumps), then add the egg and egg white and the milk powder. Beat on a medium-high speed for 2 minutes until the mixture looks foamy.

❸ Add flours, brown sugar, spices, sultanas and nuts, then mix again at medium speed for 2 minutes, stopping and scraping down the sides of the bowl after about 1 minute.

❹ Thoroughly coat the inside of a large loaf pan with non-stick spray, then pour/spoon the batter into it. Spread the batter evenly in the pan and smooth the top with an oiled spatula.

❺ Put the pan in a warm place to rise for 50–60 minutes or until the mixture has reached to top of the pan.

❻ Bake at 200°C for 15–20 minutes until golden brown and hollow sounding when tapped.

❼ Remove from the oven and cool in the pan for a few minutes before tipping onto a rack to cool completely.

Ciabatta or Pizza Base

Most gluten-free breads are made from a mixture more like a batter than a dough. This is made from a stiffer mixture which can be shaped more like a traditional dough.

For 1 ciabatta-style loaf or 1 large pizza base:

½ cup warm water

2 tsp yeast

2 tsp sugar

1 tsp salt

3 tsp guar gum

1 Tbsp canola oil

2 egg whites

1 cup (125g) tapioca starch

1 cup (140g) rice flour

¼ cup skim milk powder

up to ¼ cup warm water

Bread Machine Instructions:

1. Measure all the ingredients, including the extra water, into the bread machine.
2. Set to the Dough cycle and press Start.
3. Check the dough after 5 minutes of mixing and scrape any unmixed flour off the sides.
4. Stop the machine 30 minutes after mixing has started and shape and bake as below.

Hand-made Bread Instructions:

1. Measure the warm water, yeast, sugar and salt into the bowl of a heavy-duty mixer. Leave to stand for 5 minutes, then sprinkle in the guar gum and add the egg whites.
2. Beat at medium speed for 2–3 minutes or until the mixture is pale and slightly foamy looking.
3. Measure in the flours and milk powder, then mix on medium speed until the mixture begins to bind together.
4. Add as much of the extra water as is required to form a cohesive dough, then mix for 2–3 minutes longer.

Shaping and Baking Pizza:

1. Thoroughly oil your hands, and lightly oil a baking paper-lined baking tray.
2. Tip/scrape the dough from the mixing bowl or bread machine onto the oiled surface. Lightly sprinkle or spray the dough with oil.
3. Gently pat out the dough into an oval shape about 25 x 35cm of about 5–7mm thickness (placing a sheet of baking paper on top of the dough may make this easier).
4. Allow to rise for 5–10 minutes, then top and bake at 200°C for 12–15 minutes.

Shaping and Baking Ciabatta:

1. Thoroughly oil your hands, and lightly oil a baking paper-lined baking tray.
2. Tip/scrape the dough from the mixing bowl or bread machine onto the oiled surface. Lightly sprinkle or spray the dough with oil.
3. Pat the dough into a 25–30cm long and 5–6cm thick sausage shaped loaf.
4. Arrange the loaf on the oiled baking sheet then leave to rise in a warm place for about 1 hour.
5. Bake at 200°C until golden brown and hollow sounding when tapped, about 12–15 minutes.

Index

www.hyndman.co.nz

The home of lifestyle books and gift stationery

Hyndman
PUBLISHING

www.holst.co.nz

*for latest news, upcoming events, recipes and sales
of our books, knives and useful kitchen products*